PLANNING AND FORMING YOUR COMPANY

PLANNING AND FORMING YOUR COMPANY

GUSTAV BERLE

WILEY

JOHN WILEY & SONS

New York • Chichester • Brisbane • Toronto • Singapore

This publication is designed to provide accurate and
authoritative information in regard to the subject
matter covered. It is sold with the understanding that
the publisher is not engaged in rendering legal, accounting,
or other professional service. If legal advice or other
expert assistance is required, the services of a competent
professional person should be sought. *From a Declaration
of Principles jointly adopted by a Committee of the
American Bar Association and a Committee of Publishers.*

This book contains numerous references with addresses and
phone numbers. These were correct at press time, but the
possibility always exists that they could have changed by
the time this book gets into your hands. Should you find
such a change, please excuse any inconvenience. We would
be grateful if you would notify the publisher of any new
change that should be made in future editions.

Library of Congress Cataloging-in-Publication Data:

Berle, Gustav, 1920–
    Planning and forming your own company / by Gustav Berle.
      p.   cm.
    Includes bibliographical references.
    ISBN 0-471-51795-X
    1. New business enterprises—Handbooks, manuals, etc.   2. New
business enterprises—United States—Handbooks, manuals, etc.
3. Small business—Handbooks, manuals, etc.   4. Small business—
United States—Handbooks, manuals, etc.   I. Title.
HD62.5.B484   1989
    658.1'1—dc20   89-22430

Printed in the United States of America

10 9 8 7 6 5 4 3 2 1

". . . the heroes of our great economic expansion have not been the Fortune 500 giants, but our entrepreneurs."

President George Bush
September 19, 1988

You are not a failure until you stop trying.

PREFACE

Quite contrary to popular belief and propaganda, the entrepreneur is not a risk-taker. He or she is a risk-controller—or a risk-minimizer.

After 35 years of entrepreneurial endeavors and several years of working with SCORE, the Service Corps of Retired Executives, I have come to the conclusion that entrepreneurs are among the most cautious of businesspeople.

Individuals who truly know a business avoid all but the most calculated risks. Their knowledge of products and people gives them an edge over naive adventurers who set out expecting the success of Columbus or Edison. How many travelers did Columbus interview and how many maps did he study before he risked his westbound voyage on the high seas? How many thousands of experiments did Edison conduct before he cried, "Eureka, a light!"?

The knowledgeable entrepreneur will study, research, and interview, then test, try, and investigate a small portion of a venture before making wholesale commitments. Of course, he or she will be propelled by the fuel that made entrepreneurship attractive in the first place—ambition, imagination, confidence, enthusiasm, sufficient capital to do the job, and time to accomplish designated goals. A background of research and a backlog of information and experience will minimize the inherent risk in any new enterprise.

A military commander who commits troops to a battle plan, a driver who steers an automobile down a busy highway, or a pedestrian who crosses a high-traffic intersection takes calculated risks. The more we know about any risks, the more chance we have to translate them into success.

SCORE counselors, all 13,000 of them, are a very valuable resource for the burgeoning entrepreneur or the one who is ready for the next step up the success ladder. Their task is not to encourage risk-takers, but to help to minimize the risks that are always lurking for entrepreneurs who have not charted their future.

Entrepreneurs can take a lesson from the Boy Scouts. Their slogan, a mere two words, says it all: Be Prepared.

Good luck!

GUSTAV BERLE

Silver Spring, Maryland
December 1989

ACKNOWLEDGMENTS

Every book is the product of more than one mind. Many who have labored silently behind the scenes have been of inestimable help in providing information and expertise for this volume. It would be impossible to name all of them; they know who they are and they understand that I am grateful to them. Two, however, deserve special mention—Michael Hamilton, my editor at Wiley, who inspired this book, and Esther Pinto Rosenbloom, who provided the framework within which this writer was able to complete it. To all, thanks.

G.B.

CONTENTS

CONTENTS

CONTENTS

CONTENTS

LIST OF FIGURES

GOING INTO BUSINESS

MISCONCEPTIONS

Of the dozens of books available to you on "how to start a business of your own," which one is the most useful? Our simple answer is: all of them. The more you read, the more you research, the more you question, the better you can make a decision on your ability to go into a business of your own. If you do not have the motivation and the curiosity, you probably would be better off going to work for somebody else and letting them worry about making next week's payroll.

But here you are, reading this book. That should indicate that you *are* motivated to consider a business of your own. One of the first things we would like to do is to dispel some of the confusion that abounds on this subject, which, unfortunately, has been created by books. Remember that, besides facts, books carry the opinions of their authors—which might not coincide with yours.

For example, a misleading statement in some "how to start a business of your own" books is that entrepreneurial tests, to help clarify in your own mind whether you are indeed the right kind of person to go into a business, are a bunch of hogwash. If they're hogwash, then thousands of psychologists, personnel experts, and other authors are wrong.

Nobody is going to grade you when you take an entrepreneurial test. It's only for your own guidance and information. If the test reveals some weaknesses in your motivation, resolve, or experience, this does not necessarily mean that you should not go into a business of your own. Instead, a caution signal is saying: Maybe I should make some changes, or do a little more research, or ask some questions.

Further, a warning you might come across in other books is that 85 percent of all business start-ups go broke within the first five years. Remember the old adage that figures can lie and liars can figure. While the statistics are correct, they need to be interpreted. Of the 85 percent of new businesses that start, many are at-home businesses begun by housewives whose husbands are making a good living, and whose motivation, therefore, may not be very strong. Nevertheless, when they decide to fold up the "business," they show up as statistics in those 85 percent "failures."

A third area of confusion is about available money. Any banker, or officer at the U.S. Small Business Administration, or business counselor will tell you that the majority of would-be entrepreneurs put a line of free and easy money at the head of their needs. Conversely, the lack of free and easy money will be blamed for the business's failure.

The SBA has a national hotline called the "Answer Desk." By calling 1-800-368-5855, you can get an answer to just about any question relating to starting up a business. When we questioned the director of that handy facility, he said, "We get 85,000 calls a year and of those, 85 percent ask, 'How can we get the money?'"

In a way, the many advisory sources that say Uncle Sam gives away millions of dollars just for the asking—and that includes some highly touted television programs that sell alleged "solutions" to the money problem for $49.95 or so—are leading you up a primrose path. As former President Harry S. Truman said, "The buck stops here." You might as well know now that there is little easy money lying around in government coffers. In a forthcoming book in this down-to-earth series, you will learn the unvarnished (though not hopeless) truth about "how to get the money." Meanwhile, be assured that many a small business has succeeded with very little start-up but with a great deal of management savvy and sweat.

The key to small business success is a principal ingredient: good management.

If you do need outside capital to get started, go to a bank. But before you risk embarrassing yourself with the banker, learn all you can about the business you want to get into. The real entrepreneur is not a foolish risk-taker. He or she is a risk-minimizer. The more the entrepreneur knows about the business *before* he or she ventures into it, the less risky the enterprise will be. Money lenders—banks, the SBA, venture capitalists, savings and loans, insurance companies, even Aunt Minnie or dear old dad—will be impressed by *your* written plan and will immediately recognize its value. A business plan is as necessary to your search for outside capital as oxygen is to your breathing. It not only marks you as a professional and opens doors to investment money, but also gives you a road map to your future success. (See Chapter 2.)

Don't let anybody dissuade you from your dream. At the same time, don't let anybody paint a rose-colored picture for you without pointing out that even the prettiest roses have thorns.

WHAT KIND OF BUSINESS SHOULD YOU BUY OR START?

This question seems elementary. However, many would-be entrepreneurs don't know. They only know they want to become independent, do something worthwhile with their time, and make a living—or supplement one that is inadequate. Some business start-ups are planned by early retirees from civil service and the military, while in recent years, corporation mergers have created a whole new class of premature retirees. Either these people do not feel old enough to retire, or else they are finally seizing the opportunity they have always dreamed about. Some even see their lump-sum retirement payment as a chance to make some real money.

Whatever the motivation for the big decision, going into a business of one's own is such a major step that it might come only once in a lifetime. For people who enter their own business in mid-life or beyond, time is of the essence. At 50 or 60, you have to be even more cautious than other entrepreneurs about assuming great risks. You have to learn as much as you can about going into business in order to minimize risks, and that's why business guidebooks are written. That's why *you* are reading this one.

Go for Growth

For entrepreneurs who are looking to the future, *growth* is an important factor in considering buying or starting a business. Of course, it is generally wise to go into a business about which you know something; your own expertise is the most important ingredient. There are always exceptions, however. The thousands of Asian immigrants who come to our hospitable shores in search of freedom and wealth seem to surface running restaurants, print shops, groceries, and almost any other service businesses that are for sale at the right price. Most of them make it—by dint of extreme hard work, extreme nepotism, and extreme frugality. Born-and-bred Americans have a different enculturation and must rely more on the statistics. The figures show the following businesses exhibiting major growth during the past few years:

- Commercial savings banks
- Electronic components
- Paper containers
- Computers
- Office machines
- Other paper products
- Basic steel products
- Pharmaceuticals
- Communications equipment
- Fixtures and partitions

Commercial savings banks show the highest growth. Even their survival rating is right at the top. (Despite the bleak savings-and-loan picture, commercial savings banks survive magnificently.) But then, not too many of us open a commercial savings bank. In fact, none of the "growth" businesses are everyday, easy-to-buy enterprises. Most of these require considerable skills, labor, equipment, and money. Still, there are exceptions.

One pharmaceutical manufacturer started as an individual pharmacist, making private-label pills and syrups for a local drug chain. When the pharmacist's son grew up, he joined his father's business, and the company developed its own product line. Twenty years later, the company, having grown to nearly 50 employees, was brought out by a larger manufacturer for a neat $2 million in cash. Father is retiring to Florida with his portion; son is looking into other business opportunities with his. As Harry Golden used to say, "Only in America!"

Alternatives

But let's say that you don't want manufacturing. By temperament, experience, and capital resources, you are more inclined to consider a service or smaller business. There are opportunities for you, too. Out of a total of 236 different kinds of businesses, the top 10 (that is, the 10 kinds most frequently started up), in order of popularity, are the following*:

1. Business services
2. Eating and drinking places
3. Retail shops
4. Automobile repair shops
5. Home construction businesses
6. Equipment and machinery distributors
7. Real estate offices
8. Professional practice
9. Home furnishings retailers
10. Computer sales and services

The business services category includes consultants. It seems that every former business executive or former government official becomes a consultant, at least for a while. It looks good on a business card and prevents your friends from asking you for free advice.

While all of the foregoing businesses require expertise, in some of the categories, a good manager, by hiring experts in the field, could open and operate one of these enterprises. In the professional

* Courtesy U.S. Department of Commerce

practices category, which includes dentistry, medicine, and veterinary medicine, specialized training is required. The survival rates of these three professions are among the ten highest of all enterprises, sharing top ranking with funeral parlors, barbershops, hotels and motels, pool parlors, trailer parks, and, of course, commercial savings banks.

WHERE SHOULD YOUR BUSINESS BE LOCATED?

Most of the time, this decision is steered by family considerations—where we live, where our children live, where our friends are, where we have connections. Sometimes health factors determine our geographical choices. As happens to 250,000 people each year, the benevolent weather of Florida may beckon. For an equal number, it is the Southwest, and for even greater numbers, California. Although a more scientific approach to locating a business is to consider where there is a need for it, the migration to areas with good weather continues unabated.

Approximately 1,300,000 new business are being established each year. In order of popularity, are the 10 top metropolitan areas for business start-ups:

1. Austin, TX
2. Dallas, TX
3. Huntsville, AL
4. Orlando, FL
5. El Paso, TX
6. Atlanta, GA
7. Nashville, TN
8. San Antonio, TX
9. Charleston, SC
10. Tampa/St. Petersburg, FL

But start-up frequency is not the only important factor when looking for a geographical location. Where do start-up businesses *survive* best? Where in the country are the best economic climates for nurturing an upstart into profitable maturity? Here are the 10 top metropolitan areas for business survival:

1. Manchester/Nashua, NH
2. Raleigh/Durham, NC
3. Nashville, TN
4. Boston, MA
5. Washington, DC
6. South Bend/Benton Harbor, IN
7. Atlanta, GA
8. Fort Wayne, IN
9. Orlando, FL
10. Austin, TX

Manchester and Nashua, New Hampshire? Why should these cities enjoy the nation's number-one business-survival rate? With barely 100,000 people in Manchester and about 75,000 in nearby Nashua, this area hardly constitutes a big market. But look at its proximity to Boston's multimillion population. The sedate New Hampshire cities have become bedroom communities of Boston, New England's largest city. Never mind the snow and the rock-ribbed topography. Here is *opportunity*, and for many business start-ups, that's what counts most.

Note that Nashville, Orlando, Atlanta, and Austin are on both the top-10 start-ups and top-10 survival lists. The two factors combined make these four cities prime candidates for *your* new business (providing that personal factors are consonant with the cold statistics).

Orlando has been touted as one of the nation's "hot spots" for several years. This central-Florida metropolis (and its burgeoning suburban cities of Altamonte Springs, Longwood, Casselberry, Winter Park, Kissimmee/St. Cloud, Maitland, and others), has been spark-plugged by the Walt Disney empire. The Disney ripple effect has caused millions of visitors and tens of millions of dollars to be infused into the local economy, and there is no letup in sight. For three-quarters of the year, the weather is great. The roads are getting more crowded, but there is still plenty of real estate at prices well below

7

those in other East and West Coast metropolitan areas. And not all the migrants are elderly retirees. For every one of the latter, two younger people find jobs in the service companies and in the moderate-sized and "clean" technology industries that central Florida is so eager to attract. Lack of a personal state income tax only adds to the opportunity-package of weather, jobs (at least for the young), and available housing.

THE BUSINESS PLAN

WHY DO YOU NEED A BUSINESS PLAN?

Entire books have been devoted to the business plan. Seminars are regularly held on the subject. Its importance cannot be overestimated. Put very simply, the business plan is a road map toward business success. It is the blueprint with which you will build your business and it is the key that will open the bank's treasure chest.

It is also a pain in the neck. But you must endure this pain in order to enjoy the pleasures of entrepreneurship. One banker came up with 140 questions that he wanted answered before he would even consider a new-business loan application. Since getting a bank loan is almost as important as having a viable business plan that *you* can follow, we have taken the banker's 140 questions as gospel and turned them into a business plan designed to inspire confidence. Your accountant, lawyer, or business consultant could answer them perhaps, but these professionals still would have to come to you for many of the answers—as well as to present their bills for several thousand dollars.

We are trying to save you this expense. Start-up capital is often difficult to come by, and it vanishes like the wind. Besides, if *you* study each question and answer it, you will soon know more about your business than anybody else. And that is perhaps the most important benefit; the more you know, the less risk you will incur in the future. Remember that a good entrepreneur is less a risk-taker than a risk-minimizer. The business plan is also a guide for reading this book. Read the whole book *before* you try to construct your plan. Then come back to the plan itself.

STRUCTURE OF THE PLAN

There are five basic ideas behind our proposed business plan, which are the ingredients of a typical loan package. The five main groupings have been broken down into more detailed forms, which are presented below as Figures 1 through 10. Other important components of the business plan, such as the executive summary, which functions as a table of contents for the proposal, and the cover letter are presented later in this chapter. A sample business plan format also appears.

1. **Purpose of proposal including money needed, loan repayment, and collateral.** How much do you really need? How will you use that money? Over what period of time? Where will you get the money to repay the loan? How much can you pay back? On what time schedule? What will you use for collateral? List in detail, without fluffing, the properties and assets that will secure the loan. (Figures 1 and 9.)

2. **Personal finances.** Your own input and that of partners and/ or family is important. It proves to the banker that you, too, are willing to assume some risks. (Figure 2.)

3. **Description of the business.** Includes dates, type of organization, location, zoning, employees, product or service, history of business, future prospects, marketing area, competition, customers, and suppliers. (Figures 3 through 7.)

4. **Management.** Refers to the background and experience of each owner and those who will manage the business. (Figure 8.)

5. **Business financial projections and data.** If this is a new business, show your own equity money and provide a credible projected balance sheet. Provide projections. How much money do you expect to take in and when? What will your expenses be? How did

you arrive at these estimates? Leave yourself a cushion for unexpected ups and downs. If this is an existing business, you will need to provide balance sheets and P&L statements for the past three years, as well as current status. (Figures 9 and 10.)

Okay, then, let's get started. When you have compiled all the information requested, you'll be ready to talk to the investor, the banker, the loan officer. You'll just about be ready to go into a business of your own.

Note: Some but not all of the business plan forms (Figures 1 through 10) have comments preceding them. If they do, read the comments first, and they will help you give the best answers.

Comment on the loan request (Figure 1). How much money will you need? Consider two vital factors before you state this amount: (1) you will need "tooling up" money before you even begin your new business (deposits, legal and accounting fees, license fees, fixtures, equipment, pre-opening promotion, etc.); and (2) it will take longer to start seeing returns than you anticipate—unless this new business is an all-cash, money-up-front enterprise. Figure on at least six months' operating expenses in addition to the items in (1).

Use *long-term money* for long-term requirements (more than one year); use *short-term* money for short-term requirements (one year or less). Short-term loans generally carry lower interest rates than long-term loans. However, short-term loans are usually more difficult to pay back because the payments are higher. You have to know what your business can handle. As your business grows, you will need more money, not less, to finance your inventory, salaries, and other expenses—because payments take 30 to 90 days to collect. A rule of thumb is to have 90 days' worth of cash on hand or available to you.

Remember two truisms in making a loan application: (1) the more money *you* have, the easier it is to get additional funds; (2) the more money you borrow, the more you have to pay back. So borrow only as much as you really need, but have an open line of credit for any future needs. The best way to make sure you keep your financial lifeline open for the future is to pay back a loan according to schedule. Getting the right kind of loan, on terms that allow you to pay it back conveniently, is second in importance only to having skilled management.

Comment on your proposed business name (Figure 1). One of the first pieces of information you will need in constructing a business plan is a name for the business. The principal criteria in choosing a company are that it be memorable; easy to pronounce; pertinent to the kind of business you are operating; different enough from your competition to avoid confusion; and short enough for telephone operators and callers—as well as the sign maker—to handle.

The business name should immediately indicate what kind of business you are in. Consider, too, that customers often prefer dealing with a company rather than an individual. Also consider your future plans. Will the business name you choose now be able to cover future expansion or changes? Further, have you checked the local county clerk's office for other registered businesses to make sure there is no close similarity or duplication? For a more detailed discussion of your business name, see Chapter 8.

1. Name, description, purpose, and goals of new business:

_____

_____

_____

_____

2. (If an existing business) I want to (acquire) (expand) this business. A loan will be used for the following:

_____

_____

_____

3. My experience will enable me to successfully operate this business, because _____

_____

_____

_____

Figure 1. Purpose of the proposal and request for loan

4. The following amounts of money are needed for the operation of this business at this time:

   My own investment: $ _____

   Other private investments: $ _____

   Loan request: $ _____

   TOTAL: $ _____

5. Here is how I plan to utilize these funds:

   _____

   _____

   _____

   _____

6. This is how the money will benefit the business:

   _____

   _____

   _____

   _____

7. I realistically feel that I can repay the loan in the following manner (amounts and time schedule):

   _____

   _____

8. I will be able to repay the loan by offering this assurance:

   _____

9. The collateral for the loan that I can offer is as follows (include verification by appraisal or other means):

   _____

   _____

10. In a case where the above collateral is owned by others or pledged to others, these are extenuating circumstances:

   _____

   _____

   _____

   _____

Figure 1. (*Continued*)

PERSONAL FINANCIAL STATEMENT

OMB Approval No. 3245-0188
Exp. Date: 10-31-89

As of _____ 19 ____

Complete this form if 1) a sole proprietorship by the proprietor; 2) a partnership by each partner; 3) a corporation by each officer and each stockholder with 20% or more ownership; 4) any other person or entity providing a guaranty on the loan.

Name	Residence Phone

Residence Address

City, State, & Zip

Business Name of Applicant/Borrower

ASSETS	(Omit Cents)	LIABILITIES	(Omit Cents)
Cash on hand & in Banks . . . .$_____		Accounts Payable . . . .$_____	
Savings Accounts . . . . _____		Notes Payable (to Bk & Others	
IRA . . . . _____		(Describe in Section 2) . . . . _____	
Accounts & Notes Receivable		Installment Account (Auto)	
(Describe in Section 6) . . . . _____		Mo. Payments $_____	
Life Insurance—Cash		Installment Account (Other)	
Surrender Value Only . . . . _____		Mo. Payments $_____	
Stocks and Bonds		Loans on Life Insurance . . . . _____	
(Describe in Section 3) . . . . _____		Mortgages on Real Estate . . . . _____	
Real Estate		(Describe in Section 4) . . . . _____	
(Describe in Section 4) . . . . _____		Unpaid Taxes	
Automobile—Present Value . . . . _____		(Describe in Section 7) . . . . _____	
Other Personal Property		Other Liabilities	
(Describe in Section 5) _____		(Describe in Section 8) . . . . _____	
Other Assets			
(Describe in Section 6) . . . . _____		Total Liabilities . . . . _____	
		Net Worth . . . . _____	
Total . . . .$_____		Total . . . .$_____	

Section 1. Source of Income		Contingent Liabilities
Salary . . . . $_____	As Endorser or Co-Maker . . . .$_____	
Net Investment Income . . . . _____	Legal Claims & Judgments . . . . _____	
Real Estate Income . . . . _____	Provision for Fed Income Tax . . . . _____	
Other Income (Describe)* . . . . _____	Other Special Debt . . . . _____	

Description of Items Listed in Section I _____

*(Alimony or child support payments need not be disclosed in "Other Income" unless it is desired to have such payments counted toward total income.)

Section 2. Notes Payable to Banks and Others

Name & Address of Noteholder	Original Balance	Current Balance	Payment Amount	Terms (Monthly-etc.)	How Secured or Endorsed—Type of Collateral

SBA Form 413 (10-87)   Use 10-86 edition until exhausted   Refer to SOP 50   10

(Response is required to obtain a benefit)

Figure 2. Personal data

Section 3. Stocks and Bonds: (*Use separate sheet if necessary*)

No. of Shares	Names of Securities	Cost	Market Value Quotation/Exchange	Date Amount

Section 4. Real Estate Owned. (*List each parcel separately. Use supplemental sheets if necessary. Each sheet must be identified as a supplement to this statement and signed*).

Address—Type of property	Title is in name of	Date Purchased	Original Cost	Present Value	Mortgage Balance	Amount of Payment	Status of Mortgage

Section 5. Other Personal Property. (*Describe, and if any is mortgaged, state name and address of mortgage holder and amount of mortgage, terms of payment, and if delinquent, describe delinquency.*

Section 6. Other Assets, Notes & Accounts Receivable (Describe)

Section 7. Unpaid Taxes. (*Describe in detail, as to type, to whom payable, when due, amount, and what, if any, property the tax lien attaches*)

Section 8. Other Liabilities. (*Describe in detail*)

Section 9. Life Insurance Held (*Give face amount of policies—name of company and beneficiaries*)

SBA/Lender is authorized to make all inquiries deemed necessary to verify the accuracy of the statements made herein and to determine my/our creditworthiness.
(I) or (We) certify the above and the statements contained in the schedules herein are a true and accurate statement of (my) or (our) financial condition as of the date stated herein. This statement is given for the purpose of: (*Check one of the following*)

☐ Inducing S.B.A. to grant a loan as requested in the application, to the individual or firm whose name appears herein.
☐ Furnishing a statement of (my) or (our) financial condition, pursuant to the terms of the guaranty executed by (me) or (us) at the same time S.B.A. granted a loan to the individual or firm, whose name appears herein.

Signature	Signature	Date

SOCIAL SECURITY NO.	SOCIAL SECURITY NO.

SBA Form 413 (10-87)

GPO 931-151

Figure 2. (*Continued*)

Comment on description of business (Figure 3). Read Chapters 7 and 8 on the legal structure of your business and on the naming of it. While these choices are not graven in stone, they are vital to the success of the business and your own happiness. Any changes can be very costly and traumatic.

The starting or opening date should, if at all possible, coincide with the peak period of the year for your particular business. By catching the upward curve, you will have a better chance to start out with the best possible income and traffic flow. However, do not rush into an opening ill-prepared—especially when the business involves a lot of traffic, as with a restaurant. A bad start can force an early closing.

Operating hours are determined at times by your competion, by customary hours in the neighborhood or, if the business is located in a shopping mall, by your lease mandates. Your personnel and utility costs will be directly affected by your operating hours.

Comment on suppliers' credit terms (Figure 3). It is possible that you have previous experience with one or several suppliers. If you have a track record with them, it will be a great boon to future relations. Also, the supplier(s) might be eager to have you as an outlet in your particular area or market. Establishing a personal rapport with the sales representative or with a key employee will be beneficial. Well-financed suppliers have been known to extend terms, especially during the formative months; to offer merchandise on consignment or at special introductory prices; or even to take an equity position in your business (this will make them a "silent partner," but it will also reduce the amount of your loan from other sources). Your supplier need not always be the lowest bidder in order to be the best resource. Check out all the possibilities before you sign on the dotted line.

1. The legal description of the business:
   Proprietorship _____
   Partnership _____
   Corporation _____
2. If a corporation, in which state has it been or is it being incorporated?
   _____
3. For tax purposes, is this a regular or a subchapter S corporation?
   _____
4. What classification of business is this?
   Retail _____
   Wholesale _____
   Service _____
   Manufacturing _____
   Professional _____
5. Are you starting a new business? _____
   Expanding an existing business? _____
   Taking over another business? _____
6. What is your projected starting or opening date?
   _____
7. If this is an existing business, attach a detailed history of the business to this page.
8. What is or will be the normal operating schedule of your business?
   Months of operations: _____
   Days: _____
   Hours: _____
9. Is this a seasonal or a year-round business? _____
   If this business is seasonal, how will you adjust your lease, employees, inventory, stock?
   _____
   _____
   _____

10. Who are your suppliers and what will they be supplying?
    _____
    _____
    _____

Figure 3. In-depth description of the business

_____

_____

_____

11. What kind of credit or terms will you be able to get from your suppliers?

_____

_____

_____

12. Will these suppliers give you any help?
    Training? _____
    Managerial training? _____
    Promotional support? _____

_____

13. What assistance can you expect from other trade or professional resources?

_____

_____

_____

14. If some or all of the work you expect to sell is contracted out to others, who are the contractors? What are their terms? What contracts do you have with them? What references do you have on them? (Attach a page with details if you need more space.)

_____

_____

_____

_____

15. If your new business is going to be located in a structure that requires remodeling, expansion, or even building, what are the specifications? Who are the contractors? What are the costs and terms? Attach plans and additional details, if applicable.

_____

_____

_____

_____

16. What do you think is so special about this business?

_____

Figure 3. (*Continued*)

17. Why do you expect this business to be successful and profitable?

18. What research can you offer that verifies your optimism?

19. What competition do you have, and where is it located?

20. Do you have any plans for R&D (research and development) for new products or processes? _____
21. If so, give a brief description and estimated cost and time frame.

22. Will you require additional financing for this R&D?

23. Are there any patents, patents pending, or trademarks that you own already or that you will apply for?

24. Do you know of any government regulations that could affect your R&D program or product-marketing efforts?

Figure 3. (*Continued*)

Comment on the size of your market (Figure 4). Determining the area or "market" for a new business is something like guessing where the little steel ball on a roulette wheel will come to rest. The U.S. Census Bureau, however, has come up with some figures that tell us approximately how many residents a local business needs in order to "make it." Here is a random selection:

Kind of Business	Pop.
Neighborhood Grocery	1,200
Retail Bakery	10,700
Meat or Fish Market	12,600
Dairy Store	25,700
Fruit/Vegetable Market	27,100
Restaurant, Cafeteria	776
Tavern	2,275
Women's Fashions	4,750
Shoe Store	7,650
Men's/Boys' Clothing	9,400
Variety Store	12,300
Women's Specialty Store	31,300
Furniture Store	5,250
Radio/TV Store	8,600
Records/Tapes	15,500
Drapery/Upholstery Store	18,700
Building Materials	7,400
Hardware Store	8,100
Paint/Wallpaper	18,300
Automobile Accessories	4,500
Auto Dealer (used)	5,800
Auto Dealer (new)	6,900
Gas Stations	1,200
Optical Store	2,200
Drugstore	4,300
Jewelry Store	6,300
Gifts/Novelties/Cards	6,300
Florist Shop	7,300
Sporting Goods	6,800

Kind of Business	Pop.
Hobbies/Toys	11,500
Bookstore	16,800
Stationery Store	33,200

1. How would you identify your primary audience?
   Neighborhood _____
   Ethnic composition _____
   Age groups _____
   Sex _____
   Economic level _____
   Social level _____
2. What is the size of your market?
   Area _____
   Population _____
3. How much of this market will you be able to sell or service?

4. What do you estimate as the growth potential of this market?

5. If there is growth potential, how will you be able to share in it?

6. Would such market growth mean that you would need more working capital? If so, when and how much?

7. How do you plan to price your product and/or service?

8. Will you be able to make a fair profit with such pricing?

9. How do such price projections compare with your existing competitors? Can you give some examples?

Figure 4. Analysis of your market

10. How do you plan to advertise and promote your business?

_____

_____

11. What advertising media are available in your market? What are their best rates or costs? Which do you plan to use?

_____

_____

_____

12. What is your first-year budget for advertising?

_____

13. What is your advertising timing or calendar?

_____

_____

14. Who will help you in the preparation of your promotions?

_____

15. If your business will require much servicing, how will you meet and beat your competition in this area?

_____

16. Are you going to offer credit? What type?

_____

17. Will you accept credit cards? Which ones?

_____

18. What are you going to do about slow-paying customers?

_____

19. If you have any ideas as yet for logos, slogans, advertisements and promotions, attach photocopies of several of them.

_____

_____

_____

Figure 4. (*Continued*)

1. Who are your nearest competitors and how far are they located from your planned location? _____

_____

_____

2. How much business do they do in relation to the total market? What is their "market share"?

_____

3. How do you plan to gain some of that "market share"?

_____

_____

_____

4. What advantages over them will you have to offer?

_____

5. What are their evident weaknesses and strengths?

_____

_____

6. Do you have any verifiable information on how your competitors are doing? _____

_____

_____

7. Can you describe your competitors in some detail? Their management? History? Principals? Financial strength? Anything that identifies them clearly.

_____

_____

_____

_____

_____

Figure 5. Your competition

Comment on your location (Figure 6). Often, the success of your business or lack of it comes down to the location you choose. The rental or mortgage payments are major expense factors, secured by a lease or mortgage agreement. It is truly a monumental decision and commitment. To help you make sure you're on the right track, here is a 25-point checklist of factors you need or need to know:

1. Central location to reach your market
2. Physical suitability of building
3. Type, length, and cost of lease
4. Provision for future expansion
5. Estimated suitability of site for next 10 years
6. Adequacy of utilities (sewer, water, power, gas)
7. Parking facilities for customers and employees
8. Public transportation availability and rates
9. Nearby competition
10. Traffic flow and count
11. Local taxation on property, inventory, utilities
12. Quality of police and fire protection
13. Environmental factors (chamber of commerce, schools, cultural and community activities)
14. Availability of employees
15. Customary pay scales in area
16. Housing availability for employees
17. Availability of merchandise or raw materials
18. Security of building (display windows, doors, skylights, fences, and gates)
19. Economic/social trend of neighborhood in the last few years
20. Zoning and licensing for your type of business
21. Other businesses that can be magnets for your business
22. Receiving and shipping facilities
23. Convenient, nearby eating facilities
24. Cost of needed improvements
25. Identification or signage requirements and restrictions

1. Why have you chosen the location? _____
   _____
   _____

2. What kind of a neighborhood is the site in?
   _____
   _____
   _____

3. What are the zoning regulations here? How do they affect your
   lease or ownership? _____
   _____
   _____

4. What other businesses are located in this area?
   _____
   _____
   _____

5. Are any of them in direct competition with you?
   _____
   _____

6. What other areas, if any, have you considered and decided
   against?
   _____
   _____
   _____

7. Are the rent and cost of operating in this location in line with
   your ability to pay? _____
   _____

8. How permanent will this location be? Will you plan to move
   and if so, when? _____
   _____

9. Are the premises leased or do you own them?
   _____

Figure 6. Your location

205598

10. What are the physical features of your location? Attach a floor plan or plat to this page.

_____

_____

_____

_____

11. Will your facility need any renovations? If so, do you have plans and estimates of their cost? If you do, attach a copy of them.

_____

_____

_____

_____

Figure 6. (*Continued*)

Comment on employees (Figure 7). In some businesses this item can comprise the major expenditure. In areas that approach full employment, finding and retaining good employees can be a major problem. In Washington, DC, for example, it is not unusual to find 36 pages of Help Wanted ads in the Sunday newspaper, and salaries are paced by the high, steady wages of the federal government. The bank's loan officer will be concerned with your solution to this problem. If yours is a one-person business, he or she will also be concerned with your plans for the enterprise's continuity in the event that anything should happen to you (at least during the term of the proposed loan). Therefore, a "succession policy" will be needed—unless your loan is fully covered by tangible collateral. (Also see Chapter 9.)

Comment on management and outside management resources (Figure 8). This section is one of the most important in the business plan, both for the loan officer and for you. *The lack of good management is the single most frequent cause of business failure.* Not only must the loan officer be satisfied with your answers, but, most important, *you* must be satisfied. You've got your resources, hopes, time, and reputation riding on this gambit.

Among the many available outside management resources available to you is one that deserves to be emphasized—SCORE, the Service Corps of Retired Executives. This 13,000-strong volunteer

1. What are the positions for which you will have to hire people?
   _____
   _____
   _____
   _____

2. When do you have to hire them? _____

3. What are the skills they should have? _____
   _____

4. How will you find these employees? _____
   _____

5. What training will they need? _____
   _____

6. Who will provide it? _____

7. Can some or all of the positions be filled with part-time employees? Commissioned employees? Independent contractors?
   _____

8. What will pay in wages? On what time basis? Will there be percentages or commissions? _____
   _____
   _____

9. Will there be an overtime policy? Fringe benefits?
   _____
   _____

10. What do you estimate these "extras" will cost?
    _____
    _____

11. Will any of your employees be family members?
    _____
    _____
    _____

Figure 7. Employees

association is the largest in the world. Its members range from Fortune 500 vice presidents to momma-and-poppa restaurant owners. They all have two things in common: (1) they are volunteers, and (2) their services are free. Because they are located in offices of the Small Business Administration (the SBA subsidizes SCORE), chambers of commerce, and colleges in more than 750 cities throughout the United States, you will be able to avail yourself of their counsel at any time and should do so before you take any major and potentially costly steps.

1. The principals of the new business are the following:

_____

_____

_____

(Attach résumés for all of the above.)
2. These principals have experience related to the proposed new business, as follows:

_____

_____

_____

3. The proposed duties and job descriptions of each above-named principal are as follows:

_____

_____

_____

4. The starting salaries, or salary ranges, and fringe benefits of the above-named are as follows:

_____

_____

_____

5. Outside management resources that we can draw on if needed, including their locations, are the following:

_____

_____

_____

Figure 8. Management

Comment on financial information (Figures 9 and 10). This is the portion of the business plan the loan officer will scrutinize most (if only because it represents familiar ground). It is also the most difficult for most entrepreneurs to compile. This is where your intimate knowledge of your business and of outside trends comes into play. Take your time on this section because it has to be thorough and accurate. If you are uncomfortable with it, get the help of a competent accountant or business attorney.

In getting credible appraisals, work with an appraiser who is approved by the bank. Even so, you will still have to provide all sorts of corroborating documents, which may include the following:

- Sales records
- Income statements, state and federal tax returns for the last three years
- State sales tax reports for the last three years
- Personal or nonbusiness expenses
- List of tangible assets
- List of intangible assets
- List of contractual obligations
- Other appraisals, leases, and/or deeds of trust

For more information on buying a business, with special focus on establishing the purchase price, see Chapter 3.

---

1. *Balance Sheet*: If this is a new business, supply a current balance sheet; if an established business, supply a balance sheet for the past three years.
2. *Operating Statement*: Do the same for this document.
3. *Projection*: Attempt to determine how your business will fare in the future—month by month for the first year; quarter by quarter for the second year; an annual projection for the third year.
4. *Cash Flow*: Provide an analysis of your projected cash needs for the first year, on a month-by-month basis.

Figure 9. Financial information for starting or expanding a business

5. *Break-Even Analysis*: Provide an analysis of what you will need to break even for the first year of operation, on a month-by-month basis. (The above analyses each should be on a separate sheet, attached to this page.)
6. What capital equipment do you already have or will you have to acquire? Indicate the cost or value for each item and whether the acquisition will be by purchase or lease.

_____

_____

_____

_____

_____

_____

7. *Major Asset Appraisals*: Attach appraisals (made by a bank-approved appraiser) and machinery in your possession.
8. *Individual Financial Statements*: Attach a statement for each individual who is a principal, cosigner, or guarantor involved with this loan application.
9. *Tax Returns*: Attach personal or business tax returns or any other documentation that will verify the value of your business and/or collateral.
10. *Other Collateral*: Are there any other assets, present or future, that might be of importance?

_____

Figure 9. (*Continued*)

PRESENTATION OF THE BUSINESS PLAN

There are no doubt many ways a business plan can be presented. Bear in mind, however, that *your* presentation will be your representative—and the only representative that the bank's or investors' loan committee will see. The quality of the paper and typing, the neatness of the folder, the way you bind the material, all add up to a "look" that will impress or turn off the readers. Put yourself into the shoes of these potential readers. They will get to look over

1. If you are buying somebody else's business, who started it and when? _____

2. What do you think is the real reason this business is for sale? _____

3. How was the purchase price determined? _____

4. Is this a customary method in the industry? _____
5. Was an appraiser or broker employed? _____
6. How much will you be paying for "good will"? How much for "key money"? _____
7. Will the seller take back any of the purchase price in the form of a loan? If so, on what terms? _____
8. What documentation do you have about the seller's past performance, sales, trends? _____
_____

9. If the sales are down over past years, what can you do to compensate for this decline? _____
_____

10. What can you or your management do to make this acquisition successful? _____
_____

11. What, specifically, are you buying? _____
_____

12. Attach balance sheets and P&L statements, as well as cash flow and break-even analyses.

Figure 10. Financial information for buying an existing business

dozens of other presentations. Yours needs to be appropriate to your business, flawlessly written, typed without error, organized for easy comprehension, and bound for easy handling; and it must exude the look of success and confidence. Professionalism is perhaps a good overall word for your business plan presentation. Put adequate effort and time into it, and get the best professional help you can afford if you need it. A yes or no from the reader could spell the fulfillment or the end of your dreams.

What follows in this section are two other components of the business plan, the executive summary (Figure 11) and the cover letter (Figure 13), as well as the MIT Enterprise Forum's example of the ideal business plan (Figure 12).

Comment on the executive summary (Figure 11). This summary is a sort of table of contents for the business plan presentation. It is of great importance, because it will determine whether the loan officer will read further in your proposal. It should be concise and cover the topics shown in Figure 11, following at least generally the order of items in the business plan. The summary is the key to the first door. Before other doors can be opened, the loan officer—whether at a bank, Small Business Administration, or other lending institution—has to step through this one.

Name of Business:	The Permanent Press
	711 Main Street
	Pikesville, Maryland 21208
	Telephone: (301) 486-1234
Contact:	Jack J. Entrepreneur
Type of Business:	Producing publications for small- to medium-sized businesses and shopping centers; handling preparation and production only; operating out of street-level offices (three rooms) in a prominent suburban four-story office building.
Purpose of Business:	To service small- to medium-sized businesses and shopping malls, helping them promote themselves in their local/ regional markets.
Loan Requested:	A credit line of $60,000 a year for five years, available at $15,000 per quarter.
Purpose of Loan:	To enable company to hire one additional person and furnish one office, in order to take in additional business.

Figure 11. The executive summary

Existing Assets: Principal has a private residence with a current value of $100,000, against a mortgage balance of $23,500. Current collectibles (all less than 90 days) total $38,458 as of this date. One paid-up motor vehicle is owned by the principal ($6,000).

Product/Market: Publications are primarily tabloid newsprint papers, containing advertising and public relations material. The limited-area distribution, in a previously defined market area, is either by carrier or by mail, although some are distributed in take-with receptacles (on street corners or traffic locations like supermarkets) or at trade shows and large public events. All public media are in a sense competitive; however, our product is direct, targeted, and flexibly adjusted to the local client's requirements and budget. In the approximately 20-mile radius defined, we have no competition as uniquely qualified to handle these publications, from the creative stage through distribution to the home or business.

Management: Our expertise is due to the fact that the principal owner has academic and practical background in advertising, public relations, and publishing. He has taught these subjects at the Maryland Business College; he has worked as public relations director of three of the area's major shopping centers, and he has edited a newspaper and a magazine. His two assistants have worked in some of these areas and have been with the

Figure 11. (*Continued*)

33

Financial Projections:

Growth and Profit Goals:

company for three and five years, respectively.

Because of the proved expertise of the staff, considerably more business could be obtained. Growth is limited only by availability of additional talent and of funds to defray the additional salary and workplace expansion. For this purpose, short-term financing is needed to ensure growth of an estimated 20% annually for the next five years. With present gross between $250,000 and $300,000, our financial projection calls for an availability of another $60,000 on an annual basis.

To expand by an annual 20%, which is the growth estimated in the local market. It is estimated that this 20% annual growth will continue for the next five years. The profit of the company will rise above this figure, as many basic functions are already underwritten by existing business. It is estimated that financial growth will be 20%, 25%, 30%, 35%, 35% in the next five years.

Figure 11. (*Continued*)

Comment on the ideal business plan format (Figure 12). The MIT Enterprise Forum is a brain trust of business managers that holds seminars in nine locations: Cambridge, MA; Kenilworth (Chicago), IL; Littleton, CO; Pasadena, CA; Coral Gables (Miami), FL; New York City; Seattle, WA; Houston, TX; and Washington, DC. Hundreds of business plans have been submitted to these seminars, and from them a model plan has evolved.

According to the forum panelists, the business plan they found to be the best featured the following elements:

- No more than 40 pages in length
- Spiral binding
- A cover bearing the company name
- A title page bearing the company name, address, and copy number
- A two-page executive summary to open the presentation, which capsulized the company's current operation and future plans
- A table of contents
- A body of text providing details on the officers and investors
- Professional editing that eliminated cumbersome language and grammatical and spelling errors
- Statements by legal and accounting advisers, especially on disclaimers of forecasts

This number-one business plan had another feature that made it stand out in the minds of the MIT Forum panelists: Each page was typed only on the right side. The left side was blank except for a small paragraph. This small paragraph listed the highlights of the right-hand presentation in brief, bulleted sentences. Thus, the reader could get an immediate overview of the content on the facing page. In ten minutes, financial officers could get an idea of what the business plan was all about. Then, if they were interested, they could go back and read the right-hand pages in detail. All the panelists did. Figure 12 shows the value of this format.

- Principals: _____ is sole principal and CEO.

- Experience: 30 years in the export business in the United States and abroad.

- Duties: Management, new business, overseas contacts, document preparation, financing, trade events.

- Salary: $4,000 a month. Other profits reinvested in company.

- Outside management: Overseas contacts and four-language capability; lower salary demands of principal create ready personnel availability.

Figure 12. Ideal business plan format

1. Principals: At this time only one principal manages this business, assisted by two full-time and two part-time employees. The principal is _____ , who is also president of this incorporated enterprise, as well as its managing officer. (Résumé attached.)

2. Experience: The above principal (myself) has been in the export business for 30 years, both in the United States and overseas. My experience can be divided into three phases: (a) a training and practical period in Cairo and Alexandria, Egypt, for 10 years, as employee of a large custom broker doing business primarily with the United States, followed by three years of independent exporting of Egyptian finished textiles to the United States. It was through this activity that contact was made with the XYZ Company in New York. The latter induced this principal to move to New York in 1968 as assistant export manager. In this position I moved up to export manager after three years and remained for seven more years before launching my own business in the Washington, DC, area. I am functioning as export manager for a number of companies, primarily in the health field, for which ready dollar currency is available abroad, especially in lesser developed countries (LDCs).

3. Duties: Principal duties include managing a staff of four people, developing new business contacts, exploring favorable overseas sales for numerous clients, overseeing details in the exporting and financing of U.S. shipments, and attending domestic and overseas trade events where contacts can be made for resources, customers, sales, etc.

4. Salary: This principal draws a regular monthly salary of $4,000. Tax-approved business expenses are drawn separately as needed. Surplus funds have been reinvested in the business during the past three years. All other staff members are on salary; occasional outside professionals are engaged on a per-assignment basis.

5. Outside management: Primary outside assistance is obtained in major overseas markets. Much overseas contact is continuous, and I can only absent myself for two to three weeks at a time. Overseas personnel are less expensive than U.S. personnel, readily available, and highly motivated. Sound relations are enjoyed because of common language proficiency (particularly in Cairo–Alexandria, Naples, and Marseilles because this principal speaks Arabic, Italian, and French).

Figure 12. (*Continued*)

Comment on the cover letter (Figure 13). While the cover letter is the first message from you a loan officer sees, it is usually the last component you write. At this point, your business plan is ready to go.

A letter on your own stationery introduces you to the loan officer of the bank, SBA, or other financial entity whom you might approach for a loan. It should look good, with a well-printed letterhead, good paper, neat typing, and proper spacing. After all, this *is* your first introduction to the person who can make your new business a reality. There is an old adage that says: "When you put your best foot forward, make sure your shoe is well shined." The letter should be brief, to the point, and businesslike. The recipient should become interested in reading the proposal or business plan to follow.

The cover letter should contain three principal paragraphs, which should cover the following:

1. The amount of money you request and for what purpose,
2. The terms and timing you seek that will make it possible for you to pay back the loan,
3. The type of collateral you can put up and what you estimate this security is worth.

Figure 13 shows how such a letter might be worded.

Your Letterhead

Date

Name of Bank Officer
Address

———————————

———————————

Name of Bank Officer:

This is a request for a loan in the amount of $ —————————— . Having researched the need for this business and having determined that this business is needed and can be exceptionally profitable, I wish to establish a (description of proposed business).

It is my intention to open this business on or about (date). I will need funds commencing (00) days prior to the projected opening. I expect that within (00) months I will be in a position to start paying back this loan. My projections further indicate that the business will generate a cash flow that will make it feasible to pay back the loan within (00) years.

The collateral that I have available at this time consists of (description of real estate, investments, savings, valuables, etc.), which has an appraised value of $ —————————— .

Attached is a detailed business plan and supporting documents. It will be appreciated if you can schedule a meeting to discuss this request for a business loan as soon as possible.

Very cordially,

(signature)

encl:

Figure 13. Sample cover letter

HOW TO BUY
A GOING BUSINESS

3

DON'T BUY A PIG-IN-A-POKE

If you are buying a going business, both you and the banker or other loan officer will want to make sure you are not buying a pig-in-a-poke. Strangely, many entrepreneurs will buy another's business much more readily than start one of their own. Of course, it is easier. But, as with buying a used car, you might be buying somebody else's headache.

Figure 14 is a checklist that can serve as a cautionary guide. In many cases, these are items you will need to back up your business plan and loan application. In all cases, *you* will want to make sure you have these details in your head or in your possession. Figure 15 will help you determine the current financial status of the business you hope to buy.

ARRIVING AT A PURCHASE PRICE

No matter what the asking price of a business is, there is another price that the seller will ultimately accept. Much, of course, depends on the psychological factors: Is the business being sold under duress? Was there a death in the family, a divorce, an estate settlement?

You should have the following items (those that are pertinent) when you plan to take over another's business:

The plat plan _____
Deed to the land _____
Blueprint or layout _____
Zoning permit _____
Property lease, option to renew _____
Building contracts _____
Business agreements (corporation or partnership papers) _____
Licenses, options to renew _____
Franchise agreement _____
Management contracts _____
Maintenance agreements _____
List of major customers and trading terms _____
List of principal suppliers and trading terms _____
Credit card agreements _____
Check approval system _____
Marketing and promotional literature and art work _____
Publicity articles _____
Annual reports _____
Buy-and-sell, purchase-and-sell agreements _____
Insurance policies _____
Waiver agreements (with landlord or mortgage company) _____
Patents and copyrights _____
Any other pertinent legal documents _____

Figure 14. Checklist for buying a business

Does the old owner want to retire? If heirs exist are they disinterested in the business? Has the business shown a steady decline in gross revenues or net profits? Has new competition surfaced? Has the merchandise or service become obsolete? Was there a legal, sanitary, union, or other problem? All these factors will directly affect your decision and your offer.

There are some other points to consider: If you were to liquidate this business and invest the money in a Treasury bill, what would your after-tax return be? Compare that with the income you could draw from the proposed business if you were to run it. Take into

1. List of creditors who have sold merchandise and services to the business
2. Terms on which the above have been sold
3. Value and age of inventory
4. Accounts receivables (and age)
5. Capital assets and condition (machinery, fixtures, etc.)
6. Debts of the business
7. Who will be responsible for the above?
8. Have the above assets been properly appraised?
9. Have you made your own appraisal?
10. Have you taken any photos of the property? Business? Rolling stock?

Figure 15. Checklist for determining financial status of business to be purchased

account the subjective value of "goodwill," or reputation. If it is substantial—if customers and prospects think highly of the company and product, if employees speak well of it—than an addition of 10 percent to the net liquidation estimate will be appropriate. Further, what is the psychological benefit to *you* of owning this business?

Figure 16 is an essential aid in arriving at a fair offering price of your own.

Example of Arriving at a Purchase Price

A service business was for sale. Run by an owner who was retiring, it had been operating for 23 years with moderate success. Most people in the area thought well of it. While there was always competition, two years ago a bigger competitor opened a few miles up the road. The effect of this new presence was to reduce the gross income of the business for sale from $300,000 a year to $250,000. The owner compensated by not replacing one retiring full-time employee, assuming her functions himself, and replacing another full-time employee with a part-time worker. Three other employees remained. This savings, or belt-tightening, allowed the owner to retain the salary he had been paying himself previously—about 15 percent of the gross—plus some fringe benefits (a car and health insurance) worth about $6,000. The seller/owner showed no taxable profit during the past three years.

Accounts receivables less than 90 days old: $ _____ .
    Take 80% of this sum (any account over 90 days
    old, write off or return to seller for action; figure
    that you can collect at least 80% of all current ac-
    counts): $ _____

Value of raw material and/or finished goods in the
current inventory (at cost): $ _____ .
    Take 50% of this sum as current value in case of
    liquidation: $ _____

Value of all machinery, equipment, and land included
in the sale (get a written appraisal): $ _____ .
    Take 40% of this value as a secure liquidation price
    you can pay: $ _____

Current market value of any buildings that are to be
included in the sale: $ _____ .
    Take 25% of this property estimate (which is what
    the bank would figure in the event of any liquidation,
    though you might feel that you can offer more if
    the property if ideally located and in good condition: $ _____

Now add up the percentage items: $ =====

Note: This is how the bank would figure the liquidation price for the
business.

Figure 16. Buy-a-business work sheet

After many years in the community, the business was well established; however, the personal-relations factor was unknown. How
much of the business would be retained by a new owner? This
uncertainty cast some doubt on the future earnings and had a negative
effect on the sale value. Having no visible net earnings, the only
ways the business could generate payoff money would be either to
reduce the new owner's income or to increase the business's income.
Accounts receivables amounted to 10 percent of the gross, and 80
percent of them were due within 90 days. Vendor contracts were
stable for the year and customer relations were good. At least one
new cost would be incurred in the form of a moderate increase due
one employee of $500 to $750 for the year. Now for some figures.

The seller was asking one-time gross, or $250,000. He wanted 20 percent down, or $50,000, with the balance of $200,000 to be paid over five years at $40,000 a year, without interest; the payments would be rendered monthly starting 12 months from the settlement date. The seller would give an agreement for the term of the payout that he would not compete with the purchaser. In case of any default in excess of 90 days, the deal would be off and the business would be returned to the seller. Upon sale, all accounts receivables would be retained by the new owner. Cash on hand and insurance policy proceeds, if any, would be retained by the seller. All equipment, of which there was very little other than files and office machinery, went with the sale. The car was leased up to the date of sale. The property lease was valid for at least one year beyond the sale. The seller would be available to consult personally for three months after settlment. Here, then, is the purchaser's work sheet:

Accounts receivables: $25,000.

80% collectible:	$20,000
Equipment value on books:	1,000
Owner's net income (salary plus end-of-year profit): $37,500.	
$37,500 × 5 years (an average):	187,500
Total estimated value:	$208,500

Based on these calculations, the purchaser's offer to the seller was $200,000, with $40,000 down and $30,000 a year for four years and $40,000 paid during the fifth year ($40,000 + [$30,000 × 4 =] $120,000 + $40,000 = $200,000). If the status quo was maintained, the new owner would actually work for nothing during the first five years. However, he was optimistic and figured he would be able to increase revenues with new ideas, harder and smarter work, and some expected growth of the community.

HOW TO BUY
A FRANCHISE

ADVANTAGES AND DISADVANTAGES OF BUYING A FRANCHISE

Nearly half-a-million franchised businesses exist, and their percentage, in comparison with independently started businesses, is growing steadily. Each year *Venture* magazine, among others, publishes a franchising directory, and throughout the country, franchisors hold periodic exhibits designed to attract potential buyers of franchises. By the end of this decade, it is estimated that fully one-half of all retail product and service businesses will be franchises.

As with buying any business, acquiring a franchise is a calculated risk, although in the case of a franchise, the risk factors have been lessened because a franchise is actually part of a chain. The downside is that, as the owner of the local franchise, you are not completely independent. Being part of a larger business, you are bound to that business by a legal agreement, and you have to operate under its rules and regulations.

Definition

Here, then, is a definition: *Franchising is a plan of distribution under which an individually owned business is operated as though it were part of a large chain.*

The ingredients of a franchise are as follows:

- All services or products of the franchise are standardized.
- The services or products of the franchise have been tested and proved workable by one or more prototype operations.
- The franchise business is administered by supposedly knowledgeable and competent managers.
- The franchisor has created a recognizable style of management and marketing on a local, regional, or national basis.
- The franchisor will provide training and continued supervision to ensure optimum effectiveness.
- Uniform trademarks, symbols, signs, designs, and equipment are used to ensure quality control and customer confidence.
- The franchise holder will have territorial protection, and no other franchisee in that chain may operate there.
- The purchaser of a franchise buys the franchise's name, reputation, selling technique, and continued supply of standardized materials.

The advantageousness of these arrangements to the purchaser has been proved by the fact that franchises survive far longer than individually owned businesses. In fact, only about 4 to 5 percent of franchises fail during any one year, compared with four times that rate for independent businesses.

Disadvantages

Before you conclude that the only way to go into a retail service or product business is via the franchise route, you need to look at the inevitable disadvantages. The drawbacks to buying a franchise are as follows:

- It takes a good bit of up-front cash. Some nationally renowned franchises, especially in the fast-food industry, can require upward of $100,000 before you have opened your doors.
- You have to operate under tight standards that will often seem restrictive and may irritate you.

- Having to continue buying the franchisor's products and paying royalties or fees on your income might start to feel like paying alimony forever and ever.
- Your expansion will be limited to the territory assigned to you by the franchise agreement.
- You might be prohibited from stocking any products or rendering any services that are not specifically spelled out in the franchise agreement.
- Similarly, promotions are limited to those approved or administered by the franchisor, and you may be charged for them whether you participate in the campaigns or not.
- Training given by the franchisor is sometimes inadequate, and the continuing counsel you had expected might not be there.

Not all of these factors have to be disadvantages, and some may not arise, but forewarned is forearmed, and now you can discuss them with the franchisor before you sign on the dotted line.

Other Factors

A few more factors you should be informed about before deciding on the franchise route are the following:

- Service franchises (quick-print shops, maid services, automobile rentals) have a higher return on investment than product franchises (fast food, appliances, clothing).
- There are more than 1300 sellers of franchises, and most of them are anxious to get you and your money. Take your time and do your research before you commit yourself. No matter how great the reputation of the franchisor, *you* are the main ingredient in your own success; the franchise key has to fit *your* door.
- The less money you are required to put up for a franchise, the greater your return on investment will be. This is especially true after the first year, when entry costs are out of the way.
- If initial investigation proves that the franchise you want to buy is among the fast-growers in the nation, then you will likely get above-average profits from your franchise.

• Fast-food and restaurant franchises are among the most popular. However, in relation to their considerable investment and labor intensity, they are not necessarily the most profitable.

The U.S. Department of Commerce publishes a "Franchise Opportunities Handbook," which goes into great detail on what a franchise is and should be, what questions to ask, and how to protect yourself. On the subsequent pages is a list taken from this handbook of the information the Federal Trade Commission requires in any complete disclosure statement—the document that the franchisor must give to you. Check it over point by point. Then go through the checklist of precautions that appears as Figure 17.

Even being this prepared, you would be ill-advised to enter into an agreement with a franchisor without a lawyer at your side who has had experience in franchise agreements. Look upon the agreement as if it were a marriage contract, but leave out the emotional aspect that propels a groom or bride into saying "I do."

THE FRANCHISOR   Check if Answer is YES

1. Has the franchisor been in business long enough (five years or more) to have established a good reputation? _____
2. Have you checked Better Business Bureaus, chambers of commerce, Dun and Bradstreet, or bankers to find out about the franchisor's business reputation and credit rating? _____
3. Did the above investigations reveal that the franchisor has a good reputation and credit rating? _____
4. Does the franchising firm appear to be financed adequately so that it can carry out its stated plan of financial assistance and expansion? _____
5. Have you found out how many franchises are now operating? _____
6. Have you found out the "mortality" or failure rate among franchises? _____
7. Is the failure rate small? _____

Figure 17. Questions to answer affirmatively before going into franchising

THE FRANCHISOR (Continued)   Check if Answer is YES

8. Have you checked with some franchisees and found that the franchisor has a reputation for honesty and fair dealing among those who currently hold franchises? _____

9. Has the franchisor shown you certified figures indicating exact net profits of one or more going operations, which you have personally checked yourself? _____

10. Has the franchisor given you a specimen contract to study with the advise of your legal counsel? _____

11. Will the franchisor assist you with:
    a. A management training program? _____
    b. An employee training program? _____
    c. A public relations program? _____
    d. Obtaining capital? _____
    e. Good credit terms? _____
    f. Merchandising ideas? _____
    g. Designing store layout and displays? _____
    h. Inventory control methods? _____
    i. Analyzing financial statements? _____

12. Does the franchisor provide continuing assistance for franchisees through supervisors who visit regularly? _____

13. Does the franchising firm have an experienced management trained in depth? _____

14. Will the franchisor assist you in finding a good location for your business? _____

15. Has the franchising company investigated *you* carefully enough to assure itself that you can successfully operate one of its franchises at a profit both to it and to you? _____

16. Have you determined exactly what the franchisor can do for you that you cannot do for youself? _____

THE PRODUCT OR SERVICE

17. Has the product or service been on the market long enough to gain good consumer acceptance? _____

18. Is it priced competitively? _____

19. Is it the kind of item or service that the same consumer customarily buys more than once? _____

Figure 17. (*Continued*)

THE PRODUCT OR SERVICE (Continued) Check if Answer is YES

20. Is it an all-year seller in contrast to a seasonal one?   _____
21. Is it a staple item in contrast to fad?   _____
22. Does it sell well elsewhere?   _____
23. Would you buy it on its merits?   _____
24. Will it be in greater demand five years from now?   _____
25. If it is a product rather than a service:
    a. Is it packaged attractively?   _____
    b. Does it stand up well in use?   _____
    c. Is it easy and safe to use?   _____
    d. Is it patented?   _____
    e. Does it comply with all applicable laws?   _____
    f. Is it manufactured under certain quality standards?   _____
    g. Do these standards compare favorably with similar
       products on the market?   _____
    h. If the product must be purchased exclusively from
       the franchisor or a designated supplier, are the prices
       to you, as the franchise, competitive?   _____

THE FRANCHISE CONTRACT

26. Does the franchise fee seem reasonable?   _____
27. Do continuing royalties or percent of gross sales payment
    appear reasonable?   _____
28. Are the total cash investment required and the terms
    for financing the balance satisfactory?   _____
29. Does the cash investment include payment for fixtures
    and equipment?   _____
30. If you will be required to participate in company-spon-
    sored promotions and publicity by contributing to an
    "advertising fund," will you have the right to veto any
    increase in contributions to the "fund"?   _____
31. If the parent company's product or service is protected
    by patent or liability insurance, is the same protection
    extended to you?   _____
32. Are you free to buy the amount of merchandise you
    believe you need rather than being required to purchase
    a certain amount?   _____

Figure 17. (*Continued*)

THE FRANCHISE CONTRACT (Continued) Check if Answer is YES

33. Can you, as the franchisee, return merchandise for credit? _____
34. Can you engage in other business activities? _____
35. If there is an annual sales quota, and can you retain your franchise if it is not met? _____
36. Does the contract give you an exclusive territory for the length of the franchise? _____
37. Is your territory protected? _____
38. Is the franchise agreement renewable? _____
39. Can you terminate your agreement if you are not happy for some reason? _____
40. Is the franchisor prohibited from selling the franchise out from under you? _____
41. Can you sell the business to whomever you please? _____
42. If you sell your franchise, will you be compensated for the good-will you have built into the business? _____
43. Does the contract obligate the franchisor to give you continuing assistance after you are operating the business? _____
44. Are you permitted a choice in determining whether you will sell any new product or service introduced by the franchisor after you have opened your business? _____
45. Is there anything with respect to the franchise or its operation that would make you ineligible for special financial assistance or other benefits accorded to small business concerns by federal, state, or local government? _____
46. Did your lawyer approve the franchise contract after studying it paragraph by paragraph? _____
47. Is the contract free and clear of requirements that would call upon you to take any steps that are, according to your lawyer, unwise or illegal in your state, county, or city? _____

Source: "Franchise Opportunities Handbook" published by the U.S. Department of Commerce.

Figure 17. (*Continued*)

DISCLOSURE INFORMATION

The following information is required by the Federal Trade Commission from a franchisor. The 47 questions in Figure 17 are based on this list. There might be other questions that you wish to add or that are suggested by your attorney.

1. Information identifying the franchisor and its affiliates, and describing pertinent business experience.

2. Information identifying and describing the business experience of each of the franchisor's officers, directors and management personnel responsible for franchise services, training and other aspects of the franchise program.

3. A description of the lawsuits in which the franchisor and its officers, directors and management personnel have been involved.

4. Information about any previous bankruptcies in which the franchisor and its officers, directors and management personnel have been involved.

5. Information about the initial franchise fee and other initial payments that are required to obtain the franchise.

6. A description of the continuing payments franchisees are required to make after the franchise opens.

7. Information about any restrictions on the quality of goods and services used in the franchise and where they may be purchased, including restrictions requiring purchases from the franchisor or its affiliates.

8. A description of any assistance available from the franchisor or its affiliates in financing the purchase of the franchise.

9. A description of restrictions on the goods or services franchisees are permitted to sell.

10. A description of any restrictions on the customers with whom franchisees may deal.

12. A description of the conditions under which the franchise may be repurchased or refused renewal by the franchisor, transferred to a third party by the franchisee and terminated or modified by either party.

13. A description of the training programs provided to franchisees.

14. A description of the involvement of any celebrities or public figures in the franchise.

15. A description of any assistance in selecting a site for the franchise that will be provided by the franchisor.

16. Statistical information on the present number of franchises; the number of franchises projected for the future; and the number of franchises terminated; the number the franchisor has decided not to renew; and the number repurchased in the past.

17. The financial statements of the franchisors.

18. A description of the extent to which franchisees must personally participate in the operation of the franchise.

19. A complete statement of the basis for any earnings claims made to the franchisee including the percentage of existing franchises that have actually achieved the results that are claimed.

20. A list of the names and addresses of other franchisees.
>Source: *Franchise Opportunities Handbook, U.S. Department of Commerce*

INDIVIDUALISTIC BUSINESS APPROACHES

In searching for a business of your own, the six approaches listed below are worth considering. Some of them have been around for generations, while others are newer and are growing by leaps and bounds.

- Incubators
- Home businesses
- Flea markets
- Mail-order businesses
- Mobile or temporary-structure businesses
- Party sales and demonstrations

The above business groupings have some characteristics in common: (1) They are highly individualistic in their operation. (2) Their capital start-up requirements are either minimal or flexible. (3) They rarely include "forever" enterprises that are supposed to be around for generations; in fact, they are often quite free spirited and mobile. That does not mean they are foolproof. While these characteristics obviously appeal to some entrepreneurs (the proof is in the large number of business start-ups falling into these six categories), if they hold any dangers, it is that they often seem too easy. They are not. Each one is a full-fledged, serious approach to doing business. Each must be studied, investigated, watched. We'll take up each one in turn.

INCUBATORS

An incubator, according to the dictionary, is "an apparatus for hatching eggs by artificial warmth" or one "in which babies born prematurely can be kept under controlled conditions." If for "eggs" and "babies" you substitute "small business," you have an idea of what is meant by a business incubator.

The way it works is that an umbrella organization, such as a state university, supplies the environmental ingredients—the physical facilities, an advisory board of specialists and experts, marketing counsel, networking opportunities, and perhaps even access to operating capital. Small business start-ups that have been nurtured by the "incubator" process can be found in almost any category. However, because the host facilities are often universities, most incubated businesses have been technology-oriented.

Example

A state university located just outside a metropolitan area has a spare building formerly used as a 14-bay garage. Each space is about 15 × 15 feet, or 225 square feet. Given the installation of adequate electrical and plumbing outlets, and a central sanitary facility, each space can accommodate a small machine shop, laboratory, workshop, or small distribution facility. Each two units are joined by doorways, thus making 450 square feet available for each incubator tenant. The spaces are pegged at a per-square-foot price that is about 50 percent of what comparable new space might cost elsewhere. But there are many advantages beyond cost savings.

Once seven noncompetitive entrepreneurs are moved in and operating, they will form an effective mininetwork. Most of them will be starting from scratch. Their capital is usually limited, as is their capacity to employ specialized personnel. They will have opportunities to work with each other, and they will have access to professors from the university, and to volunteer specialists attracted by the power and prestige of the university. On the faculty staff are experts in the technologies, sciences, and marketing.

Because this is university property, utilities, roads, and parking facilities are already in place. When additional help is needed, hundreds of undergraduate and graduate students are available for part-time assistance. The university has a fine reputation, a good library, on-campus eating facilities, and fiscal stability that is not always present in normal commercial facilities. All in all, the incubator is worth checking out through your local university, SBA, SCORE, or SBDC office.

If you are unable to find out where the nearest university or other incubator facility is located, write or call the Office of Private Sector Initiatives at the U.S. Small Business Administration, 1441 L Street, NW, Washington, DC 20416 (202) 653-7880.

HOME BUSINESSES

A home business is one that is based in your home, although not necessarily carried on there. You might have fixed up a corner of the kitchen or bedroom with a desk and filing cabinet, or outfitted a spare room or the garage.

A lot of service businesses are conducted out of the home— e.g., piano tuning, consulting, sports instruction, and guided tours. The important thing is, whatever business you set up in your home should be operated discreetly. It should have proper zoning, should not attract a lot of traffic to which neighbors might object, should have space for vehicles you might be needing, should not create any noise or pollution, and, equally important, should not interfere with your own family's daily life.

An extension to your regular phone might be all that you need, although a separate business phone is more professional. An answering machine is useful, but a photocopy machine and computer are luxuries you might be able to do without at the beginning, when capital conservation is vital. Other considerations will be professional-looking stationery that reflects the identity of your business, a good typewriter, a separate business checking account tied in with a simple but efficient bookkeeping system, a post office box (this is more businesslike than a known, residential address), and—of special note—a personal, internalized time clock.

The last item is really critical. It is your determination to take your business seriously that will make it succeed. This means you can't dawdle over a second cup of coffee reading the papers, entertain the neighbor who comes calling at 11, or respond to requests for assistance from all members of your extended family at all times.

Doing business from home can be difficult because of the potential distractions. The high percentage rate of small-business bankruptcies is due primarily to the number of defections by home-based entrepreneurs. They often find that the demands of their businesses are greater than they had anticipated or are able to fulfill "on the side," so that at the end of a few months or a year, they close up shop. As Pogo said, "I have met the enemy and he is us!"

Statistics notwithstanding, some of the home-based, self-employment possibilities are as follows:

Retail. You can use your garage, basement, or spare room. You buy wholesale and sell retail (usually at a discount). You can even load merchandise into a van and visit customer groups, events, and meets. Automotive supplies are frequently sold from vans right at the various mechanics' shops. So are snacks and foods sold from vans. (See the section on mobile businesses, below.)

Mobile Businesses. Goods are stocked on a truck or van and brought to your retail customer's door. In rural areas, especially, this is a real convenience for the retailer and has taken the place of the old-time peddler.

Distribution Sales. A specific line of merchandise can be sold from a mobile vehicle both to wholesalers and retailers. Some manufacturer's reps work this way.

Professionals. This category includes dispensing consulting or other services, such as bookkeeping, professional advice, troubleshooting, counseling, and educational instruction, to others.

Services. Lawn maintenance, tree surgery, painting, carpentry, interior decorating, electrical repairs, plumbing, and domestic work are all needed services that can be based in a home—even though the actual work is done at the customer's residence.

Manufacturing. Because of zoning, space, and noise considerations, this must be limited to such relatively "quiet and clean" operations as knitting, tailoring, baking, ceramics, cabinet making, and hobby assembling.

Agriculture. If the zoning in your home location permits, the growing and selling of fresh produce or the processing of food products is a promising business and one that can involve the entire family. This category might include selling pond-raised fish, or growing herbs, flowers, and cost-effective fruits and vegetables.

Door-to-Door Sales. If you are a representative of Mary Kay, Avon, Fuller, etc., you are in business from your home.

Artistic Production. A writer or artist can create stories, paintings, and nonmonumental sculptures from a quiet, at-home studio. Travel to libraries, galleries, and art fairs will probably be required, and welcomed. Creative work can be lonely.

Teaching. Tutoring small children or students in high schools; providing dance, music, or crafts instruction; giving small seminars at home or at trade events, are all included in this category.

Telemarketing. This work always involves the telephone. You can make calls for other companies that sell merchandise, sell your own merchandise, or conduct surveys for market researchers. While you may have to field occasional unpleasant responses, telemarketing is a profitable and fast-growing business that can be carried out effectively and economically from your home.

Some organizations have been formed to educate and encourage people starting home-based businesses. You might want to contact the following to see what it can offer you, and to find out if any organization exists for your particular state.

National Association of Home-Based Businesses
Box 30220
Baltimore, MD 21270
Cynthia Brower (301) 363-3698

FLEA MARKETS

Because flea markets are often held outdoors, more of them are to be found in the good-weather states. Because flea markets are often held on weekends, entrepreneurs in this field are likely to have other jobs. Some people, however, make flea-market selling a full-time occupation; there are flea markets that are open all week, with permanent indoor locations. The business also may require considerable time during nonoperating hours for merchandise to be purchased, processed, ticketed, and transported.

Stands and facilities may or may not be furnished. But grounds maintenance, security, and publicity are always handled by the promoters. Stall owners pay only for the space they occupy, which has a surcharge built-in to take care of the centralized services. For the small distributor or retailer, or even small manufacturer and craftsperson, such a facility is a godsend. It allows him or her to test out products, get leads, and buy short lots for resale, all while investing a minimum of capital.

London and Paris have been famed for their flea markets for generations. Florida and California flea markets have proliferated into gigantic businesses that are both marketplaces and strolling destinations. Look in the Yellow Pages of any major city's telephone directory under "Flea Market," and there is probably a listing. It takes little "scratch" to become a flea-market entrepreneur.

MAIL-ORDER BUSINESSES

Buying something for $1 and selling it for three or four times that much to some unknown customer far away, sounds like a trip to a Disney wonderland, conjuring visions of mailboxes stuffed with checks and dollar bills. It ain't necessarily so.

The sad statistics indicate that this business approach has perhaps the highest bankruptcy rate of any form of entrepreneurship. It can require more know-how than normal retailing or manufacturing, along with the same amount of concentration, effort, time, and investment.

The arithmetic of the mail-order business is such that you have to make a very substantial markup in order to survive and profit. In retailing, an item manufactured for $2 will normally wholesale for $4. The retail price again doubles to $8. In mail order, you are equivalent to the manufacturer, selling directly to the retailer. Thus, if the item you make yourself or buy advantageously for $2 can be sold for $6, or even $8, you have a chance of success.

Because you do not have a retail store that customers can visit, you must rely entirely on advertising in publications and electronic media, or on direct-mail pieces and catalogs. All of these marketing tools are very expensive and are subject to tricky variables and competition. Moreover, the percentage of actual orders is so small that you must reach a huge audience to get sufficient orders to make a profit. It has been said that the average catalog return is 2 percent. If this figure is correct, then huge mailings are needed to make that average 2 percent return worthwhile (100,00 or more, depending on the exclusivity of your list, your profit margin, and your capital).

One of the biggest and least controllable expenses in mail order is the amount of inventory that must be stocked on speculation. If you buy your merchandise from outside sources, it is desirable to have a drop-ship arrangement (in which the manufacturer or supplier sends the item to your customer directly and only when a bona fide order is received), or to have merchandise-return privileges after a limited time. Unfortunately, that is not the usual case. The result is that, while some of the merchandise is sold at a high profit, more is left over and must be sold at a loss or dumped by selling it to a surplus dealer, often at 10 cents on the dollar.

There are many good books on mail-order marketing. It will behoove you to peruse some of them before jumping into this sea. At the least, make sure you get accurate figures on what it costs to produce a catalog; make up a professional mailing piece, including handling and postage; buy a good, current mailing list with a return guarantee; and insert even a small ad in a national magazine. If you use the latter, use one that has an established mail-order section, because then you know it already has an audience for this kind of merchandise, and you won't be spending your money to pioneer the market! You might even see if the publications you survey have mail-order classified pages. That way, you can test your offer at a far lower cost, especially if your product or service does not need an illustration to sell the item.

Costs for both display and classified ads can be obtained from the Standard Rate and Data Service catalog (either the newspaper or the magazine section) that most major libraries have on the reference shelf. Or you can buy a copy of the particular magazine, study it, and write to the advertising department for rates, circulation data, and deadlines.

At the beginning, don't think of producing a color catalog— unless you have beaucoup bucks, enough variety of merchandise to put into the catalog, and enough profit built into the products. Also, don't do it unless you can expect plenty of reorders in the future *without* the ads or the catalog. The latter expense can amount to half of your gross income. Eliminate that and you can show a profit on lower returns. But that will be in the future. . . .

MOBILE OR TEMPORARY-STRUCTURE BUSINESSES

Go into any major shopping mall, and you will see free-standing kiosks or stands that sell everything from junk jewelry, novelties, and import goods to art and hot dogs. These structures are rented out either for short terms or as long as a year at very substantial per-square-foot rates. However, even if you have to pay $500 to $1000 a month, this cannot compare to the $15 to $30 per-square-foot annual cost of a 1000- to 5000-square-foot store.

In a short-term situation, you will need no fixturing, or very little. Utilities are usually built into the lease. You have no storage space, but the owner might make some available to you on the premises at a small increase in rental. One person usually can handle the sales. Obviously, you must feature the kind of merchandise that has a quick turn over and, usually, that is not competitive with the long-term store tenants.

Pushcarts are available in some malls, or in the concourses of airports and train stations. These lend themselves to flowers, souvenir goods, and take-with snacks, or even to arty handmades and costume jewelry. Make entrepreneurs have a number of pushcarts operating in various locations. They hire attractive high school and college students to do the selling, and they only have to make the rounds during the morning to stock up the cart and again in the evening to remove leftover stock and collect the cash. These modern push-cart vendors have taken the place of the old-fashioned coin-op machine routes.

Mobile sales units, such as vans filled with merchandise displays and food trucks equipped both to refrigerate and heat foods, have made comfortable livings for some entrepreneurs. One man-and-wife team clears $30,000 a year working out of one food truck, and only during the early-morning-through-lunch hours. They travel to construction sites and a few factory sites. All of their foods are prepared in their own kitchen, made fresh each day. Plastic-wrapped snacks and canned drinks are bought wholesale and retailed at "keystone" (i.e., double) markups. It's not glamourous, but this pair work at their own pace; further, their only investment is in the truck—which is easily amortized, like any motor vehicle.

PARTY SALES AND DEMONSTRATIONS

Vast sales organizations have been established nationwide by Tupperware, Mary Kay Cosmetics, Avon, Fuller, and numerous other companies dealing in silver jewelry, lingerie, toys, and gourmet products. Their representatives are nominally independent, appointed entrepreneurs. Sometimes they are asked to stock a basic amount of product inventory to assure their continued participation and interest.

If you are outgoing, have a home that can accommodate enough people to make a live demonstration worthwhile, and like to entertain, then this is a quick way of going into business on the coattails of an established company.

The best way to get into one of these businesses is to ask around. Get invited to some "home parties" and watch how it's done. Observe the reactions of the guests. Count how much they spend. See what the incentives are. There is a technique to it that can maximize your income, which can be substantial without any immense investment on your part, or the detail work that other businesses mandate.

The percentages earned on at-home sales and demonstrations often are pyramidal—that is, they go up as the volume you sell rises. Sometimes incentives are offered in the form of free merchandise or premium gifts. *Example*: Mary Kay sales reps can wind up driving pink Cadillacs.

INVENTIONS AND PATENTS, COPYRIGHTS AND TRADEMARKS

6

INVENTIONS AND PATENTS

Riding on the back of an invention—either your own or one you "rent" or "borrow" from an inventor—is a traditional way of becoming an entrepreneur. It is also a risky way that might take a lot more money and time than you would like to devote to it.

There are two ways that you can latch onto an invention that is not your own: Make a percentage arrangement with the inventor, or make a royalty arrangement with a larger company that has the necessary financing and marketing capabilities.

If you try to make a deal with an inventor, you might find the person very secretive about his or her "baby." Inventors are often loath to relinquish sufficient information or a workable prototype to someone else, or to invest enough time in pragmatic research themselves to make the considerable work involved in launching a new device or process a reality. In one classic case, the inventor of a double-glazed glass panel took up the time of a marketer for three years, until the latter gave up in disgust. Within a couple of years, a very large company came out with a very similar idea, and it has since become a staple in the industry.

If you have what you believe is a feasible and marketable process or product, you can go two ways: You can invest considerable money yourself or with a financial partner to investigate and file for a patent, or you can hire a patent attorney to do the research for you—at a cost of several thousand dollars, of course.

A patent on your product or process is good for 17 years. It gives you exclusive right to manufacture and/or distribute your invention in a manner you determine. It can take many months to file and search a patent; the length of time depends on the complexity of the product or process. Brochures can be obtained from the U.S. Department of Commerce (see below) that will guide you through the process of protecting your invention and then marketing it.

In the marketplace a patent has a real value. You can sell your rights, or franchise the manufacture or process, or assign a value to the patent that will be included in the worth of your business if you should sell it. Having a patent puts you in what is called a "proprietary position." It limits competition and gives you an edge on the possible profits that may be derived from the manufacture and sale of the patent or process.

A classic case is Polaroid, which produced an instant camera in the 1950s. It was 30 years before Kodak was able to invent one that used a different enough technology that the company would not be infringing on Polaroid's proprietary position. Even so, there were costly court battles that wasted millions of dollars, and then years of marketing efforts were required before each of these giants "settled down" in this field.

Where to Get Help with Patents and Inventions

A number of government offices can help inventors or companies interested in leasing a patent and in learning how to develop, protect and market their innovations. Listed below are two sources that will steer you in the right direction:

> Department of Commerce
> National Bureau of Standards
> Building 220, Room 319A
> Gaithersburg, MD 20899
> (301) 975-5020

This bureau is located about 20 miles north of Washington, DC. Its Manufacturing Technology Center can apply automated manufacturing technology to small- and medium-sized private companies. It runs an ultra high-tech workshop that exemplifies the technology and innovations of the next decade, including robotics. The center can provide assistance of a technological or financial nature and can help with networking.

> Department of Commerce
> Patent and Trademark Office
> Washington, DC 20231
> (703) 557-4636

The Patent and Trademark Office facilitates getting information you might need for processing patent and trademark applications, and it provides forms. While the use of a patent attorney is encouraged, an inventor may file and follow up on his or her own application for registration. Under the Patent and Trademark Office, there are four basic services available to inventors and patent holders:*

Patent Subscription Service
Provides patents automatically by subclass
Patent and Trademark Office, Department of Commerce,
Attn: Vangard Technologies Corporation, 14th & Constitution Avenue, N.W., Room 1627, Washington, DC 20231
Contact Mr. Robert Sardelli at (202) 377-2481.
Assistance: Technical
By establishing a deposit account with the Patent and Trademark Office, businesses can be sent full copies of all patents as they are issued. Selection is made using any of the more than 112,000 subclasses.

Patent Depository Library Programs
Nationwide network provides access to copies of and guidance in searching U.S. patents
Patent and Trademark Office, Department of Commerce, Crystal Mall Building 2, Room 306, Washington, DC 20231
Contact (703) 557-9686.

* Reprinted from Directory of Federal and State Business Assistance 1988–1989 (U.S. Department of Commerce)

Assistance: Networking
The program office administers a nationwide network of university, state, public, and special libraries which have been designated Patent Depository Libraries (PDLs) by the U.S. Patent and Trademark Office (PTO). Through the PDLs, the PTO is able to increase dissemination of the technological information contained in U.S. patents to the users in scientific, industrial, academic, economic, patent law, historical, and general public communities around the United States. These PDLs acquire and are responsible for maintaining collections of U.S. patents and related publications which assist patrons in performing patent searches. These libraries offer to the public free access to patents and provide reference assistance and photocopy services. PDLs receive current issues of U.S. patents on microfilm; however, the retrospective scope and format of their patent collections varies from library to library. In addition, the libraries retain all publications of the PTO including the Index to the U.S. Patent Classification, Manual of Classification, Classification Definitions, and the Official Gazette as well as informational pamphlets and brochures. PDLs also purchase scientific and technical monographs and periodicals to support their patent collections.

Public Affairs Office
How to file for a patent
Patent and Trademark Office, Department of Commerce, Washington, DC 20231
Contact (703) 557-5168.
Assistance: Information/Networking
The office examines patent applications and, grants protection for qualified inventions. It also collects, assembles, and disseminates the technological information disclosed on patent grants. Printed copies of individual patents may be purchased directly from PTO. Printed collections of all new patents are issued each week in the Official Gazette which is available by subscription from the Government Printing Office. A booklet, General Information Concerning Patents, is available from the Superintendent of Documents, Washington, DC 20202 for $2.00.

Trademark Information
Patent and Trademark Office, Department of Commerce, Washington, DC 20231
Contact (703) 557-4636.
Assistance: Information/Networking
Businesses interested in registering a trademark or applying for a patent may contact this office for the information and forms required.

Two information booklets, Basic Facts about Trademarks and Basic Facts about Patents, are available. Applications for trademark registration must be filed in the name of the owner of the mark. The owner may file and prosecute his own application for registration, or he may be represented by an attorney. Applications for patents must be filed by the inventor, and applicants are encouraged to seek the services of an attorney or agent registered to practice before the Patent and Trademark Office The Office cannot aid in the selection of an attorney or agent.

Other Resources for Inventors

Aside from the services offered by the Department of Commerce, there is assistance available from the following sources:

"How to Get a Patent," is available free from the Consumer Information Center, Dept. 126E, Pueblo, CO 81009. This pamphlet tells briefly about America's patent law.

Inventors Club of America, Box 3799, Springfield, MA 01101. A nonprofit organization designed to help inventors help themselves, the Inventors Club is a valuable resource for inventors who want to develop and market their ideas themselves. Publishes "Inventors News."

Inventors Assistance League, Inc., 345 W. Cypress St., Glendale, CA 91204. The league arranges meetings with inventors and assists in the patenting process and in finding licensees.

"Patent Attorneys and Agents Registered to Practice Before the U.S. Patent Office," can be ordered from the Superintendent of Documents, U.S. Government Printing Office, Washington, DC 20402, or purchased at a government bookstore near you. This is an alphabetically and geographically arranged directory of all current patent attorneys.

Center for Innovation and Entrepreneurship, Maine Technical Center, Orono, ME 04473; attention: Prof. Ray Noddin. This Maine-based volunteer group of inventors meet to exchange ideas and help each other. The organization can serve as a prototype for comparable organizations in other states.

Many states also have bureaus that will help local inventors with technology transfers, patent information, business planning, and networking. For a state-by-state listing of these, see Chapter 15, "Free Help," under "Centers for High-Tech Assistance."

COPYRIGHTS

The protection of a copyright is available—and *automatically granted*—to any created materials in a fixed form, such as literary works; musical pieces and their words; dramatic works and their accompanying music; pantomimes and choreographic works if they have been notated or somehow recorded; pictorial, sculptural, and graphic works; motion pictures and other audiovisual creations; and sound recordings on wax, tape, or other material.

A copyright covers these materials for the life of the creator plus 50 years. This means that nobody can copy or imitate these works without written permission from the copyright owner and, sometimes, paying a fee or royalty to that owner. The main advantage of registering works is in case of a need to take legal action.

If you have published or disseminated a created work without a copyright notice and fear infringement, you can protect yourself in two ways: either by making a reasonable effort to place a copyright notice on all undistributed copies, or by registering the work with the Copyright Office within five years of publication. (A copyright notice consists of the mark © or the word "copyright," your name, and the year in which the work was originally made.)

Many professional writers and artists do not bother to copyright their works. They depend on their reputations, and on the automatic rights grants to created material. The Copyright Office recommends registering even unpublished works, just to be safe, but it is a personal choice. In the event of an infringement, if you are not registered, you can only sue for actual damages, which is a difficult and costly thing to prove.

To obtain a copyright for your printed, written, recorded, or depicted work, you need to file Form TX. With this form you send in a copy of your work (imprinted with a copyright notice) and a check for $10. You can get Form TX by writing to the Register of Copyrights, Library of Congress, Washington, DC 20559.

With more than half a million applications being filed each year, don't expect an acknowledgment before 90 days. Should there be any questions about your application, a copyright examiner will call you. The completed certificate of registration will be mailed to you in due time.

The Copyright Office will also send you Circulars R1 and R96, which explain, in typical bureaucratese, all the copyright basics, methods of affixation, etc. If you are in a hurry, you can telephone (202) 287-9100 and ask to have Form TX and the other pertinent materials mailed to you.

TRADEMARKS

A trademark is a pictorial element—a symbol, picture or stylistic device that may or may not be combined with letters or words—that identifies a manufacturer's or merchant's goods. A graphic trademark or trade name can only be registered if it is used at least once, and in interstate commerce.

One example of a trademark is the "GE" written in script and surrounded by a circle, that identifies products manufactured by General Electric Corporation. Another example is the typical fancy, handwritten names fashion designers use as their ID, incorporating them into labels, tags, packaging, signs, and ads.

Franchisors protect their trademarks jealously. Quick-print out-fits like PIP, or company branch offices like Weight Watchers, are protected by having their name trademarks registered. Lawyers usually take care of this process, but if you want to look into it yourself, you can write to the Patent and Trademark Office, Superintendent of Documents, Washington, DC 20559, for appropriate information booklets and application forms.

While a registered trademark offers legal protection against direct imitators, it also has a psychological impact. Having this pictorial and printed ID on your product establishes you as a solid enterprise; it imparts a measure of prestige and, therefore, helps to increase the profit for the item or service. It also adds to the value of the company in the marketplace, in case you decide to sell all or a portion of your company.

LEGAL STRUCTURE OF THE BUSINESS | 7 |

THE OPTIONS

The options for structuring your business are as follows:

1. **Sole proprietorship.** The business is owned by a single person, and he or she has sole responsibility, as well as liability, for its operation.

2. **Partnership.** Two or more owners, who may have different amounts of fiduciary interest in the business, finance and manage the business according to a legal agreement that spells out the responsibilities and limitations of each partner.

3. **Corporation.** A business incorporated under the laws of the state in which it is registered sells shares of stock to a number of partners and investors and is managed by a board of directors responsible to the stockholders.

General Considerations

When you start out in a new business, the most important considerations are your own needs, your personality, the purpose of the business, and the protection of your assets (and those of others if there are outside investors). At the beginning, you should remember that no business organization is graven in stone. If, in the future, circumstances change—your fledgling grows, employees are hired, more outside capital is brought in—you can then change from one legal structure to another, more suitable one.

In deciding which legal structure to choose at the beginning, you should know and take into account the answers to the following:

- Are there any legal restrictions for your kind of business?
- Do you need outside investors or loans?
- What liabilities will you be assuming?
- What other people will be associated with your venture?
- How will you divide the expected profits?
- What tax advantages or disadvantages does the proposed legal structure have?
- How will the proposed legal structure affect business continuity?

The three forms of ownership will be considered in turn.

SOLE PROPRIETORSHIP

You might want to keep your new business small and simple for any or all of the following reasons: (1) you have family and other obligations and do not want to devote too many hours to the new business; (2) you have a good income from other sources and just want to "do something" to keep busy, while adding a little cushion to your existing income; (3) you dislike complicated arrangements and don't want a lot of employees, paperwork, or other people's involvement in telling you how to run your business.

This is your privilege, and in such a situation, the sole proprietorship is certainly the structure for you. It is the easiest, least costly, and least regulated form. With this kind of setup you have 100 percent of the responsibility. The buck stops with you. But—you also have all of the liabilities, and sometimes it gets lonely up at the top. So consider the following pros and cons of the sole proprietorship (and see Figure 18):

1. Have you considered any liabilities that might arise in the conduct of your business?
2. Will anybody else be empowered to sign checks in your absence?
3. What arrangements can you make in the event that you are absent or ill?
4. What functions do other members of your family have in the operation of your business?
5. What arrangements have you contemplated for the potential succession of your business's management?
6. Have you set up a separate checking account to avoid conflicts with personal expenses?
7. Since you will be "chief cook and bottlewasher," are there functions that should be allocated to others? Family members, employees, or outside professionals?
8. What provisions have you made or will you make to protect yourself with health and retirement income insurance?
9. Are you contemplating any profit sharing in order to retain key employees?
10. Have you looked into insurance policies that protect you from employees' suits, thefts, or other claims?

Figure 18. Checklist for a sole proprietorship

Advantages

- It is the easiest structure to start up
- Offers greatest freedom to do what you want; you have all the power and authority
- There is a tax advantage as long as you remain small
- There are advantages in the Social Security benefits
- There are virtually no government restrictions

Disadvantages

- You have all the liability; if anything at all goes wrong, if employees have accidents or goof up, you're the goat
- Business growth is limited by your personal energy

- If illness or death strikes, goodbye business
- It's easy to let personal affairs get mixed up with business

PARTNERSHIPS

There are two types of partnership—general and limited. The general partnership is the most common.

General Partnerships

This form provides for two or more entrepreneurs to pool their capital, skills, and experiences. It is quite simple to set up. If a trade name is used other than your own name(s), it should be registered, of course. The biggest single problem will be to spell out at the start how the partners are expected to operate, who owns what, and how they will share both the gains and responsibilities. Here are some pros and cons of this setup:

Advantages

- Simple to set up
- Greater financial assets are available
- Credit's easier to get than with a similarly sized corporation
- Eliminates hiring others
- Share experiences, skills; "two heads are better than one"

Disadvantages

- It is difficult to delineate responsibilities and contributions
- Withdrawal of a partner for any reason jeopardizes organization
- It is often hard to get rid of a partner—as bad as getting a divorce

A written partnership agreement is not required by law, but it is useful, to prevent future misunderstandings. Transition of ownership, continuity of business operation, and protection of individual assets and dependents can be assured by such an agreement. Be aware that many states have a code on partnerships that must be followed. It probably is a good idea to have a neutral party, such as a mutually acceptable attorney, draw up the papers for each partner. Once such an agreement has been drawn up and duly signed by all participants, it is an enforceable contract.

See Figure 19 for a checklist of essential information for a partnership agreement. Consult your attorney and accountant to make sure all bases are covered before final documents are drawn up and signed!

---

1. Have you agreed on a name for the partnership?
2. What is the duration of Partnership? What is the specific number of years, or time "until dissolved"?
3. What is the address of your business office?
4. What is the capital contribution of each partner?
5. How will you handle additional contributions in the future if these should become necessary?
6. At what level will you maintain your partnership account?
7. How will each partner participate in profits and losses?
8. What salaries will each partner receive?
9. Will these salaries affect any profit distribution?
10. What fringe benefits will be available to each?
11. How much time is each partner expected to contribute?
12. What are the duties and responsibilities of each?
13. How will you handle any additional "loans" or "draws" if a partner asks for them, or if there is an emergency situation?
14. What is your policy on hiring family members?
15. What limitations on outside business activities do you place on each partner, especially if these activities can be construed as competitive or detrimental?
16. In case of dispute or impasse, whose decision will rule?
17. What procedure do you have for admitting new or junior partners?
18. In case of dissolution of the partnership for whatever reason, how will you evaluate the company's good will?
19. What is your method of liquidating the departing or departed partner's interest?

Figure 19. Checklist for a partnership agreement

20. Will you have any age limit at which a partner must retire? If so, how will his or her equity be paid out?
21. Will the surviving partner have the right to continue using the departed partner's name? If so, under what terms?
22. If a partner departs prior to retirement, will there be a noncompetition clause in your agreement?
23. If one partner's presence is harming the business, what means of termination do you have available?
24. How will you handle the long-term disability of one partner?
25. Have you agreed on the method of keeping accounts? This will affect compensation and withdrawal agreements and needs to be detailed by your accountant.
26. What is your fiscal year?
27. If a partner has a debit or credit account with the business, will interest be charged?
28. Where will the business keep its accounts?
29. Who will sign the checks?
30. Do all partners have access to all books?
31. How will you decide who to hire as your attorney, accountant, advertising person, etc.?
32. If you operate as a general or limited partnership or decide to change to that method, who will be designated as a general partner? And who will be admitted as limited partners?
33. If a partner withdraws, how will his or her interest be assigned to another partner?
34. Can a partner's interest be pledged or assigned to an outsider? Or must it be offered first to an existing partner?
35. Under what cirumstances can a partner sign contracts or make commitments that affect the liability of the business?
36. In purchasing partnership insurance, what are the amounts and who will be the beneficiary? Who will pay the premiums?

Figure 19. (*Continued*)

Limited Partnerships

The basic difference between this form of organization and the general partnership is that, in a limited partnership, only one general partner runs the business and is responsible for it. The other "partners" are in reality investors whose liability is limited to the amount of their financial participation. A share or investment in a limited partnership can be sold without the consent of the other partners.

This business structure is still quite simple to set up even though a legal agreement is required. (See Checklist, Figure 19.) It operates under general state codes and usually is registered with the secretary of state of its home state, as well as with the appropriate county recorder's office. The limited partnership is not taxed.

Because of its legal simplicity, it is quite popular in speculative enterprises, real estate developments, venture capital groups, and business/professional circles whose members have extra money to put to work. Some of the pros and cons are listed here:

Advantages

- Limited partner has liability only up to the amount of money invested
- Attracting investors is a good way to get new capital without interference
- The business is not taxed directly

Disadvantages

- Limited partner has no control over the business
- The general liability rests with one person, the general partner
- It is a more complex organization than the general partnership

CORPORATIONS

While the legal structure of all corporations is pretty much the same, there are evident differences between a General Motors Corporation and the small, closely held corporation that has three employees and does $200,000 in sales. Here we are concerned primarily with the latter kind. The closely held corporation is usually a family affair. The owner (or owners) is intimately involved with the day-to-day operation of the business. Stock is sold only to a few friends, local people, and perhaps others who have a specific interest in the new company. Usually the number of investors is 15 or less.

Definition and Rules

The most important characteristic of a corporation is that it is a legally separate entity from the individuals who own and operate it. Your personal liability is usually limited to the amount you have invested in the company. You are protected, therefore, if one of your employees fouls up, if a customer gets hurt on your premises or is harmed by one of your products, or if you have to declare bankruptcy and renege on your loan.

When you have a corporation, you have to follow certain state regulations, which vary from state to state. However, some requirements are standard, such as having at least one incorporator and one director, or, depending on the state, three officers and three directors. A meeting must be held once a year, in person or by mail or phone, and a record (minutes) book must be kept that lists the corporation's activities and any legal changes in operation and management. If the principal incorporator or incorporators should die, the business can continue. Stock shares can be transferred to other family members or outside investors (you can put this matter in your will, and the shares can be disposed of according to your wishes).

A corporation must pay taxes on its earnings. This is, in effect, double taxation because the stockholders will have to pay taxes again on any dividends they receive from their stock. A good tax attorney or accountant can advise you on minimizing this tax burden.

The cost of incorporating can be as low as $100 if you file your own papers with the state, or $500 to $1000 if you have an attorney draw up the papers for you, set up the stock certificates, etc. Corporation status does not last forever. It should be renewed each year by filing an annual report, paying a small recording fee, and thus going on record with the secretary of your state that the corporation still exists and is continuing to operate. A corporation can be dissolved by filing an application with the secretary of state, declaring an intent to dissolve and giving articles of dissolution.

More on Personal Liability

While the individual incorporator is usually safe from liability, in practice this protection does not always work. Let's say you own a small corporation that is seeking to sign a lease for $100,000 over the next five years, or to borrow money from a bank. It is unlikely that a small corporation will have sufficient liquid assets to cover the loan or lease, or can afford to tie up these assets for the duration of the commitment. To compensate for this lack of guaranteed collateral, the property owner or banker will require the principal incorporator, and perhaps other stockholders, to personally sign the documents. In this manner, despite the legal protection afforded the corporation, the individual investor becomes liable and is then no better off than a partner or owner. Sometimes this is one of the realities of doing business.

To avoid this situation, it is advantageous for a corporation, no matter of what size, to accumulate assets that can be put up as collateral in case a loan or legal commitment becomes necessary. Equipment or rolling stock with a low depreciation, or property that maintains substantial residual value, should be part of the planned assets of a closely held corporation if the owner or owners want to minimize personal risks.

To sum up, the pros and cons of a corporation are as follows:

Advantages

- Shared personal resources
- Shared financial resources
- Continuity unrelated to persons involved
- Increased management capabilities
- Easier transfer of business
- Limited personal liability
- Easier addition of outside investment
- Transfer of shares possible by sale or gifting

Disadvantages

- Greater expense in forming and operating
- Possible lulling of owners into a false sense of security
- Heavier tax load
- Limited power as detailed in corporate charter

- Vulnerability to suits
- Less freedom of activities, more government control

See Figure 20 for a countrywide list of "How and Where to File Incorporation Papers."

S Corporations

"S" can stand for *small*; actually it refers to subchapter S of the U.S. Tax Code. You have the option of incorporating as an S corporation if the following is true:

- There are fewer than 35 shareholders;
- The corporation has only one class of stock;
- It is a domestic corporation.

The S corporation is a legal device, subject to the approval of individual states, that has some advantages under specific conditions: if you anticipate high earnings (dividends) right from the start, or if you expect substantial operating losses during the formative years. The reason is that profits and losses in an S corporation shift to the stockholder(s), who claim them, instead of the corporation. If you are in a 28 percent tax bracket and the corporation is in a 35 percent tax bracket, you can see that there is an immediate 7 percent tax advantage.

During the formative stages of a corporation, therefore, the "S" factor is of considerable benefit, as it allows the corporation to retain more earnings. Such complexities make it clear that a good lawyer and accountant are needed to steer you through the tricky floes of S corporation entrepreneurship. The following is a list of advantages and disadvantages of the S corporation:

Advantages

- Lowers tax rate by shifting earnings to stockholders
- Helps new corporation to retain more earnings

State	What to File	Where to File It	Filing Fee (Domestic Corp.)	Filing Fee (Foreign Corp.)	Franchise Tax (Domestic)	Franchise Tax (Foreign)
AL	AI	County Probate Judge of county where business is located	$45	$45	$25+(1)	same
AK	AI	Department of Commerce and Economic Development Pouch D Juneau 99811	$35+	$35+	$100 (every 2 yrs.)	$200 (every 2 yrs.)
AZ	AI	Corporation Commission 2222 West Encanto Blvd. Phoenix 85009	$50	$50	NONE	NONE
AR	AI	SS Corporate Department State Capitol Bldg. Little Rock 72201	$15+	$50+	$11+(1)	same
CA	AI	SS 111 Capitol Mall Sacramento 95814	$65	$550	$200+(2)	same
CO	AI	SS 1575 Sherman Ave. Denver 80203	$22.50	$100	NONE	NONE

Figure 20. How and where to file incorporation papers

State	What to File	Where to File It	Filing Fee (Domestic Corp.)	Filing Fee (Foreign Corp.)	Franchise Tax (Domestic)	Franchise Tax (Foreign)
CT	CI	SS 30 Trinity St. PO Box 846 Hartford 06115	$50+	$150+	10% of net income	same
DE	CI	SS Dover 19901	$10+	$10+	$20+(1)	$30
FL	AI	SS Charter Section Tallahassee 32304	$35+	$45+	$10	same
GA	AI	SS 225 Peachtree St. NE Atlanta 30303	$15	$100	$10+(2)	same
HI	AI	Department of Regulatory Agencies 1010 Richards St. Honolulu 96813	$50+	$50+	NONE	NONE
ID	AI	SS State House Boise 83720	$60	$60	$20+(2)	same
IL	AI	SS Corporation Division Springfield 62706	1/10 of 1% of stated capital	1/10 of 1% of stated capital	$25+(3)	same

IN	AI	SS State House #155 Indianapolis 46204	$30+	NONE	NONE
IA	AI	SS Corporations Division Des Moines 50319	$25+	$5+(3)	same
KS	AI	SS Corporation Division Topeka 66612	$50	$20+(1)	same
KY	AI	SS Capitol Bldg. #150 Frankfort 40601	$10+	$10+(3)	same
LA	AI	SS Corporations Division PO Box 44125 Baton Rouge 70804	$10+	$1.50/$1,000 stock	same
ME	AI	SS Augusta 04333	$10+	NONE	NONE
MD	Form 1	Department of Assessments and Taxation 301 West Preston St. Baltimore 21201	$20	NONE	NONE

Figure 20. (*Continued*)

State	What to File	Where to File It	Filing Fee (Domestic Corp.)	Filing Fee (Foreign Corp.)	Franchise Tax (Domestic)	Franchise Tax (Foreign)
MA	Articles of Organization	Secretary of the Commonwealth Corporation Division 1 Ashburton Place Boston 02108	$150	$150+	NONE	NONE
MI	AI	Department of Commerce Corporation Division Box 3004 Lansing 48909	$25	$25	NONE	NONE
MN	AI	SS Corporation Division 180 Senate Office Bldg. St. Paul 55155	$62.50+	$125	NONE	NONE
MS	AI	SS PO Box 136 Jackson 39205	$25+	$25+	$10+(3)	same
MO	AI (Form 41)	SS Jefferson City 65101	$50+	$60+	$25+(1)	same
MT	AI	SS State Capitol Helena 59601	$50+	$50+	$10+(2)	same
NB	AI	SS Corporation Division 2304 State Capitol Bldg. Lincoln 68509	$20+	$20+	$10+(1)	same

NV	AI	SS Corporation Division Capitol Bldg., Capitol Complex Carson City 89710	$50+	$50+	NONE	NONE
NH	Record of Organization	SS Concord 03301	$60+	$100	$60+(1)	$150
NJ	CI	SS State House Trenton 08625	$25+	$165	$25+(4)	$50+(4)
NM	AI	State Corporation Commission Corporation and Franchise Tax Departments PO Drawer 1269 Santa Fe 87501	$50+	$100+	$10+(4)	same
NY	CI	SS Division of Corporations 162 Washington Ave. Albany 12231	$10+	$10+	10% net NY income	same
NC	AI	SS Corporations Division 116 West Jones St. Raleigh 27603	$40+	$40+	$10+(1)	same
ND	AI	SS Division of Corporations Bismarck 58505	$25+	$75+	NONE	NONE

Figure 20. (*Continued*)

State	What to File	Where to File It	Filing Fee (Domestic Corp.)	Filing Fee (Foreign Corp.)	Franchise Tax (Domestic)	Franchise Tax (Foreign)
OH	AI	SS Division of Corporations 30 East Broad St. Columbus 43215	$50+	$50+	$50+(3)	same
OK	AI	SS State Capitol Bldg., Rm. 101 Oklahoma City 73105	$3+	$18+	$10+(3)	same
OR	AI (Form 11-B)	Corporation Commission Commerce Bldg. Salem 97310	$10	$50	$10+(2)	$200
PA	AI and Registry Statement	Secretary of the Commonwealth of Pennsylvania Corporation Bureau Harrisburg 17120	$75	$150	1¢/$10 stock	same
RI	AI	SS Providence 02903	$80+	$15+	$100+(1)	same
SC	AI	SS Box 11350 Columbia 29201	$45+	$45+	$10+ (based on dividends)	same

SD	AI	SS State Capitol Pierre 57501	$40+	$50+	NONE	NONE
TN	Charter	SS Corporation Division Nashville 37219	$10+	$300	$10+(1)	$25+ (based on gross receipts in TN)
TX	AI	SS Corporation Division Sam Houston State Office Bldg. Austin 78711	$100	$500	$55+(3)	same
UT	AI	SS State Capitol Bldg., Rm. 203 Salt Lake City 84114	$25+	$25+	$25+(2)	same
VT	Articles of Association	SS Montpelier 05602	$20+	$60	NONE	NONE
VA	AI	State Corporation Commission Box 1197 Richmond 23209	$20+	$60+	$20+(1)	same
WA	AI	SS Corporation Division Legislative Bldg. Olympia 98504	$50+	$50+	$30+(1)	same

Figure 20. (*Continued*)

State	What to File	Where to File It	Filing Fee (Domestic Corp.)	Filing Fee (Foreign Corp.)	Franchise Tax (Domestic)	Franchise Tax (Foreign)
WV	AI	SS Corporation Division Charleston 25305	$30+	$260+	$20+(1)	$35+(1)
WI	AI (Form 2)	SS Corporation Division State Capitol Bldg. Madison 53702	$55+	$55+	2.3% or more of income	same
WY	AI	SS Division of Corporations Cheyenne 82002	$50+	$50+	$10+(4)	same

AI = Articles of Incorporation
CI = Certificate of Incorporation
SS = Secretary of State

Figure 20. (Continued)

- Limits number of shareholders and thus reduces operating costs and some liabilities
- Requires only one filing form with IRS (Form 2553), signed by all stockholders

Disadvantages

- Paying out profits to shareholders makes surpluses unavailable for corporate expansion
- The limiting of investors to 35 in number limits the attraction of more capital
- Excludes foreign residents as stockholders
- Does not allow subsidiaries
- Limits "passive" income from investments, and taxes this if such income exceeds 25 percent of gross receipts

THE PERSONAL SIDE OF BUSINESS START-UPS

8

WHO WILL BE WITH YOU?

A small enterprise usually starts with one person. It might develop into a giant conglomerate, as a small oak seed develops into a mighty tree, but, large or small, it has to start with the seed—that one intrepid, skilled, ambitious individual. That is *you*.

And yet, you are not alone. "No man is an island." The most successful enterprise will become burdensome and boring after a while if it is conducted in total isolation and in a social vacuum. The entrepreneur who is about to embark on the most demanding endeavor of his or her life cannot survive unless he or she has the support of friends and family. If you have ideas, you want to bounce them off someone else. If you are successful, you want to share your achievement with a close friend or spouse. If you have a long-range vision, you might want to ensure the survival of your dream through your children or other family members.

Before you start a new business or decide to make a major expansion in an existing business, think of how your goals and rewards fit into your family life. If your friends and family are with you, if they support and encourage your efforts, if they understand that what you are doing is for them as well—then your enterprise will indeed be crowned with success and rewards.

But if your business is successful and yet is not supported by your family, it ceases to be worthy and pleasurable. The hermetic entrepreneur is no paragon, to be emulated, but, rather, someone to be pitied, because he or she has not learned that the fruits of entrepreneurship are in the enhancement of the human being.

YOUR E.Q.

Since you are reading this book, you evidently are considering a monumental decision: becoming an entrepreneur. You want to start a business or buy a business. The most important, the most vital, the most irreplaceable ingredient is a three-letter word: *you*. So take twenty minutes to make sure about the you-factor. Figure 21 is a quick test—just for your eyes. It will give you an approximate idea of your own "E.Q."—your Entrepreneurial Quotient. If you "pass" it with high marks, you can be happy indeed. If you detect weaknesses in some areas, you may want to work on shoring up those weaknesses before you invest a lot of money, effort, and time. The items in this test add up to a prescription for success. What do you have to lose?

YOUR ENTREPRENEURIAL QUOTIENT TEST
There are 20 questions. Give each positive reply 5 points. Some of the questions are no doubt more important than others, but in this "test," nobody but you judges the answers. You can take this test as often as you wish. The closer you can come to 100 percent, the surer your success will be. This is one test in which only you are the evaluator!

1. Being an optimist is a good characteristic for an entrepreneur. Do you think you are one?

2. Personalities that go into businesses of their own are usually restless; they are quickly bored by routine and repetitive tasks. Are you?

3. Surveys have shown that many successful entrepreneurs are the children of immigrants. Are you? (Not much you can do about this one if you're not! But it is one of the facts uncovered in national surveys.)

Figure 21. Your Entrepreneurial Quotient Test

4. When you were in high school or college, were you very much involved in team and club activities? Or were you pretty self-contained, and even aloof? Entrepreneurial types were almost uniquely independent while in school.

5. How good a student were you in school? Were you an academic superachiever—a straight-A student or a Phi Beta Kappa? Most successful entrepreneurs were not.

6. If you can remember your very young years, did you play by yourself often? Entrepreneurs have often been unusually self-sufficient at a very early age.

7. While in junior and senior high school, did you have a newspaper route? Did you sell salve or cookies to your neighbors or baby-sit, or work after school at the local soda shop or pharmacy? Entrepreneurial spirit manifests itself during these formative teen years.

8. If you were self-sufficient and ambitious as a youngster, you probably were quite determined and even stubborn. Do you recall showing these traits?

9. How were you at managing your own money or your allowance? If you were skilled at this during your early years, you had good self-training in entrepreneurship.

10. When you have ideas and plans, do you make notes, write them down, go over them, check them off as you complete them? Writing things down makes them real—it is the mark of an organized person.

11. Do you consider yourself a little adventurous when it comes to trying new things? It's a good trait for people who plan to go into a business of their own.

12. Would you say you follow the advice and paths of others? Or do you prefer to strike out on your own and take a less conservative course? Venturers are usually *ad*venturers.

13. Getting started in a new business usually takes long hours and involves uncertain remuneration. Would you be willing to take that chance in a business of your own?

14. Most entrepreneurs have a mind that is always racing ahead of their ability to complete a project. Are you like that? Do you

Figure 21. (*Continued*)

sometimes start a new project before you even have completed the previous one?

15. Many entrepreneurs get started in a business because they were bored in their job situations. Did this happen to you?

16. Financing a new business is always risky. Do you have the faith in your new venture to risk your own capital?

17. If you were a bank loan officer, would you extend a loan to an entrepreneur such as you?

18. Would you be willing to convince family and friends that your new business is a worthwhile investment—and try to borrow from them?

19. How would you react if your new business failed after a while? Would you give up entrepreneurship, or would you start up another business, having learned from your past errors? You are only a failure when you stop trying.

20. Do you consider yourself a pragmatist? Do you research your ideas before implementing them? Do you read, ask questions, investigate, develop a business plan, check the competition before venturing forth? A successful entrepreneur is not a gambler, but a risk-minimizer.

Figure 21. (*Continued*)

NAMING THE BUSINESS: PERSONAL AND PRACTICAL CONSIDERATIONS

If you are buying somebody else's business and the name retention is not important for business, *you* get to choose your new business name. If you are starting from scratch, you *have* to choose a name. In a partnership, two or more partners will have to agree. In a corporation, the choices are up to the managing partners. (See also Chapter 2, the Comment preceding Figure 1.)

This part can be fun. Your business identity is like your ideal mirror image. You can be whoever you want in your business. You can express yourself. But don't get carried away. You also can and should enlist the opinions of your family and friends, because how your business name strikes other people is of great importance.

There are many practical, as well as personal, considerations in choosing a business name, and you could be living with the one you choose for a long time.

The company name is a selling tool, and the main concerns are to make it descriptive, appropriate to the kind of business you will conduct, and memorable to potential customers. The biggest practical consideration is what a name costs you: signs will have to be made up at a hefty expense; stationery will have to be printed; bags or other packaging will have to be imprinted; and vehicles will have to be lettered with the name. It is truly a major investment.

Name Promotion

The most costly aspect of your company name, however, is promoting its recognition by your customers. You have to sell even the most memorable name before it begins to sell you. It will take a great deal of advertising and networking to get your name across. Big companies spend millions on brand recognition, and this "consumer franchise" is worth many dollars in the appraised value of a business. Sometimes it is called "goodwill."

Name Duplication

Another important matter is name duplication. What are the names of your neighbors or competitors? You don't want any name for your business that is too close to one of theirs and might confuse customers. Of course, there is the story of the small shopkeeper whose little store was situated between two big, busy, and highly competitive stores. He knew he could not compete with them on their level. So he had a sign painter make a large canvas sign, which he had fastened over his store entrance. The sign read: MAIN ENTRANCE.

Jokes aside, you have to make sure the name you select hasn't already been taken. Registered names are protected, and you don't want a lawsuit. A search of local county records and area phone books and business directories can give you some assurance. It would be embarrassing, not to mention costly, to have signs and stationery made up, have your grand opening, and then get a letter from some corporation lawyer informing you that you cannot use your chosen name—even if it is your own!

A call to the office of your state's secretary of state or to the local chamber of commerce is also advised. Someone who is not even operating a business could have registered the same name years ago. If in doubt, first find out.

Name Registration

A new business name should be registered according to the laws of the state in which you do business. Your lawyer will advise you on what steps must be taken. Figure 20 in the previous chapter will tell you where in each state a corporate name is to be registered. Usually the office of the secretary of state receives the application for the registration of your business name. It is also advisable (and in many states mandatory) to publish the name of your new business in the Legal Notices columns of a local newspaper. This is even more important if your business name is a name other than your personal name.

Name Recognition

A factor that relates to all four categories of name choice discussed below is ease of recognition. You don't want a name that is too long or too difficult to pronounce, or that means something totally different from the kind of business you conduct. If yours is a service business, the listing you have in the Yellow Pages could make a difference. Some businesses have contrived a name like "AAAA-1" in the hope that they will be placed on top of the "A" listings.

Think of cost in this regard, too. Making a difficult name stick requires a lot more advertising and promotional dollars than selling a memorable name. It stands to reason that if you have a simple, vivid name that demands no further explanation, customers will recall you more quickly. The public is fickle enough, and competition is always around the corner. So don't complicate your business life with an impossible name.

The choice of a company name falls into one of four categories, which will be taken up in turn:

- Your personal name or names
- Descriptive names
- Geographic names
- Contrived, or artificial, names

Personal names. Some business owners, especially developers of residential real estate, have a penchant for using their children's or grandchildren's names, or the combined first syllables of their own and their spouse's names. This cutesy approach does not suit a professional enterprise and should be avoided.

However, if your new business is a professional practice, then your own name, and the names of your partners if you have any, is entirely appropriate, dignified, and even necessary. You can also use part of your name in conjunction with the kind of business you are setting up. For example: "Joe the Bootmaker," "Tom the Tailor," or "Claude's French Restaurant." If your business is some kind of design service, your name, if it is known in the trade, can be an asset. Sometimes a personal name becomes the name of the product. Henry Ford fared quite well with this approach. The magazines called *Forbes*, *Lear's*, and *Mirabella* are other examples. A fictitious character may even be created around a name, as in the cases of Mrs. Campbell, Sara Lee, and Betty Crocker. If the shoe fits, wear it.

Descriptive names. Avoid initials, even though many businesses use this device. The nationally known book chain B. Dalton is an example. Do you look this up in the phone book under "B" or "D"? The customer may decide to forget it. Perhaps B. Dalton can spend enough on advertising so that it doesn't worry whether some customers are confused, but can you afford this attitude? We feel that this kind of name works against ease of recognition at the lowest cost.

Apostrophes and articles of speech before names also add difficulty. "L'Hotel," "A Flower Shop," and "The French Bakery" are some examples. Will you look them up under "L," "A," and "T"? Or under "H," "F," and "F"?

Trendy names are problematic, too. Today's fad is tomorrow's attic treasure. Trendy, clever names might make you smile, or attract you for the duration of the fad, but what happens then? Perhaps these people only plan to be in business for a relatively short time, so that it doesn't really matter.

Geographic names. Place names have some advantages, especially with local businesses. However, if you have the kind of business that goes beyond the borders of your town or state, then a geographic name tends to parochialize you. It might even prevent an out-of-state customer from doing business with you, because your service sounds too far away. For a business with a limited local market, however, a geographic name is okay.

Contrived names. These are difficult to judge or recommend. Of course, there are always the examples of "Kodak" and "Xerox." These are known worldwide. They mean nothing by themselves; they are simply trade names for gigantic enterprises. And these enterprises have spent countless billions of dollars in getting the kind of name recognition they enjoy today. Artificial business names that have no meaning by themselves, that need long subtitles or massive advertising campaigns to become recognized and accepted, are best left to the giant corporations.

EMPLOYEES

If you are going to be a consultant, or are going to start a business that includes only you, and perhaps your spouse and kids on occasion, so be it; you will not be hiring anyone. But if your new business is the kind that is labor intensive, you'll need some policy regarding personnel, even if you start with one employee.

Hiring even one person is serious; it is almost like saying "I do" at the altar. After the honeymoon is over, problems can arise. If you then hire a second employee, and you do something extra for the first one but not the second, watch out. You might be accused of, and sued for, discrimination. Not only is the employer belabored with all kinds of taxes—federal, state, county, municipal—but he or she is also supposed to be an expert on and conform to all sorts of regulations that involve safety, discrimination, environment, etc. Check out the pros and cons of hiring carefully.

At least in the early, formative stages, consider using part-time workers who are employed 20 hours a week or less, or workers from a temporary employment agency, or specialized workers who can legitimately be called independent contractors. That route might be a trifle more costly in the short run, but it could be cheaper in the long run and save you time and grief.

MANAGING YOUR EMPLOYEES

In planning for your personnel needs, there are several factors to consider:

1. *What employees do you actually need?* Some entrepreneurs, especially those who come out of large organizations, tend to overstaff their fledgling businesses at the beginning. Getting and training employees is a costly and time-consuming process. It is vital to make sure you do not take on more personal and financial responsibilities than are absolutely necessary. To help you take a realistic approach, write a job description for each potential employee, showing what each one is supposed to achieve. (See Figure 22.)

2. *How are you going to find these employees?* Use the following:

   - Local classified newspaper columns—both placing Help Wanted ads and reading Situation Wanted ads
   - Supermarket and copy-shop bulletin boards
   - Networking with other entrepreneurs and local service providers
   - Local educational institutions
   - Public and private employment agencies (know what you commit yourself to when contacting private employment agencies!)
   - Current employees, if you have any already
   - Sign in the window or outside if you have an exposed location
   - Trade magazines, if you are looking for a specialized person

3. *Prepare an employees' manual.* Even if you hire only one person, a single sheet that spells out in nitpicking detail what your house rules are, is a necessary adjunct to your business. Figure 23 gives a possible format. It could save you grief later on. It would not be a bad idea to have the new employee sign one copy of the employment agreement. The impact and importance might be purely psychological, but it could also be a legal lifesaver at some unexpected moment in the future. In our lawsuit-happy society, the wise entrepreneur looks ahead. Remember—knowledge minimizes risk!

Job title: _____

Department (if any): _____

Reports to: _____

Function: _____

Remuneration: _____

Major duties and approximate time spent on each: _____

_____

_____

_____

_____

Other employees reporting to above: _____

_____

_____

_____

_____

Special requirements and conditions (including training):

_____

_____

_____

_____

Goals for position over next one to five years:

_____

_____

_____

_____

Figure 22. Job description

Working hours: _____

Vacation time: _____

Overtime: _____

Lunch period: _____

Meetings: _____

Sick leave: _____

Health benefits: _____

Insurance: _____

Training: _____

Other educational provisions: _____

Figure 23. Company policy statement

Dress code: _____

Addressing of supervisors/executives: _____

Employee discounts: _____

Other employee benefits: _____

Outside telephone calls: _____

Personal property provisions: _____

Parking arrangements: _____

Check-in/check-out procedure: _____

Employee bonding: _____

Layoff or dismissal policy: _____

Severance-pay policy: _____

Smoking/drinking on the job: _____

Outside visitors: _____

Add to or substract from this list to suit your own special requirements.

Figure 23. (*Continued*)

4. *Train your employees.* Some provision must be made. Who will do it? What is to be taught? How long should it take? What incentives will you offer for successful training and performance?

SOME CAUTIONS FROM PERSONNEL EXPERTS

- Always check references—but don't talk to personnel departments. They only have bare facts, but no face-to-face experience with the worker. Try to talk to the boss, supervisor, co-workers. Study the applicant's Personal Data Sheet and Application for Employment (Figures 24 and 25), or other equivalent forms.
- Prepare a written proposal to the employee so that you both have in writing what the job is all about.
- If you are ready to hire, make a verbal and written offer and have the latter signed by the employee—with a copy to him or her.
- If you have a contractual agreement, have your lawyer prepare it or check out the one you prepare.

SOME CAUTIONS

Name_____ Date of birth _____

Address _____

_____

Telephone number _____ Years there _____

Marital Status _____ Name of spouse _____ Dependents _____

Education   Grade completed/

	Name and address	diplomas/degrees obtained
High school		
Other		

Military service _____ Years _____

Highest rank obtained _____

Relevant training or work experience _____

_____

Work Experience

Business and address	Job title and duties	Supervisor	Dates

Trade, professional or civic membership and activities _____

_____

Hobbies, interests, other relevant information _____

_____

_____

Use another sheet if necessary.

Figure 24. Personal data sheet

APPLICATION FOR EMPLOYMENT
(PRE-EMPLOYMENT QUESTIONNAIRE)   (AN EQUAL OPPORTUNITY EMPLOYER)

PERSONAL INFORMATION

DATE

SOCIAL SECURITY NUMBER

NAME _____
LAST   FIRST   MIDDLE

PRESENT ADDRESS _____
STREET   CITY   STATE

PERMANENT ADDRESS _____
STREET   CITY   STATE

PHONE NO. _____   ARE YOU 18 YEARS OR OLDER   Yes ☐   No ☐

SPECIAL QUESTIONS

DO NOT ANSWER **ANY** OF THE QUESTIONS IN THIS FRAMED AREA UNLESS THE EMPLOYER HAS **CHECKED** A **BOX PRECEDING** A QUESTION, THEREBY INDICATING THAT THE INFORMATION IS REQUIRED FOR A BONA FIDE OCCUPATIONAL QUALIFICATION, OR DICTATED BY NATIONAL SECURITY LAWS, OR IS NEEDED FOR OTHER LEGALLY PERMISSIBLE REASONS.

☐ Height _____ feet _____ inches   ☐ Citizen of U.S. ____ Yes ____ No

☐ Weight _____ lbs.   ☐ Date of Birth* _____

☐ What Foreign Languages do you speak fluently? _____ Read _____ Write _____

☐ _____

*The Age Discrimination in Employment Act of 1967 prohibits discrimination on the basis of age with respect to individuals who are at least 40 but less than 70 years of age.

EMPLOYMENT DESIRED

POSITION _____   DATE YOU CAN START _____   SALARY DESIRED _____

ARE YOU EMPLOYED NOW? _____   IF SO MAY WE INQUIRE OF YOUR PRESENT EMPLOYER? _____

EVER APPLIED TO THIS COMPANY BEFORE? _____   WHERE? _____   WHEN? _____

EDUCATION	NAME AND LOCATION OF SCHOOL	*NO. OF YEARS ATTENDED	*DID YOU GRADUATE?	SUBJECTS STUDIED
GRAMMAR SCHOOL				
HIGH SCHOOL				
COLLEGE				
TRADE, BUSINESS OR CORRESPONDENCE SCHOOL				

*The Age Discrimination in Employment Act of 1967 prohibits discrimination on the basis of age with respect to individuals who are at least 40 but less than 70 years of age.

GENERAL

SUBJECTS OF SPECIAL STUDY OR RESEARCH WORK _____

U.S. MILITARY OR NAVAL SERVICE _____   RANK _____   PRESENT MEMBERSHIP IN NATIONAL GUARD OR RESERVES _____

(CONTINUED ON OTHER SIDE)

Figure 25. Application for employment

108

FORMER EMPLOYERS [LIST BELOW LAST FOUR EMPLOYERS, STARTING WITH LAST ONE FIRST].

DATE MONTH AND YEAR	NAME AND ADDRESS OF EMPLOYER	SALARY	POSITION	REASON FOR LEAVING
FROM				
TO				
FROM				
TO				
FROM				
TO				
FROM				
TO				

REFERENCES: GIVE THE NAMES OF THREE PERSONS NOT RELATED TO YOU, WHOM YOU HAVE KNOWN AT LEAST ONE YEAR.

	NAME	ADDRESS	BUSINESS	YEARS ACQUAINTED
1				
2				
3				

PHYSICAL RECORD:

DO YOU HAVE ANY PHYSICAL LIMITATIONS THAT PRECLUDE YOU FROM PERFORMING ANY WORK FOR WHICH YOU ARE BEING CONSIDERED?   □ Yes   □ No

PLEASE DESCRIBE:

IN CASE OF EMERGENCY NOTIFY

NAME   ADDRESS   PHONE NO.

"I CERTIFY THAT THE FACTS CONTAINED IN THIS APPLICATION ARE TRUE AND COMPLETE TO THE BEST OF MY KNOWLEDGE AND UNDERSTAND THAT, IF EMPLOYED, FALSIFIED STATEMENTS ON THIS APPLICATION SHALL BE GROUNDS FOR DISMISSAL.

I AUTHORIZE INVESTIGATION OF ALL STATEMENTS CONTAINED HEREIN AND THE REFERENCES LISTED ABOVE TO GIVE YOU ANY AND ALL INFORMATION CONCERNING MY PREVIOUS EMPLOYMENT AND ANY PERTINENT INFORMATION THEY MAY HAVE, PERSONAL OR OTHERWISE, AND RELEASE ALL PARTIES FROM ALL LIABILITY FOR ANY DAMAGE THAT MAY RESULT FROM FURNISHING SAME TO YOU.

I UNDERSTAND AND AGREE THAT, IF HIRED, MY EMPLOYMENT IS FOR NO DEFINITE PERIOD AND MAY, REGARDLESS OF THE DATE OF PAYMENT OF MY WAGES AND SALARY, BE TERMINATED AT ANY TIME WITHOUT ANY PRIOR NOTICE."

DATE   SIGNATURE

DO NOT WRITE BELOW THIS LINE

INTERVIEWED BY   DATE

HIRED: □ Yes   □ No   POSITION   DEPT.

SALARY/WAGE   DATE REPORTING TO WORK

APPROVED: 1.   2.   3.

EMPLOYMENT MANAGER   DEPT. HEAD   GENERAL MANAGER

This form has been designed to strictly comply with State and Federal fair employment practice laws prohibiting employment discrimination.

Figure 25. (*Continued*)

- Never quote a weekly, biweekly, or monthly salary—and certainly not an annual salary—unless that is the way you pay the salary. *Example*: If the weekly salary is $300, don't tell the employee that you are paying $15,600. It could be construed as a verbal contract and be held against you if the employee is fired or dismissed before the year is up.
- Do not make any casual statements regarding future benefits, a long relationship, or anything that might be taken as a contractual commitment.
- Once you make a written offer, append a deadline to this offer. If the applicant does not accept by your terminal date, work on another prospect. The negligent one is not interested, is disorganized, or is waiting for another offer to come through.
- If the prospective employee refuses to have a satisfactory background check made that is needed for possible bonding or insurance, forget him or her.
- If personal habits during the interview annoy you—such as overwhelming perfume, sloppy clothes, outlandish or inappropriate dress, smoking, offensive odors, disturbing mannerisms—forget the applicant. It can only get worse once this person is within your premises.

TAXES, LICENSES, AND OTHER RED TAPE

10

TAXES: ALMOST EVERYTHING YOU WANTED TO KNOW BUT MIGHT HAVE BEEN AFRAID TO ASK

Taxes are a necessary evil and a part of business life. In order to have national, state, and local services, we must pay taxes. We might disagree with the method of taxation and the amount that we pay—but it does not seem to matter whom we elect. The need, or the temptation, of levying taxes transcends political boundaries. Next to inflation, taxes are the entrepreneur's biggest external, or "life," problem.

The small businessperson generally has less access to additional capital than the large operator. Hence every dollar he or she can save on taxes is retained income. It could be used to build up capital funds to improve and expand the business; it could be used to increase personal profits.

Tax planning is an important aspect of financial planning. Good tax accountants are literally worth their weight in gold; the goal is to find one who has the proper empathy and whom you can afford. Make sure you and your accountant examine every opportunity for depreciation, tax credits, tax shelters, real estate investments, alternative forms of expenditures, and any other legal means available to you for avoiding taxes. If the government did not want you to utilize tax incentives, it would not have written them into the tax statutes. It is your job, with the help of your accountant, to keep what is yours.

Here are some suggestions that your accountant will recognize as being wise to consider:

- Many tax shelters will be offered to you once it is known that you have surplus cash. There will be enticing ones in oil explorations, motion-picture production and farm syndicates. Unless they contribute to the direct welfare of your business, or enhance the business you are in, stay away from them—or at least study them until you, too, become an expert in them.
- Don't try to take a tax-shelter deduction for more than the amount of cash or property that is at risk and could be lost.
- If you buy equipment, invest only in the kind that will produce additional income and on which you can take investment tax credits. Don't buy just for the sake of tax credits. It won't pay off.
- Have excess capital? Invest in income-producing property, especially if you can use part of the space yourself. If you have no use for the space, or are short on capital, don't buy—lease.
- Before 1990 a sole proprietor had some payroll tax advantages over the employee of a corporation. However, as of 1990 these advantages have virtually been eliminated. Similarly, other tax advantages of proprietorship over incorporation disappear after 1989.

Hiring Noncitizens

The temptation is often great to hire one or more of the many aliens who either overstayed their visits here, or who crossed the borders illegally. The alien's anxiety and willingness to work for you, at virtually whatever pay rate you determine, are enticements to a start-up entrepreneur. This is especially true in industries that are labor intensive, seasonal, or involved with farming.

However, the Immigration and Naturalization Service (425 I St., NW, Washington, DC 20536) takes a very dim view both of transgressors and those who abet them.

You are advised to follow legal procedures and protect yourself from possible fines or worse. Figure 26 shows Form I-9, which the alien job applicant should fill out—perhaps with your assistance. In helping the alien to execute this form, you are acting just as a CPA or tax preparer does in countersigning income tax returns.

FAVORED TAX STATES

If you are going into business but have not yet settled on the location, you will want to survey the tax climate of the various states. There are five major taxes that can make a difference in your profit picture: (1) personal income tax, (2) corporate income tax, (3) inventory tax, (4) real property tax (machinery, factory, land), and (5) manufacturing sales and use tax.

Personal income tax. This one is important for you personally, especially if you are a sole proprietorship or partnership. There are a few states that have NO personal income tax. They are Connecticut, Florida, Nevada, New Hampshire, South Dakota, Tennessee, Washington, and Wyoming.

Corporate income tax. Only five states give incorporated businesses a break: Nevada, South Dakota, Texas, Washington, and Wyoming.

Inventory tax. This is one of the more insidious forms of fiscal bloodletting. Only 16 states see fit to levy this tax, while 34 states do not levy tax on a company's inventory. The 16 states that DO have an inventory tax are Arkansas, California, Colorado, Florida, Kansas, Kentucky, Louisiana, Missouri, Montana, New Mexico, North Carolina, Ohio, Oklahoma, Tennessee, Texas, and West Virginia.

Real property tax. This tax that is paid on commercial real estate and the residual value of your machinery is assessed in all states except four: Delaware, Massachusetts, Pennsylvania, and Vermont. In the other 46 states you have to pay.

Manufacturing sales and use tax. Only a baker's dozen states hit manufacturers with a sales and use tax, which could be interpreted

---

1 **EMPLOYEE INFORMATION AND VERIFICATION:** (To be completed and signed by employee.)

Name: (Print or Type) Last	First	Middle	Maiden

Address: Street Name and Number	City	State	ZIP Code

Date of Birth (Month Day Year)	Social Security Number

I attest, under penalty of perjury, that I am (check a box):

☐ A citizen or national of the United States.

☐ An alien lawfully admitted for permanent residence (Alien Number A _____).

☐ An alien authorized by the Immigration and Naturalization Service to work in the United States (Alien Number A _____ .
or Admission Number _____ , expiration of employment authorization, if any _____).

I attest, under penalty of perjury, the documents that I have presented as evidence of identity and employment eligibility are genuine and relate to me. I am aware that federal law provides for imprisonment and/or fine for any false statements or use of false documents in connection with this certificate.

Signature	Date (Month/Day Year)

PREPARER TRANSLATOR CERTIFICATION (If prepared by other than the individual) I attest, under penalty of perjury, that the above was prepared by me at the request of the named individual and is based on all information of which I have any knowledge.

Signature	Name (Print or Type)		
Address (Street Name and Number)	City	State	Zip Code

---

2 **EMPLOYER REVIEW AND VERIFICATION:** (To be completed and signed by employer.)

Examine one document from those in List A and check the correct box, **or** examine one document from List B **and** one from List C and check the correct boxes. Provide the **Document Identification Number** and **Expiration Date,** for the document checked in that column.

List A Identity and Employment Eligibility	List B Identity	**and**	List C Employment Eligibility
☐ United States Passport ☐ Certificate of United States Citizenship ☐ Certificate of Naturalization ☐ Unexpired foreign passport with attached Employment Authorization ☐ Alien Registration Card with photograph	☐ A State issued driver's license or I.D. card with a photograph, or information, including name, sex, date of birth, height, weight, and color of eyes. (Specify State)_____) ☐ U.S. Military Card ☐ Other (Specify document and issuing authority) _____		☐ Original Social Security Number Card (other than a card stating it is not valid for employment) ☐ A birth certificate issued by State, county, or municipal authority bearing a seal or other certification ☐ Unexpired INS Employment Authorization Specify form # _____
Document Identification # _____	**Document Identification** # _____		**Document Identification** # _____
Expiration Date (if any) _____	**Expiration Date (if any)** _____		**Expiration Date (if any)** _____

CERTIFICATION: I attest, under penalty of perjury, that I have examined the documents presented by the above individual, that they appear to be genuine, relate to the individual named, and that the individual, to the best of my knowledge, is authorized to work in the United States.

Signature	Name (Print or Type)	Title
Employer Name	Address	Date

Form I-9 (03 20 87)
OMB No. 1115-0136

U.S. Department of Justice
Immigration and Naturalization Service

Figure 26. Employment eligibility verification

NOTICE: Authority for collecting the information on this form is in Title 8, United States Code, Section 1324A. It will be used to verify the individual's eligibility for employment in the United States. Failure to present this form for inspection to officers of the Immigration and Naturalization Service or Department of Labor within the time period specified by regulation, or improper completion or retention of this form may be a violation of 8 USC §1324A and may result in a civil money penalty.

Section 1. Employee's/Preparer's instructions for completing this form.

Instructions for the employee.

All employees, upon being hired, must complete Secton 1 of this form. Any person hired after November 6, 1986 must complete this form. (For the purpose of completion of this form the term "hired" applies to those employed, recruited or referred for a fee.)

All employees must print or type their complete name, address, date of birth, and Social Security Number. The block which correctly indicates the employee's immigration status must be checked. If the second block is checked, the employee's Alien Registration Number must be provided. If the third block is checked, the employee's Alien Registration Number *or* Admission Number must be provided, as well as the date of expiration of that status, if it expires.

All employees must sign and date the form.

Instructions for the preparer of the form, if not the employee.

If the employee is assisted with completing this form, the person assisting must certify the form by signing it, and printing or typing his or her complete name and address.

Section 2. Employer's instructions for completing this form.

(For the purpose of completion of this form, the term "employer" applies to employers and those who recruit or refer for a fee.)

Employers must complete this section by examining evidence of identity and employment authorization, and:
- checking the appropriate box in List A *or* boxes in both Lists B and C;
- recording the document identification number and expiration date (if any);
- recording the type of form if not specifically identified in the list;
- signing the certification section.

NOTE: Employers are responsible for reverifying employment eligibility of aliens upon expiration of any employment authorization documents, should they desire to continue the alien's employment.

Copies of documentation presented by an individual for the purpose of establishing identity and employment eligibility may be copied and retained for the purpose of complying with the requirements of this form and no other purpose. Any copies of documentation made for this purpose should be maintained with this form.

Employers may photocopy or reprint this form, as necessary, for their use.

RETENTION OF RECORDS.

After completion of this form, it must be retained by the employer during the period beginning on the date of hiring and ending:
- three years after the date of such hiring, or;
- one year after the date the individual's employment is terminated, whichever is later.

U.S. Department of Justice
Immigration and Naturalization Service

OMB #1115-0136
Form I-9 (03 20 87)

Figure 26. (*Continued*)

as double taxation on the same product. These 13 hungry states are Arizona, California, Hawaii, Louisiana, Maine, Maryland, Mississippi, Missouri, Nebraska, Nevada, New Mexico, Vermont, and Washington.

LICENSES AND PERMITS

No matter what kind of business you plan to start, chances are excellent that some kind of license or permit will be required. If you have a lawyer or certified accountant in the family, or a close friend who is one or the other, count yourself blessed. If you don't, you still might want to consult one of each—and consider the fee for each consultation well spent.

Is your new business going to be a one-man band? Will you be working out of your home at this stage? If so, there is little to worry about, except to make sure that your residence's zoning permits you to conduct a business there. If you have a consulting business, do outside sales, do someone's books at home, or have extended your hobby of dressmaking or making preserves into a business, you have little to worry about. But anything that generates traffic, makes noise, requires a truck to be parked in your driveway, or involves machinery or chemicals will hardly be welcome in a quiet residential neighborhood.

Generally, any business that entails deducting expenses from your year-end taxes will require some federal permit or license. (Sometimes small business are exempt from federal licensing; check this, however, with the local U.S. tax office.) More obviously, if you conduct trade or manufacture for interstate purposes, you will need a license. If you hire employees, or set up a business with a partner or as part of a corporation, you will need a license. Figure 27 shows the Application for Employer Identification (Form SS-4). You must file an SS-4 if you plan to hire any employees. If you have just a one-person business, the IRS will let you get away with making expense deductions on your taxes, providing you show a profit in two out of the first five years in business. If you don't show a profit in five years, you might be better off going to work for someone else anyway.

Department of the Treasury
Internal Revenue Service

Instructions for Form SS-4
(Rev. August 1988)
Application for Employer Identification Number
(Section references are to the Internal Revenue Code, unless otherwise noted.)

General Instructions

Paperwork Reduction Act Notice.—We ask for this information to carry out the Internal Revenue laws of the United States. We need it to ensure that taxpayers are complying with these laws. You are required to give us this information.

The estimated average time needed to complete Form SS-4, depending on individual circumstances, is 43 minutes. If you have comments concerning the accuracy of this time estimate or suggestions for making this form more simple, we would be happy to hear from you. You can write to the **Internal Revenue Service**, Washington, DC 20224, Attention: IRS Reports Clearance Officer TR:FP; or the **Office of Management and Budget,** Paperwork Reduction Project, Washington, DC 20503.

Purpose.—Use this form to apply for an employer identification number (EIN). Return this form to the Internal Revenue Service. You will receive your EIN in the mail.

Note: *The information you provide on this form will establish your filing requirements.*

Who Must File.—You must file this form if you have not obtained an EIN before and:

(a) You pay wages to one or more employees;

(b) You are required to have an EIN to use on any return, statement, or other document, even if you are not an employer; or

(c) You are required to withhold taxes on income, other than wages, paid to a nonresident alien (individual, corporation, partnership, etc.). For example, individuals who file **Form 1042,** Annual Withholding Tax Return for U.S. Source Income of Foreign Persons, to report alimony paid to nonresident aliens must have EINs.

Individuals who file **Schedule C,** Profit or Loss From Business, or **Schedule F,** Farm Income and Expenses, of **Form 1040,** U.S. Individual Income Tax Return, must use EINs if they are required to file excise, employment, or alcohol, tobacco, or firearms returns.

The following must use EINs even if they do not have any employees:

• Trusts (not IRA trusts unless the IRA trust is required to file **Form 990-T,** Exempt Organization Business Income Tax Return, to report unrelated business taxable income or is filing Form 990-T to obtain a refund of the credit from a regulated investment company.)

• Estates
• Partnerships
• REMICs (Real estate mortgage investment conduit)
• Corporations
• Nonprofit organizations (churches, clubs, etc.)
• Farmers' cooperatives
• Plan administrators

New Business.—If you become the new owner of an existing business, you cannot use the EIN of the former owner. If you already have an EIN, use that number. If you do not have an EIN, apply for one on this form. If you become the "owner" of a corporation by acquiring its stock, use the corporation's EIN.

If you incorporate a sole proprietorship or form a partnership, you must get a new EIN.

File Only One SS-4.—File only one Form SS-4, regardless of the number of businesses operated or trade names under which a business operates. However, each corporation in an affiliated group must file a separate application.

If you do not have a number by the time a return is due, write "Applied for" and the date you applied in the space shown for the number. If you do not have a number by the time a tax deposit is due, send your payment to the Internal Revenue Service Center. (See "Where To File" below.) Make it payable to Internal Revenue Service and show your name (as shown on Form SS-4), address, kind of tax, period covered, and date you applied for an EIN.

For more information about EINs, see **Pub. 583,** Information for Business Taxpayers.

When To File.—File this form early enough to allow time for us to process Form SS-4 and to send you an EIN before you need the number for a return or deposit. If possible, file 4 weeks before you will need the number. Make sure you sign and date the application.

Where To File.—

If your principal business, office or agency, or legal residence in the case of an individual, is located in:	File with the Internal Revenue Service Center at:
Florida, Georgia, South Carolina	Atlanta, GA 39901
New Jersey, New York City and counties of Nassau, Rockland, Suffolk, and Westchester	Holtsville, NY 00501
Connecticut, Maine, Massachusetts, New Hampshire, New York (all other counties), Rhode Island, Vermont	Andover, MA 05501
Illinois, Iowa, Minnesota, Missouri, Wisconsin	Kansas City, MO 64999
Delaware, District of Columbia, Maryland, Pennsylvania, Virginia	Philadelphia, PA 19255
Indiana, Kentucky, Michigan, Ohio, West Virginia	Cincinnati, OH 45999
Kansas, New Mexico, Oklahoma, Texas	Austin, TX 73301
Alaska, Arizona, California (counties of Alpine, Amador, Butte, Calaveras, Colusa, Contra Costa, Del Norte, El Dorado, Glenn, Humboldt, Lake, Lassen, Marin, Mendocino, Modoc, Napa, Nevada, Placer, Plumas, Sacramento, San Joaquin, Shasta, Sierra, Siskiyou, Solano, Sonoma, Sutter, Tehama, Trinity, Yolo, and Yuba), Colorado, Idaho, Montana, Nebraska, Nevada, North Dakota, Oregon, South Dakota, Utah, Washington, Wyoming	Ogden, UT 84201
California (all other counties), Hawaii	Fresno, CA 93888
Alabama, Arkansas, Louisiana, Mississippi, North Carolina, Tennessee	Memphis, TN 37501

If you have no legal residence, principal place of business, or principal office or agency in any Internal Revenue District, file your form with the Internal Revenue Service Center, Philadelphia, PA 19255.

Specific Instructions

The instructions that follow are for those items that are not self-explanatory. Enter N/A (nonapplicable) on the lines that do not apply.

Line 1.—Enter the legal name of the entity applying for the EIN.

Individuals.—Enter the first name, middle initial, and last name.

Trusts.—Enter the name of the trust.

Estate of a decedent, etc.—Enter the name of the estate.

Partnerships.—Enter the legal name of the partnership as it appears in the partnership agreement.

Corporations.—Enter the corporate name as set forth in the corporation charter or other legal document creating it.

Plan administrators.—Enter the name of the plan administrator. A plan administrator that has been assigned an EIN for other purposes (such as the filing of income or employment tax returns) should use the same number.

Line 2.—Enter the trade name of the business if different from the legal name.

Line 3.—Trusts enter the name of the trustee. Estates enter the name of the executor, administrator, or other fiduciary. If the entity applying has a designated person to receive tax information, enter that person's name as the "care of" person. When entering names, print or type first name, middle initial, and last name.

Lines 4 and 4a.—Enter the complete mailing address. Include room number, apartment number, or suite number.

Line 5 and 5a.—If the physical location of the business is different from the mailing address (lines 4 and 4a), enter the address of the physical location on lines 5 and 5a.

Line 7.—Enter the first name, middle initial, and last name of a principal officer if the business is a corporation; of a general partner if a partnership; of a grantor if a trust.

Line 8.—Check the box that best describes the type of entity that is applying for the EIN. If not listed, check the "other" box and enter the type of entity. Do not enter N/A.

Figure 27. Instructions for Form SS-4

Individual.—Check this box if the individual files Schedule C or F (Form 1040) and is required to file excise, employment, or alcohol, tobacco, or firearms returns. If this box is checked, enter the individual's SSN (social security number) in the space provided.

Plan administrator.—The term plan administrator means the person or group of persons specified as the administrator by the instrument under which the plan is operated. If the plan administrator is an individual, enter the plan administrators's SSN (social security number) in the space provided.

New withholding agent.—If you are a new withholding agent required to file Form 1042, check the "other" box and enter in the space provided "new withholding agent."

REMICs.—Check this box if the entity is a real estate mortgage investment conduit (REMIC). A REMIC is any entity:

1. To which an election to be treated as a REMIC applies for the tax year and all prior tax years,

2. In which all of the interests are regular interests or residual interests,

3. Which has one (and only one) class or residual interests (and all distributions, if any, with respect to such interests are pro rata),

4. In which as of the close of the 4th month ending after the startup date and each quarter ending thereafter, substantially all of its assets consist of qualified mortgages and permitted investments, and

5. Which has a tax year that is a calendar year.

For more information about REMICs see the **Instructions for Form 1066,** U.S. Real Estate Mortgage Investment Conduit Income Tax Return.

Personal service corporations.—Check this box if the entity is a personal service corporation. An entity is a personal service corporation for a tax year only if:

1. The entity is a C corporation for the tax year,

2. The principal activity of the entity during the testing period (as defined in Temporary Regulations section 1.441-4T) for the tax year is the performance of personal service,

3. During the testing period for the tax year, such services are substantially performed by employee-owners, and

4. The employee-owners own 10 percent of the fair market value of the outstanding stock in the entity on the last day of the testing period for the tax year.

For more information about personal service corporations, see the instructions to **Form 1120,** U.S. Corporation Income Tax Return, and Temporary Regulations section 1.441-4T.

Other corporations.—This box is for any corporation other than a personal service corporation. If you check this box, enter the type of corporation (such as insurance company) in the space provided.

Other nonprofit organizations.—Check this box if the nonprofit organization is other than a church or church-controlled

organization and specify the type of nonprofit organization (for example educational organization.)

Group exemption number (GEN).—If the applicant is a nonprofit organization that is a subordinate organization to be included in a group exemption letter under Revenue Procedure 80-27, enter the GEN in the space provided. If you do not know the GEN, contact the parent organization for it. GEN is a four-digit number. Do not confuse it with the nine-digit EIN.

Line 9.—Check only one box. Do not enter N/A.

Started a new business.—Check this box if you are starting a new business that requires an EIN. If you check this box, enter the type of business being started. Do not apply if you already have an EIN and are only adding another place of business.

Changed type of organization.—Check this box if the business is changing its type of organization, for example, if the business was a sole proprietorship and has been incorporated or has become a partnership. If you check this box, specify in the space provided the type of change made, for example "from sole proprietorship to partnership."

Purchased a going business.—Check this box if you acquired a business through purchase. Do not use the former owner's EIN. If you already have an EIN, use that number.

Hired employees.—Check this box if the existing business is requesting an EIN because it has hired or is hiring employees and is therefore required to file employment tax return for which an EIN is required. Do not apply if you already have an EIN and are only hiring employees.

Created a trust.—Check this box if you created a trust, and enter the type of trust created.

Created a pension plan.—Check this box if you have created a pension plan and need this number for reporting purposes. Also, enter the type of plan created.

Banking purpose.—Check this box if you are requesting an EIN for banking purpose only, and enter the banking purpose (for example, checking, loan, etc.,).

Other (specify).—Check this box if you are requesting an EIN for any reason other than those for which there are checkboxes and enter the reason.

Line 10.—If you are starting a new business, enter the starting date of the business. If the business you acquired is already operating, enter the date you acquired the business. Trusts should enter the date the trust was legally created. Estates should enter the date of death of the decedent whose name appears on line 1.

Line 11.—Enter the last month of your accounting year or tax year. An accounting year or tax year is usually 12 consecutive months. It may be a calendar year or a fiscal year (including a period of 52 or 53 weeks). A calendar year is 12 consecutive months ending on December 31. A fiscal year is either 12 consecutive months ending on the last day of any month other than December

or a 52-53 week year. For more information on accounting periods, see **Pub. 538,** Accounting Periods and Methods.

Individuals.—Your tax year generally will be a calendar year.

Partnerships.—Partnerships generally should conform to the tax year of either its majority partners, its principal partners, or a calendar year in that order, unless it can establish a business purpose for a different tax year.

REMICs.—Remics must have a calendar year as their tax year.

Personal service corporations.—A personal service corporation generally must adopt a calendar year unless:

(1) it can establish to the satisfaction of the Commissioner that there is a business purpose for having a different tax year, or

(2) it elects under section 444 to have a tax year other than a calendar year.

Line 12.—If the business has or will have employees, enter on this line the date on which the business began or will begin to pay wages to the employees. If the business does not have any plans to have employees, enter N/A on this line.

New withholding agent.—Enter the date you began or will begin to pay income to a nonresident alien. This also applies to individuals who are required to file Form 1042 to report alimony paid to a nonresident alien.)

Line 15.—Generally, enter the exact type of business being operated (for example, advertising agency, farm, labor union, real estate agency, steam laundry, rental of coin-operated vending machine, investment club, etc.).

Governmental.—Enter the type of organization (state, county, school district, or municipality, etc.)

Nonprofit organization (other than governmental).—Enter whether organized for religious, educational, or humane purposes, and the principal activity (for example, religious organization—hospital; charitable).

Mining and quarrying.—Specify the process and the principal product (for example, mining bituminous coal, contract drilling for oil, quarrying dimension stone, etc.).

Contract construction.—Specify whether general contracting or special trade contracting. Also, show the type of work normally performed (for example, general contractor for residential buildings, electrical subcontractor, etc.).

Trade.—Specify the type of sales and the principal line of goods sold (for example, wholesale dairy products, manufacturer's representative for mining machinery, retail hardware, etc.).

Manufacturing.—Specify the type of establishment operated (for example, sawmill, vegetable cannery, etc.).

Signature block.—For a trust, the trustee should sign this form. For an estate of a decedent, insolvent, etc., the administrator or other fiduciary should sign it. If the business is a partnership, a general partner should sign. For a corporation, a principal officer should sign this form.

Figure 27. (*Continued*)

YOUR BUSINESS AND COMPUTERS | 11

WHAT IS A COMPUTER?

Since the majority of business start-up entrepreneurs are in their 40s and 50s (in the next decade many more will probably be in their 60s) and may not be computer literate, a few basic words about computers are in order.

The human brain is said to consist of ten million parts (cells and such). The best computers are said to have at most 100,000 parts. Damage a small portion of the brain, and it can still function reasonably well. Damage one vital part of a computer—and the computer stops.

The greatest single difference between a computer and a human brain is *intelligence*. Scientists are working on artificial intelligence, of course, and in Hollywood they have been creating intelligent computers for the past 15 years.

Intelligence is the ability to understand information and gain knowledge, use existing knowledge to solve problems, and store knowledge in our memory. As a result of experience, we can improve or change our thinking. We can even create new ideas and combinations of ideas. The computer cannot create either data or functions; you must put the information into it and tell it what to do (program it).

This reminder of the superiority of the human brain is intended to make you feel better. A modern generation is growing up to regard the computer as indispensable—i.e., to venerate it as an "artificial intelligence" without which the new information age could not function.

To some extent, this is true, but we should not lose sight of the fact that the computer is a machine, developed by humans, and placed in the service of humans. Nor should we hope that the computer will replace the human capacity to reason, to philosophize, and to create—or even merely to spell correctly and add up a column of figures.

Particularly sad is the decline of the human brain as a tool in arriving at relatively simple mathematical functions. Minor additions, subtractions, divisions, and multiplications—like figuring a 5 percent sales tax on a $2.98 purchase—now must be done on a cash register or calculator. The clerk or cashier has forgotten that $2.98 is close to $3 and that $3 \times 5 = 15$—thus, the total charge will be $2.98 + .15 = $3.23. Heaven forbid if the computer should be down!

TO USE OR NOT TO USE COMPUTERS?

With an entire new generation growing up on computers, to deny the need for these technological marvels is tantamount to denouncing motherhood and apple pie. But let a small businessperson step into the neighborhood bank to make a deposit or into a local store to check out a purchase, only to hear the clerk say, "Sorry, I can't do that just now because the computer is down," and he or she will realize that the use of computers for everything but flushing the toilet has become debatable.

In an office of our government a computer expert had been laboring mightily for two months (at $450 per week) to come up with an alphabetical roster. The idea was brilliant, but there was one problem: Three-quarters of the way through the task, the programmer left. A new expert came on board, and before you could say "Give me a printout of the roster from New Jersey," the entire input to that point was lost. LOST!

In a magazine office the writer was laboring on a deadline story. Some new material was rushed in, unearthed by a researcher. No problem: All one needed to do was move the cursor about six lines up on the screen and insert the additional paragraph. Problem: Somehow a wrong button got pushed and the entire "page" was erased from the screen. The writer had concocted this story out of her brain and hadn't printed it out yet. It didn't exist anywhere else, and thus she had to start all over again, trying to remember what she had written.

In the annals of small business failures, there is one about a publisher who started a new magazine by investing in a multi-thousand-dollar desktop computer setup. He spent so much time and money on his new gadgetry that he forgot to go out and sell the advertising that would have made his business successful. Within six months he was out of money, and the computer was reclaimed by the company that had financed its purchase.

This is the danger with computers: overreliance on them. We expect an electronic apparatus to do our thinking for us. Still, millions are in use and their utility and proliferation increases by leaps and bounds. The computer age *is* here, and we may do better to join it, intelligently, than to fight it.

In answer, then, to the question, to or not to computer, let's say that it depends on the kind of business you are doing—on its complexity and on the number of names, items, or prices you need to keep track of. It depends most of all on your ability to understand what is going on. You can't run a successful business without being in control of every phase of it. It would be like relying on hired help that might be gone tomorrow to become entirely dependent on computers that can go "down" and stop you dead in your tracks. If you are going to use a computer, it only makes sense to understand it, so that it can be treated as a helpmate and not as a crutch.

Reading an introductory book on computer operation (the most recent you can find), visiting a computer show, getting in-depth explanations of various equipment in a computer store, or even taking a basic computer course in the adult education department of the local college are all steps in the right direction. Just like buying a new car and resorting to "kicking a few tires," you need to go out and explore the vast and confusing world of the computer and ask a few questions. Remember: *Illegitimis non carborundum* ("Don't let the bastards wear you down").

COMPUTERIZATION PITFALLS

What are some of the problems you might encounter in opting for a computer system for your small business?

1. The initial investment can be substantial. If you are not totally familiar with the field, you will be well advised to hire a consultant who can guide you to the right equipment for your needs, train you in its operation, and recommend the kind of software programs that make sense for your particular business.

2. Installation is not always easy. The system must be coded correctly and then tested and debugged.

3. Personnel must be trained to use the system. If you fail to solve that problem, you might wish that you had never heard of a computer.

4. Software must be acquired that does what you expect your computer to do, providing the right kind and amount of information you need. And don't try to change the software package, or the software manufacturer's warranty and service goes up in smoke.

5. A computer is a machine, and machines sometimes break down. Then, unless you have a maintenance contract, you need to call an expert to fix it. Computer experts, like plumbers, are expensive. Nevertheless, you'll need to be prepared for this eventuality and have some names at the ready. You also need to learn simple troubleshooting to keep these calls at a minimum.

HOW TO BUY A COMPUTER

Considering the transitory technology of many computers and the fact that the computer industry comes out with new, improved models every year, weigh the pros and cons of buying versus leasing. If you are well financed, buying is probably more economical. If money

is tight (start-ups are always more cash intensive than you anticipated) and you have to take out a loan to get started, then a lease
program could be more advantageous. You will probably pay 25
percent or more on your purchase than its actual cost (adding on
interest, maintenance-contract charge, instruction charge, etc.), but
three or four years down the road, if you do well, it could be worth
the premium.

The proliferation of computer stores today makes it easier to
"shop around"—shopping for a computer becoming more and more
like looking for a new car. Do make comparisons, not only of models
and prices, but of performance and capability; the goal is to choose
a computer system that does what you need it to do.

Another way of conserving initial start-up capital is to rent computer time from a time-sharing company. Your accountant will probably be able to guide you in this move.

For entrepreneurs already familiar with some computer terms,
experts offer this advice:

- Disk Operating Systems (DOS) will continue to dominate the
  business market, including IBM PCs and the various compatibles
  and clones.
- First find the software that is compatible with your business.
  Then buy the hardware that can run those programs.
- One reason for buying (or leasing) newer models is that they
  are more economical, run faster, and are more compact.
- Hard disks are now being used more and more, because they
  have greater storage capacity.
- With greatly reduced prices for PCs, look for models that offer
  at least 640K random access memory (RAM).
- If you are considering buying a laptop computer, take into consideration their weakest characteristic: low resolution of the
  monitor that makes it difficult to read.
- When buying a printer, chances are you will have no compatibility
  problem with DOS or Apple Macintosh, but you might have
  problems with other systems. Check it out.
- Check your power supply. Buy a good surge protector.
- Attend one or more computer shows. This is often where you
  can get the best buys.

INSURANCE

This part of your business planning is a "winners-pay-losers" game. You pay premiums on more than a dozen different types of insurance policies, but you hope that you will never collect. If you never have an occasion that calls for indemnity, then you are in luck—you are a winner. Those, however, who have an accident, a fire or a nasty law suit on their hands, will be indemnified by the insurance company. In that case you are helping to pay for the damage that the insurer pays the "loser."

The premiums are the price you pay for your security—your freedom from worry. The more you pay, the more secure you can be. On the other hand, you can insure yourself right out of business. You've heard the old adage, "Cash poor, insurance rich." It is essential, therefore, to analyze your insurance program carefully. Several thousand dollars are riding on your decision, but worse than that—if you do not have the right kind of insurance, if you are not familiar with your policies or understand the fine print, you can get stuck with a pittance of a payoff instead of the full reimbursement you had expected.

Insurance companies are full of tricks. They seem to have invented *caveat emptor*—let the buyer beware. If you have a friend in the insurance business, you are fortunate. Learn all you can from this agent; lean on her or him.

MENU OF POLICIES

The following menu of policies is available to you, and you can buy all of them if you have the money to pay the premiums. If you can place all or most of the policies through one general agent, you usually can save some money. Also important is the fact that this one agent knows you are a good customer and will protect your interests both in front, when you buy the policies, and afterward, if you need to collect on any of them. Here are your choices:

- *Fire insurance:* Includes such other possible perils as windstorms, hail, floods, smoke, snow, explosions, and mischief. Get either full replacement value or a specific amount. And don't forget the contents!
- *Liability insurance*: Besides bodily injury, should include libel, slander, defamation, and all those subjective "injuries" that lawsuit-happy people dream up these days. This must extend to vendors and employees whom you hire or have under contract, and cover legal costs in defending and suit, no matter how frivolous.
- *Automobile insurance*: Should include liability of employees or contractors performing tasks on your behalf (five or more vehicles are insurable under a fleet policy). Should also include merchandise or equipment inside any of the insured vehicles.
- *Workmen's compensation*: Find out what the requirements are in your state. They vary. Even if your state does not require you to carry this insurance, it is wise to carry a policy.
- *Business interruption insurance*: Should cover such exigencies as fire, flood, lightning, explosion, interruption by utilities, even strikes—compensating you and key employees for the time work is interrupted.
- *Crime insurance*: Should include merchandise, tools, paper or computer records, showcase contents, contents of your safe, and even employee theft and robbery of goods from facilities outside of your store or office. If you are in an urban high-crime area and have problems getting this kind of insurance, contact your state's insurance commissioner's office.

- *Glass insurance*: Should cover *all* glass such as store fronts, signs, showcases, and the lettering that goes on them.
- *Rent insurance*: To continue payments during periods when your premises are not usable due to fire, flood, explosion, etc.
- *Group life insurance*: Available if 75 percent of your employees opt for it. Coverage up to $50,000 per employee is deductible from your federal income tax, even if it is not taxable income to your employees.
- *Group health insurance*: A good tool to increase employee retention. If you pay only a portion of each policy, employees can take the policy with them if they should leave; if you pay the entire cost, then employees cannot be dropped from the group plan even if they leave.
- *Disability insurance*: Picks up where workmen's compensation leaves off, up to lifetime payments.
- *Retirement income insurance*: A good policy for yourself as proprietor, as well as for longtime key employees. This policy can be either fixed or variable, taking into account future inflation.
- *Keyman insurance*: Premiums are not tax deductible, but neither is the income from such a policy taxable. Accumulated assets in such a policy are carried as an asset of the company. This is especially valuable in a small company or partnership.
- *Umbrella coverage*: Take $1,000,000 in coverage in excess of what you have in the other policies. In this age of malpractice mayhem, everybody in business should have such a policy.

It is a good idea to get quotations from at least two different insurance agencies. There can be some remarkable differences. Agents make their living by selling you the most insurance you can handle. They get about 55 percent for the first year of life insurance; 10 to 15 percent on other kinds of insurance.

You can finance the entire insurance package by paying lump sum premiums monthly. However, find out how much interest or carrying charge you pay for this privilege. It could be more than you would have to pay if you were to borrow the money elsewhere.

Each year as your policies come up for renewal, check over the coverage you are getting. Has the value of the property or goods that are being insured gone up? Has inflation made income replacement policies inadequate? Have you made improvements that need to be added to the coverage?

By all means talk to other business owners about their insurance policies and any claims and settlements they have had. Don't overlook your own trade or professional association, if you belong to one. They might have valuable advice, or even a lower-cost package that suits your needs. And do take your lawyer and/or accountant into your confidence before you buy that insurance package. This field is too complicated for one person to know all the answers.

INTERNAL SECURITY

THE SILENT BANKRUPTCY PROBLEM

Numerous SCORE chapters in many parts of the country have given and are continuing to give seminars on inside theft. In some instances such employee skulduggery has cost companies as much as 20 percent of their profits and helped to put others out of business.

The American Management Association confirms this estimate, adding that as many as 20 percent of all businesses fail because of internal theft. Fatal business losses can come from professional burglars, as well as customers, suppliers, or employees.

One important precaution that is often ignored is the bonding of any employee who handles substantial sums of money—especially when these employees are not directly supervised. There are companies that send undercover investigators to check up on cashiers, salesclerks, deliverypeople, and bartenders, but the ingenuity of some of these money handlers is astounding—a fact to which the following cases will attest.

Temptation is one human frailty for which no amount of training, incentives, and insurance has been able to compensate. That is why it is necessary to check the background of any employees who handle money prior to employment, to have theft insurance, and to get these employees bonded.

One Cash Register More

A few years ago in Baltimore, a tavern owner's accountant flagged a discrepancy between liquor purchases (and presumably sales) and the tavern's gross income. The accountant knew that the markup on alcoholic beverages was substantial. He also knew there were about 30 "shots" in an average bottle of liquor. Multiplying the number of bottles of liquor purchased, less inventory on hand, by 30 shots gave the accountant the total number of drinks dispensed. He multiplied the average price per drink by the number of shots per bottle to get an approximate total sales figure for drinks. Then he added beer, soft-drink, and miscellaneous sales (snacks available at the bar) and came up with a grand total (gross income). It was far higher than the actual amount of money that had been collected in the two cash registers.

The owner decided to hire an investigator who would seat himself at the bar during the evening hours when the proprietor was away. The investigator duly reported the number of transactions for each of the three cash registers on the long counter. Upon hearing this, the owner said to the investigator, "How much did you drink while you were there? I only have *two* cash registers!" The sleuth, however, insisted that there were three cash registers. They agreed that he would go back on another evening to look again and verify his previous report. Once again, he counted sales rung up on *three* cash registers. This time, on a hunch, the investigator stayed till closing time. He told the bartender goodnight and got into his car, but he only moved it to where he could keep an eye on the tavern's rear door. Within a short time, the lights dimmed and the bartender came out. Sure enough, he was carrying a cash register, which he proceeded to wrestle into the trunk of his car. The next day the bartender was caught red-handed and arrested. The case of the missing "gross" was solved, and the business was saved.

Alcoholic beverage businesses are particularly vulnerable to internal larceny. A bar is principally a cash business. Its customers stay a long time and occasionally become friendly with the bartender. The latter may slip a good customer a free drink, overpour to show generosity, or upgrade the brand—moves that are all designed to increase tips. Sometimes a transaction is not rung up; sometimes cash left on the counter finds its way into the "subway" (the receptacle underneath the counter).

Runaway Steak

Another classic example occurred in New York at a popular steak restaurant. Employees shipped so much food out the back door into waiting vehicles that the owners soon .would have faced bankruptcy—but finally they discovered the cause of their deficit. The irony in this case was that the four owners were all partners in a major law firm and were very sharp professionals in their own arena. But they were naive lambs in the restaurant business, and they ended up being fleeced.

Don't Use Pencil

Customers, rather than employees, were the culprits in another example. A large, sparsely clerked ladies' clothing store marked the high-turnover merchandise with penciled price tickets. This was for convenience's sake, because of a progressive markdown policy. Some clever customers saw an opportunity for saving even more money and either erased prices, substituting lower ones by merely writing on the tickets, or switched tickets. Eventually the management caught on, and after that the tickets were rubber-stamped.

Popularity Killed the Cat

One saleslady in a big store was unusually popular; she enjoyed many repeat customers, who always asked for her. Having so many of these "personal" customers, she made a higher income than other salespeople because of her commissions. Her luck ran out, however, when one of the owners compared the sales she rang up on the cash register with the portion of the ticket stubs retained for inventory records. It turned out that while the saleslady was making $50 a week more in commissions on her "special" sales, the store lost $500 a week in what she took off the ticket prices. No wonder she was so popular!

Someone Smelled a Rat

In another store a similar scam was operated by a less magnanimous salesperson. The store enjoyed brisk sales and high paper volume, yet profits were quite marginal. Comparisons of individual sales rung up by the several cashiers with actual prices of merchandise pointed to one cashier whose sales were consistently lower than the price tickets on the merchandise she sold. She was marking down the merchandise and pocketing the difference.

Other Examples

Internal fraud can be as simple as picking up cash that a customer lays on the counter and not ringing it up on the cash register, or as sophisticated as fudging large money transfers in a bank or debiting wealthy old widows' in-and-out deposits, assuming the customers will never try to balance their accounts.

Sometimes a delivery person is in cahoots with a warehouse receiver; they simply shortchange the delivery and split the payments made by the bookkeeper, who, of course, does not count the merchandise received.

A sales manager makes a deal with a salesperson. The latter makes phony sales, gets paid commissions on them, and the two buddies split the commissions.

The petty cash account gets lots of small vouchers for expenses or mileage allowances that are phony and are never checked. Over a year, or years, these can mount up to thousands of dollars.

In another case, goods are "returned," and money is paid out for them or credit given for new merchandise. But the clerk's prearranged "customer" gets the merchandise, and the store gets nothing for its credit.

A collector supposedly collects receivables, but he or she merely writes the debts off as "uncollectibles," and the collector and debtor "settle" for a lesser amount.

Payments are issued to temporary laborers or clerks from a petty cash fund and "receipted." However, the temp employees never worked. They are phantoms, and the crew boss pockets the real money.

OUTSMART THE CROOKS

Abuses by employees can be positively ingenious. Wherever there is temptation, there will be somebody to rise to the occasion and take advantage of it. If all the clever methods to milk companies out of money were converted into productive energy, many a small company would be profitable and rich. It is important, therefore, for employees who handle money and merchandise to be bonded and, even then, to be watched. Management must make sure that foolproof systems are installed to compensate for the deviousness of the white-collar crook.

It is discouraging. But why mope? It simply means that if you want to be in business, and if you have employees, you've got to be smarter than they are. And you are, because you're the one who started the business. You just have to apply those "smarts" and not be too trusting and naive. Not to have a good internal security system can be detrimental to your wealth. Figure 28 gives you a checklist to help ensure that you are secured against the people on your payroll and the ones with whom you do business.

---

1. Check all premises for easy entrance or exit. Install safety locks, alarms, mirrors, visible surveillance cameras, etc.
2. Limit access to warehouse or other inventory storage areas with special entry codes or devices.
3. Install foolproof inventory recording and control procedures.
4. Have a safe for your cash and valuables, preferably anchored to the floor.
5. Create a tight goods-receivable system.
6. Keep a close eye on all cash operations and hire only bonded people to handle cash.
7. Have a step-by-step cash-handling procedure, extending from the cash register to the bank.

Figure 28. A security checklist

8. Money-handling functions of employees should be separated so that you have a checks-and-balances system in case of discrepancies.
9. Paying out money should be under a controlled system just like the receipt of funds.
10. Purchasing functions should be checked not only for value received, but for competitive pricing.
11. Have all checks, price tickets, sales slips, requisitions, and other merchandise forms marked in sequentially numbered order, so that a foolproof review system can be used.
12. For unexplained increases that could point to "padding" or unauthorized payouts, check cost of goods received.
13. Make sure that all shipping cartons are flattened before discarding them. Make periodic after-hours checks of them.
14. Have incoming merchandise and supplies checked in by a person other than the regular warehouse or receiving clerk.
15. Do not have any employee parking near your receiving door.
16. Distribute keys to your establishment, especially to the receiving or back door, sparsely.
17. Change locks regularly if you have frequent employee turnover.
18. Make periodic floor checks, especially on cashiers' stations, looking for clusters of people around cashiers, visible signals passed between clerks and customers, unusual popularity of certain clerks, etc.
19. Be alert for too many "00" rings on the cash register to cover errors or overrings.
20. Watch for items that the cashier might bypass and not ring up.
21. Employ an unknown "shopper" on occasion to check sales and cashiering procedures.
22. Portion-control as much of your food and drink inventory as possible and relate purchases to income.
23. Make sure that customers have actually received money refunds by making periodic spot checks.
24. Make refund inspections in person or through an employee who did not handle the transaction.
25. Have a system in which returned merchandise is matched to the return voucher and put back in stock immediately.

Figure 28. (*Continued*)

FREE HELP AND OTHER ASSISTANCE

14

GENERAL RESOURCES

Forget the old adage that anything free is worth exactly that. There *are* some real aids that you can get for no cost. Learn about them and take advantage of them. In a roundabout way, of course, you are paying for these services anyway through your taxes.

If you go into any kind of small business, you will find a whole treasure of resources at your fingertips. If you check these resource categories out, one by one, you cannot fail to find some stimulation and positive help.

Libraries. Local and regional libraries have become amazingly sophisticated. If you can't find something in the film templates that most libraries have these days, ask the information librarian. If a particular branch doesn't have the book you are looking for, they'll either find it listed in their computer in another branch or let you know of its availability. Libraries also keep back issues of magazines, newspapers, and government publications. And, except for special computer searches, this help costs you nothing.

Trade publications. There are about 2500 business, trade, and technical publications in the United States. The information contained in them is prodigious. Some of them might be in your local library, but even if they are not, the major libraries have the Standard Rate and Data Service catalog (the green business publications edition), which lists most of these business magazines with their addresses, ad rates, personnel, etc. Then there is the MMP catalog (the Magazine Marketplace), which concentrates more on editorial information. Reading a few issues of the ones in your field can be a short course in your specialization. Among the most pertinent publications for the start-up entrepreneur are the following:

Business Age, Box 11597, 4060 N. Oakland, Milwaukee, WI 53211 (monthly)

Entrepreneur and New Business Opportunities, 2392 Morse Ave., Irvine, CA 92714

In Business, Box 323, 18 S. 7th St., Emmaus, PA 18049 (bi-monthly)

Inc., 38 Commercial Wharf, Boston, MA 02110 (monthly)

Venture Magazine, 521 Fifth Ave., New York, NY 10175 (monthly)

Trade Associations. The library also has a Trade Associations Directory that lists thousands of professional, commercial, and trade associations throughout the United States. You can also look in your local Yellow Pages under "Associations," or in the directory for the local chamber of commerce (if you do local business, a membership would be a good investment!). In addition, see the sections, "National Business Organizations" and "Selected National, Professional, and Trade Organizations," below.

Government Assistance. Numerous government bureaus have booklets and brochures, either free or at very little cost, as well as counselors to guide you. This is especially true in the high-tech, energy, and small-business-opportunities fields. (See "Free Help from Uncle Sam to Start Your Own Business" by William Alarid and Gustav Berle, Puma Publishing Co., 1670 Coral Dr., Santa Maria, CA 93454, 1989.) Small businesses going into export will find much help in the Department of Commerce.

SCORE. The most prolific all-around small business assistance can be obtained free of charge through SCORE, the Service Corps of Retired Executives. There are nearly 13,000 volunteer counselors, all former entrepreneurs, industrial executives, retired teachers, or military. They work out of 385 offices, usually located in chambers of commerce, federal buildings, or community colleges. If you cannot find the local SCORE office in your telephone book's blue section (under U.S. Government/Small Business Administration), call the free national information line at 1-800-368-5855. One-on-one appointments with a SCORE counselor are free. All counselors are quite knowledgeable, although you may ask for one who has *your* kind of business experience. SCORE does charge between $5 and $20 for workshops that can last from two to six hours and include useful materials. Offices of the SBDC (Small Business Development Corporation), also operating under SBA auspices, are usually located in universities. They are staffed mostly by graduate students, have very sophisticated resources (computers, research, statistics), and will charge user fees after the initial session.

FREE HELP FROM STATE AGENCIES

Uncle Sam is not the only one who offers free help to start-up entrepreneurs. Each of our 50 states has a substantial interest in helping new businesses get started. States are actively helping entrepreneurs in five areas: business development, financial assistance, procurement assistance, minority/women opportunities, and international trade. If you are planning to open a business, contact your state's bureau for information and assistance. These agencies all have complimentary publications available, especially in the areas of business development and international trade. Inquire about any such publications when you make your initial contact. The following is a list of individual state development offices, their locations, and principal phone numbers:

ALABAMA:	Development Office, State Capitol, Montgomery, AL 36130, 1-800-248-0033 or (205) 263-0048
ALASKA:	Division of Business Development, P.O. Box D, Juneau, AK 99811, (907) 465-2017
ARIZONA:	Department of Commerce, 1700 W. Washington St., 4th Fl., Phoenix, AZ 85007, (602) 255-5705
ARKANSAS:	Small Business Information Center, One State Capitol Mall, Rm.4C300, Little Rock, AR 77201, (501) 682-3358

CALIFORNIA:	Office of Small Business, 1121 L St., Suite 600, Sacramento, CA 95814, (916) 445-6545
COLORADO:	Business Information Center, 1525 Sherman St., Rm. 110, Denver, CO 80203, (303) 866-3933
CONNECTICUT:	Small Business Services, 210 Washington St., Hartford, CT 06106, (203) 566-4051
DELAWARE:	Development Office, 99 King's Highway, P.O. Box 1401, Dover, DE 19903, (302) 736-4271
DISTRICT OF COLUMBIA:	Office of Business and Economic Development, 7th Fl., 1111 E St., NW, Washington, DC 20004, (202) 727-6600
FLORIDA:	Bureau of Business Assistance, 107 Gaines St., Tallahassee, FL 32339-2000, 1-800-342-0771 or (904) 488-9357
GEORGIA:	Department of Industry and Trade, 230 Peachtree Rd. NW, Atlanta, GA 30303, (404) 656-3584
HAWAII:	Small Business Information Service, 250 S. King St., Rm. 727, Honolulu, HI 96813, (808) 548-7645
IDAHO:	Economic Development Division, Department of Commerce, State Capitol, Rm. 108, Boise, ID 83720, (208) 334-3416
ILLINOIS:	Small Business Assistance Bureau, 620 E. Adams St., Springfield, IL 62701, 1-800-252-2923 or (217) 785-6282
INDIANA:	Division of Business Expansion, Department of Commerce, One North Capital, Suite 700, Indianapolis, IN 46204-2288, 1-800-824-2476 or (317) 232-3527
IOWA:	Bureau of Small Business Development, 200 E. Grand Ave., Des Moines, IA 50309, 1-800-532-1216 or (515) 281-8310

KANSAS:	Division of Existing Industry Development, 400 S.W. Eighth St., 5th Fl., Topeka, KS 66603, (913) 296-5298
KENTUCKY:	Small Business Division, Capitol Plaza, 22nd Fl., Frankfort, KY 40601, 1-800-626-2250 or (502) 564-4252
LOUISIANA:	Development Division, Office of Commerce and Industry, P.O. Box 94185, Baton Rouge, LA 70804-9185, (504) 342-5365
MAINE:	Business Development Division, State Development Office, State House, Augusta, ME 04333, 1-800-872-3838 or (207) 289-2659
MARYLAND:	Office of Business and Industrial Development, 45 Calvert St., Annapolis, MD 21401, 1-800-654-7336 or (301) 974-2946
MASSACHUSETTS:	Small Business Assistance Division, 100 Cambridge St., 13th Fl., Boston, MA 02202, (617) 727-4005
MICHIGAN:	Business Ombudsman, Department of Commerce, P.O. Box 30107, Lansing, MI 48909, 1-800-232-2727 or (517) 373-6241
MINNESOTA:	Small Business Assistance Office, 900 American Center, 150 E. Kellogg Blvd., St. Paul, MN 55101, 1-800-652-9747 or (612) 296-3871
MISSISSIPPI:	Small Business Bureau, 3825 Ridgewood Rd., Jackson, MS 39211-6453, (601) 982-6231
MISSOURI:	Small Business Development Office, P.O. Box 118, Jefferson City, MO 65102, (314) 751-4981/8411
MONTANA:	Business Assistance Center, 1424 Ninth Ave., Helena, MT 59620, 1-800-221-8015 or (406) 444-3923

NEBRASKA:	Small Business Division, P.O. Box 94666, 301 Centennial Mall S., Lincoln, NE 68509, (402) 471-4167
NEVADA:	Office of Community Service, 1100 East William, Suite 116, Carson City, NV 89710, (702) 885-4602
NEW HAMPSHIRE:	Office of Industrial Development, 105 Loudon Rd., Prescott Park, Bldg. 2, Concord, NH 03301, (603) 271-2591
NEW JERSEY:	Office of Small Business Assistance, 1 W. State St. (CN-835), Trenton, NJ 08625, (609) 984-4442
NEW MEXICO:	Economic Development Division, 1100 St. Francis Dr., Santa Fe, NM 87503, 1-800-545-2040 or (505) 827-0300
NEW YORK:	Division for Small Business, 230 Park Ave., Rm. 834, New York, NY 10169, (212) 309-0400
NORTH CAROLINA:	Small Business Development Division, Dobbs Bldg., Rm. 2019, 430 N. Salisbury St., Raleigh, NC 27611, (919) 733-7980
NORTH DAKOTA:	Small Business Coordinator, Economic Development Commission, Liberty Memorial Bldg., Bismarck, ND 58505, 1-800-472-2100 or (701) 224-2810
OHIO:	Small and Developing Business Division, P.O. Box 1001, Columbus, OH 43266-0101, 1-800-282-1085 or (614) 466-1876
OKLAHOMA:	Oklahoma Department of Commerce, 6601 Broadway Ext., Oklahoma, OK 73116, (405) 521-2401
OREGON:	Economic Development Department, 595 Cottage St. NE, Salem, OR 97310, 1-800-233-3306 or 547-7842; or (503) 373-1200
PENNSYLVANIA:	Small Business Action Center, Department of Commerce, 404 Forum Bldg., Harrisburg, PA 17120, (717) 783-5700

PUERTO RICO:	Commonwealth, Department of Commerce, Box S, 4275 Old San Juan Station, San Juan, PR 00905, (809) 758-4747
RHODE ISLAND:	Small Business Development Division, 7 Jackson Walkway, Providence, RI 02903, (401) 277-2601
SOUTH CAROLINA:	Business Development M Assistance Division, P.O. Box 927, Columbia, SC 29202, 1-800-922-6684 or (803) 737-0400
SOUTH DAKOTA:	Governor's Office of Economic Development, Capital Lake Plaza, Pierre, SD 57501, 1-800-952-3625 or (605) 773-5032
TENNESSEE:	Small Business Office, 320 Sixth Ave. N., 7th Fl., Rachel Jackson Bldg., Nashville, TN 37219, 1-800-922-6684 or (803) 737-0400
TEXAS:	Small Business Division, P.O. Box 12728 Capitol Station, 410 E. Fifth St., Austin, TX 78711, (512) 472-5059
UTAH:	Small Business Development Center, 660 S. Second St., Rm. 418, Salt Lake City, UT 84111, (801) 581-7905
VERMONT:	Agency of Development and Community Affairs, The Pavillion, Montpelier, VT 05602, 1-800-622-4553 or (802) 828-3221
VIRGINIA:	Small Business and Financial Services, 1000 Washington Bldg., Richmond, VA 23219, (804) 786-3791
WASHINGTON:	Small Business Development Center, 441 Todd Hall, Washington State University, Pullman, WA 99164, (509) 335-1576
WEST VIRGINIA:	Small Business Development Center Division, Governor's Office, Capital Complex, Charleston, WVA 25305, (304) 348-2960
WISCONSIN:	Small Business Ombudsman, Department of Development, 123 W. Washing-

ton Ave., P.O. Box 7970, Madison, WI 53707, 1-800-435-7287 or (608) 266-0562

WYOMING: Economic Development and Stabilization Board, Herschler Bldg., 3rd Fl. E., Cheyenne, WY 82002, (307) 777-7287

CHAMBERS OF COMMERCE

While chambers of commerce charge membership dues, the benefits are worth it. Some of these benefits are practical—such as networking with other members, attending meetings and seminars, participating in local trade events, and receiving literature. But membership also has a certain psychological effect, both on you and your customers. When the "member" sticker goes up on your window or door, or the membership certificate hangs on your office wall, you show that you are a part of an established institution. A certain "approval" is conferred. Many businesses, especially sales organizations, make it a point to join the local chamber, the Better Business Bureau, or other respected local associations right from the start. Nearly 5000 local chambers exist in the United States. If there is none in your immediate community, find out from other businesspeople where the nearest one is located and make contact. Here is a complete list of state chambers; you can write or call them for membership information, either on a statewide or local basis:

ALABAMA: Business Council of Alabama, 468 South Perry St., P.O. Box 76, Montgomery, AL 36195, (205) 834-6000

ALASKA: Alaska State Chamber of Commerce, 310 Second St., Juneau, AK 99801, (907) 586-2323

ARIZONA: Arizona Chamber of Commerce, 1366 E. Thomas Rd., Suite 202, Phoenix, AZ 85012, (602) 248-9172

ARKANSAS: Arkansas State Chamber of Commerce, P.O. Box 3645, 100 Main St., Suite 510, Little Rock, AR 72203-3645, (501) 374-9225

CALIFORNIA:	California Chamber of Commerce, 1027 10th St., P.O. Box 1736, Sacramento, CA 95808, (916) 444-6670
COLORADO:	Colorado Association of Commerce & Industry, 1860 Lincoln St., Suite 550, Denver, CO 80295-0501, (303) 831-7411
CONNECTICUT:	Connecticut Business & Industry Association, Inc., 370 Asylum St., Hartford, CT 06103, (203) 547-1661
DELAWARE:	Delaware State Chamber of Commerce, Inc., One Commerce Center, Suite 200, Wilmington, DE 19801, (302) 655-7221
FLORIDA:	Florida Chamber of Commerce, 136 S. Bronought St., P.O. Box 11309, Tallahassee, FL 32302, (904) 222-2831
GEORGIA:	Business Council of Georgia, 1280 S. CNN Center, Atlanta, GA 30303-2705, (404) 223-2264
HAWAII:	The Chamber of Commerce of Hawaii, Dillingham Bldg., 735 Bishop St., Honolulu, HI 96813, (808) 531-4111
IDAHO:	Idaho Association of Commerce & Industry, 805 Idaho St., P.O. Box 389, Suite 200, Boise, ID 83701, (208) 243-1849
ILLINOIS:	Illinois State Chamber of Commerce, 20 N. Wacker Dr., Chicago, IL 60606, (312) 372-7373
INDIANA:	Indiana State Chamber of Commerce, Inc., Indiana Commerce Center, One N. Capitol, Suite 200, Indianapolis, IN 46204-2248, (317) 634-6407
IOWA:	Iowa Association of Business & Industry, 706 Employers Mutual Bldg., 717 Mulberry St., Des Moines, IA 50309, 1-800-532-1406 (Toll Free—Iowa Only), (515) 244-6149

KANSAS: Kansas Chamber of Commerce & Industry, 500 Bank IV Tower, One Townsite Plaza, Topeka, KS 66603, (913) 357-6321

KENTUCKY: Kentucky Chamber of Commerce, Versailles Rd., P.O. Box 817, Frankfort, KY 40602, (502) 695-4700

LOUISIANA: Louisiana Association of Business & Industry, P.O. Box 80258, Baton Rouge, LA 70898-0258, (504) 928-5388

MAINE: Maine Chamber of Commerce & Industry, 126 Sewall St., Augusta, ME 04330, (207) 623-4568

MARYLAND: Maryland Chamber of Commerce, 60 West St., Suite 405, Annapolis, MD 21401, (301) 269-0642

MASSACHUSETTS: Massachusetts Association of Chamber of Commerce Executives, % Wellesley Chamber of Commerce, 287 Linden St., P.O. Box 715, Wellesley, MA 02181, (617) 235-2446

MICHIGAN: Michigan State Chamber of Commerce, 600 S. Walnut St., Lansing, MI 48933, (517) 371-2100

MINNESOTA: Minnesota Chamber of Commerce & Industry, 300 Hanover Bldg., 480 Cedar St., St. Paul, MN 55101, (612) 292-4650

MISSISSIPPI: Mississippi Economic Council, 656 N. State St., P.O. Box 1849, Jackson, MS 39215-1849, (601) 969-0022

MISSOURI: Missouri Chamber of Commerce, P.O. Box 149, Jefferson City, MO 65102, (314) 634-3511

MONTANA: Montana Chamber of Commerce, 110 Neill Ave., P.O. Box 1730, Helena, MT 59624, (406) 442-2405

NEBRASKA:	Nebraska Association of Commerce & Industry, 1320 Lincoln Mall, P.O. Box 95128, Lincoln, NE 68509, (402) 474-4422
NEVADA:	Nevada Chamber of Commerce Association, P.O. Box 3499, Reno, NV 89505, (702) 786-3030
NEW ENGLAND:	New England Council, Inc., 120 Boylston St., 8th Fl., Boston, MA 02116, (617) 542-2580
NEW HAMPSHIRE:	Business and Industry Association of New Hampshire, 23 School St., Concord, NH 03301, (603) 224-5388
NEW JERSEY:	New Jersey State Chamber of Commerce, 5 Commerce St., Newark, NJ 07102, (201) 623-7070
NEW MEXICO:	Association of Commerce & Industry of New Mexico, 4001 Indian School Rd., N.E., Suite 333, Albuquerque, NM 87110, (505) 265-5847
NEW YORK:	Business Council of New York State, 152 Washington Ave., Albany, NY 12210, (518) 465-7511
NORTH CAROLINA:	North Carolina Citizens for Business and Industry, 336 Fayetteville St. Mall, P.O. Box 2508, Raleigh, NC 27602, (919) 828-0758
NORTH DAKOTA:	Greater North Dakota Association/State Chamber of Commerce, P.O. Box 2467, Fargo, ND 58108, (701) 237-9461
OHIO:	Ohio Chamber of Commerce, 35 E. Gay St., 2nd Fl., Columbus, OH 43215-3181, (614) 228-4201
OKLAHOMA:	Oklahoma Chamber of Commerce & Industry, 4020 N. Lincoln Blvd., Oklahoma City, OK 73105, (405) 424-4003

OREGON:	Associated Oregon Industries, Inc., 1149 Court St., N.E., P.O. Box 12519, Salem, OR 97309, (503) 588-0050
PENNSYLVANIA:	Pennsylvania Chamber of Business & Industry, 222 N. Third St., Harrisburg, PA 17101, (717) 255-3252
PUERTO RICO:	Chamber of Commerce of Puerto Rico, 100 Tetuan St., Old San Juan, PR 00904, (809) 721-6060
RHODE ISLAND:	Rhode Island Chamber of Commerce Federation, 91 Park St., Providence, RI 02908, (401) 272-1400
SOUTH CAROLINA:	South Carolina Chamber of Commerce, Bankers Trust Tower, 1301 Gervais St., Suite 520, P.O. Box 11278, Columbia, SC 29211, (803) 799-4601
SOUTH DAKOTA:	Industry and Commerce Association of South Dakota, P.O. Box 190, Pierre, SD 57501, (605) 224-6161
TENNESSEE:	Tennessee Manufacturers and Taxpayers Association, 226 Capitol Blvd., Suite 800, Nashville, TN 37219, (615) 256-5141
TEXAS:	Texas State Chamber of Commerce*, 206 W. 13th, Suite A, Austin, TX 78701, (512) 472-1594 * A federation of four regional chambers of commerce in Texas East Texas Chamber of Commerce, P.O. Box 1592, Longview, TX 75606, (214) 757-4444 Rio Grande Valley Chamber of Commerce, P.O. Box 1499, Weslaco, TX 78596, (512) 968-3141 South Texas Chamber of Commerce, 6222 N.W. Interstate 10, Suite 100, San An-

tonio, TX 78201, (512) 732-8185

West Texas Chamber of Commerce, 155 Hickory St., P.O. Box 1561, Abilene, TX 79604, (915) 677-4325

VERMONT: Vermont State Chamber of Commerce, P.O. Box 37, Montpelier, VT 05602, (802) 223-3443, (802) 229-0154

VIRGINIA: The Virginia Chamber of Commerce, 9 S. Fifth St., Richmond, VA 23219, (804) 644-1607

WASHINGTON: Association of Washington Business, P.O. Box 658, Olympia, WA 98507, (206) 943-1600

WEST VIRGINIA: West Virginia Chamber of Commerce, 1101 Kanawha Valley Bldg., P.O. Box 2789, Charleston, WV 25330, (304) 342-1115

WISCONSIN: Wisconsin Association of Manufacturers & Commerce, 501 E. Washington Ave., P.O. Box 352, Madison, WI 53701, (608) 258-3400

NATIONAL BUSINESS ORGANIZATIONS

Numerous other business organizations exist that you will want to know about and perhaps investigate for membership. Below are the 13 of most interest to the small business entrepreneur. Following this list is another valuable group organizations, the trade associations in various fields. From among the thousands that exist, we have selected just 48 of the major associations, representing a cross-section of commerce and industry. Each one holds meetings, often in local chapters or councils, where opportunities exist to learn about your business, and who publish newsletters and trade journals that are often of inestimable value in the continuing education and success of the entrepreneur.

General

American Entrepreneurs Association, 2392 Morris Ave., Irvine, CA 92714, (714) 261-2325.

A privately promoted and managed organization built around *Entrepreneur Magazine*, has published more than 250 detailed "how to" manuals on specific small businesses.

National Association of Development Companies, 1730 Rhode Island Ave., NW, Suite 209, Washington, DC 20036, (202) 785-8484.

A union of certified development companies that participate in SBA lending programs (Section 503 companies), providing small entrepreneurs with long-term fixed-asset financing.

National Association of Entrepreneurs (NAE), 2378 S. Broadway, Denver, CO, 80210, (303) 426-1166.

A private networking organization for small business operators, to exchange ideas, information, and support. Chartered chapters exist in many cities of 25,000 or more population. Offers workshops, books, tapes, annual conference.

National Association of Manufacturers (NAM), 1331 Pennsylvania Ave., Suite 1500, Washington, DC 20004-1703, (202) 637-3000.

National Association of Small Business Investment Companies, 1156 15th St., NW, Suite 1101, Washington, DC 20005, (202) 833-8230.

A group of over 400 SBICs, privately capitalized and owned, licensed by the SBA. Provides long-term financing and assistance with equity capital and management. Focuses heavily on job creation.

The National Federation of Independent Business (NFIB), 600 Maryland Ave., SW, Suite 700, Washington, DC 20024, (202) 554-9000.

Boasts a membership of more than 500,000 small and independent businesses. Conducts surveys and studies, lobbies, produces educational materials, holds conferences.

National Small Business United, 1155-15th St., NW, Suite 710, Washington, DC 20005, (202) 293-8830.

An umbrella group representing semi-independent business organizations in Ohio, Wisconsin, New England, Pennsylvania, Michigan, Texas, Denver area, Illinois, Kentucky, Georgia, and California. Founded in 1937, it provides regional networking information, newsletters, legislative liaison.

Women and Minority

National Association of Black and Minority Chambers of Commerce, 654 13th St., Oakland, CA 94612-1241, (415) 451-9231.

Funded by the U.S. Department of Commerce in 1979. Operating primarily in the tourist and convention field, it networks through 350 chambers of commerce.

National Association of Investment Companies (NAIC), 915 15th St., NW, Suite 700, Washington, DC 20005, (202) 347-8600.

A trade association representing minority enterprises that invest in small businesses owned by socially or economically disadvantaged entrepreneurs.

National Association of Minority Contractors, 806 15th St. NW, Suite 340, Washington, DC 20005, (202) 347-8259.

Founded in 1969 to support the needs of minority contractors. Offers newsletters, films, education, seminars, networking.

National Association of Women Business Owners, 600 S. Federal St., Suite 400, Chicago, IL 60605, (312) 922-0465.

Has about 3000 members in 37 local chapters nationwide. Offers monthly local programs, national annual conference.

National Business League, 4324 Georgia Ave., NW, Washington, DC 20011, (202) 829-5900.

The voice of black business on Capitol Hill. Has 127 local chapters covering a variety of industries. Established in 1900.

U.S. Hispanic Chamber of Commerce, 4900 Main Street, Suite 700, Kansas City, MO 64112, (816) 531-6363.

Represents interests of over 400,000 Hispanic-owned enterprises. Develops opportunities with major corporations and governments. Has over 200 chambers.

SELECTED NATIONAL PROFESSIONAL AND TRADE ASSOCIATIONS

American Bankers Association, 1120 Connecticut Ave., NW, Washington, DC 20036, (202) 663-5000.

American Farm Bureau Federation, 225 W. Touhy Ave., Park Ridge, IL 60068, (312) 399-5700.

American Council of Life Insurance, 1001 Pennsylvania Ave., NW, Ste. 500, Washington, DC 20004-2599, (202) 624-2000.

American Electronics Association, 5201 Great America Parkway, Santa Clara, CA 95054, (408) 987-4200.

American Financial Services Association, 1101 14th St., NW, 4th Floor, Washington, DC 20005, (202) 289-0400.

American Health Care Association, 1200 15th St., NW, 8th Floor, Washington, DC 20005, (202) 833-2050.

American Hotel and Motel Association, 888 Seventh Ave., New York, NY 10106, (212) 265-4506.

American Institute of Certified Public Accountants, 1211 Avenue of the Americas, New York, NY 10036, (212) 575-6200.

American Insurance Association, 85 John St., New York, NY 10038, (212) 669-0400.

American Petroleum Institute, 1220 L St., NW, Washington, DC 20005, (202) 682-8000.

American Retail Federation, 1616 H St., NW, Ste. 600, Washington, DC 20006, (202) 783-7971.

American Society of Association Executives, 1575 Eye St., NW, Washington, DC 20005, (202) 626-2723.

American Society of Travel Agents, 1101 King St., Alexandria, VA 22314, (703) 739-2782.

American Trucking Association, 2200 Mill Rd., Alexandria, VA 22314, (703) 838-1800.

Association of American Publishers, 220 E. 23rd Street, New York, NY 10016, (212) 689-8920.

Associated Builders and Contractors, Inc., 729 15th St., NW, Washington, DC 20005, (202) 637-8800.

Associated General Contractors of America, 1957 E St., NW, Washington, DC 20006, (202) 393-2040.

Automotive Parts and Accessories Association, 5100 Forbes Blvd., Lanham, MD 20706, (301) 459-9110.

Automotive Service Association, P.O. Box 929, Bedford, TX 76021, (817) 283-6205.

Automotive Service Industry Association, 444 N. Michigan Ave., Chicago, IL 60611, (312) 836-1300.

Computer & Business Equipment Manufacturers Association, 311 First St., NW, Suite 500, Washington, DC 20001, (202) 737-8888.

Computer Software and Services Information Industry, 1300 N. 17th St., Suite 300, Arlington, VA 22209, (703) 522-5055.

Electronic Industries Association, 2001 Eye St., NW, Washington, DC 20006, (202) 457-4900.

Food Marketing Institute, 1750 K St., NW, Suite 700, Washington, DC 20006, (202) 452-8444.

Grocery Manufacturers Association, 1010 Wisconsin Ave., NW, Suite 800, Washington, DC 20007, (202) 337-9400.

Health Industry Distributors Association, 1701 Pennsylvania Ave., NW, Suite 470, Washington, DC 20006, (202) 659-0050.

Health Industry Manufacturers Association, 1030 15th St., NW, Suite 1100, Washington, DC 20005, (202) 452-8240.

Independent Insurance Agents of America, Inc., 100 Church St., Suite 1901, New York, NY 10007, (212) 285-2500.

Independent Petroleum Association of America, 1101 16th St., NW, 2nd Floor, Washington, DC 20036, (202) 857-4722.

Information Industry Association, 555 New Jersey Ave., NW, Suite 800, Washington, DC 20001, (202) 639-8262.

International Association for Financial Planning, Two Concourse Parkway, Suite 800, Atlanta, GA 30328, (404) 395-1605.

International Communications Industries Association, 3150 Spring St., Fairfax, VA 22031-2399, (703) 273-7200.

National Association of Broadcasters, 1771 N St., NW, Washington, DC 20036, (202) 429-5300.

National Association of Chain Drug Stores, P.O. Box 14177-49 Alexandria, VA 22314, (703) 549-3001.

National Association of Convenience Stores, 1605 King St., Alexandria, VA 22314-2792, (703) 684-3600.

National Association of Home Builders, 15th and M Sts., NW, Washington, DC 20005, (202) 822-0200.

National Association of Realtors, 403 N. Michigan Ave., Chicago, IL 60611, (312) 329-8200.

National Association of Truck Stop Operators, P.O. Box 1285, Alexandria, VA 22313-1285, (703) 549-2100.

National Association of Wholesaler-Distributors, 1725 K St., NW, Suite 710, Washington, DC 20006, (202) 872-0885.

National Automobile Dealers Association, 8400 Westpark Dr., McLean, VA 22102, (703) 821-7000.

National Business Incubators Association, 114 N. Hanover St., Carlisle, PA 17013, (717) 249-4508.

National Forest Products Association, 1250 Connecticut Ave., NW, Suite 200, Washington, DC 20036, (202) 463-2700.

National Home Furnishing Association, 220 W. Gerry Drive, Wood Dale, IL 60191, (312) 595-0200.

National Industrial Transportation League, 1090 Vermont Ave., NW, Suite 410, Washington, DC 20005, (202) 842-3870.

National Lumber & Building Materials Dealers Association, 40 Ivy St., SE, Washington, DC 20003, (202) 547-2230.

National Restaurant Association, 311 First St., NW, Washington, DC 20001, (202) 638-6100.

Printing Industries of America, Inc., 1730 N. Lynn St., Arlington, VA 22209, (703) 841-8100.

Travel Industry Association of America, 1133 21st St., NW, Washington, DC 20036, (202) 293-1433.

CENTERS FOR HIGH-TECH ASSISTANCE

A number of selected states offer specialized help to companies in high-technology fields, research and development, and biological sciences—the so-called "clean industries." Here are 43 such centers, councils, and programs that can help new or expanding high-tech businesses with advice, research, networking, and even financial assistance.

ALABAMA: Alabama High Technology Assistance Center, University of Alabama, 336 Morton Hall, Huntsville, AL 35899, (205) 895-6409

ARKANSAS: Arkansas Science and Technology Authority, 100 Main St., Suite 450, Little Rock, AR 72201, (501) 371-3554

Center for Technology Transfer, University of Arkansas, 49 Engineering Research Center, Fayetteville, AR 72701, (501) 575-3747

CALIFORNIA: Western Research Application Center, University of Southern California, 3716 S. Hope St., Los Angeles, CA 90007-4344, (213) 743-2371

COLORADO: Business Advancement Center, Colorado University, 1690 38th St., Room 101, Boulder, CO 80301, (303) 444-5723

CONNECTICUT: Connecticut Product Development Corp., 93 Oak St., Hartford, CT 06106, (203) 566-2920

FLORIDA: Product Innovation Center, The Progress Center, One Progress Blvd., Box 7, Alachua, FL 32615, (904) 462-3942

NASA/Southern Technology Application Center, University of Florida, Box 24, Alachua, FL 32615, (904) 392-0854

GEORGIA: Advanced Technology Development Center, 430 Tenth St., NW, Suite N-116, Atlanta, GA 30318, (404) 894-3575

ILLINOIS:	I-Tec Program, Illinois Dept. of Commerce, 100 W. Randolph St., Chicago, IL 60601, (312) 917-3982
	Inventor's Council, 53 W. Jackson St., Suite 1041, Chicago, IL 60604, (312) 939-3329
	Venture Capital and Direct Loan Program, Illinois Development Finance Authority, 2 N. Vasant St., Chicago, IL 60602, (217) 782-6861
INDIANA:	Business and Industrial Development Center, Purdue University, Engineering Administration Building, West Lafayette, IN 47907, 1-800-821-8261
	Innovators Forum, Rose-Hulman Institute of Technology, 5500 Wabash Ave., Terre Haute, IN 47803, (812) 877-1511
	Inventors and Enterpreneurs Society, Purdue University, Hammond, IN 46323, (219) 989-2354
IOWA:	Center for Industrial Research and Service, Iowa State University, 205 Engineering Annex, Ames, IA 50011, (515) 294-3420
KANSAS:	Kansas Technology Enterprise Corporation, 400 S.W. 8th St., Topeka, KS 66603, (913) 296-5272
KENTUCKY:	Business and Technology Office, Kentucky Commerce Cabinet, Capital Plaza Tower, Frankfort, KY 40601, (502) 564-7670
MAINE:	The New Enterprise Institute, Center for Research and Advanced Study, University of Southern Maine, 246 Deering Ave., Portland, ME 04102 (207) 780-442-
MARYLAND:	Technology Extension Service, University of Maryland, Engineering Research Cen-

	ter, College Park, MD 20742-3261, (301) 454-7941
MASSACHUSETTS:	Massachusetts Technology Development Corp., 84 State St, Suite 500, Boston, MA 02109, (617) 723-4920
MICHIGAN:	Industrial Technology Institute, P.O. Box 1485, Ann Arbor, MI 48106, (313) 769-4000
	Technology Transfer Network, Michigan Department of Commerce, P.O. Box 30225, Lansing, MI 48909, (517) 335-2139
MINNESOTA:	Science and Technology Office, 900 American Center Building, 150 E. Kellogg Blvd, St Paul, MN 55101, (612) 297-1554
MISSOURI:	High Technology Program, Missouri Department of Economic Development, P.O. Box 118, Jefferson City, MO 65102, (314) 751-4241
MONTANA:	Montana Science and Technology Alliance, Department of Commerce, 46 N. Last Chance Gulch, Room 2B, Helena, MT 59620, (406) 449-2778
NEW JERSEY:	Commission on Science and Technology, 122 W. State St. (CN 832), Trenton, NJ 08625 (609) 984-1671
NEW MEXICO:	Technological Innovation Program, Anderson School of Management, University of New Mexico, Albuquerque, NM 87131, (505) 277-5934
NEW YORK:	Centers for Advanced Technology Programs, N.Y. State Science and Technology Foundation, 99 Washington Ave., Suite 1730, Albany, NY 12210, (518) 474-4349
NORTH CAROLINA:	Technological Development Authority, N.C. Department of Commerce, 430 N.

Salisbury St., Raleigh, NC 27611, (919) 733-7022

Science and Technology Research Center, P.O. Box 12235, Research Triangle Park, NC 27709-2235, (919) 549-0671

OHIO: Ohio Technology Transfer Organization, 1712 Neil Avenue, Columbus, OH 43210, (614) 292-5485

Technology Information Exchange (TIE-IN), Department of Development, Ohio Data Users Center, P.O. Box 1001, Columbus, OH 43266-0413, (614) 466-2115

OKLAHOMA: Technology Transfer Center, Oklahoma State University District Office, P.O. Box 1378, Ada, OK 74820, (405) 332-4100

PENNSYLVANIA: NASA Industrial Applications Center, University of Pittsburgh, 823 William Pitt Union, Pittsburgh, PA 15260, (412) 648-7000

PUERTO RICO: Scientific Community Council, Inc., P.O. Box 2284, Hato Rey, PR 00918, (809) 751-1815

SOUTH CAROLINA: Research and Information Resources Division, S.C. State Development Board, P.O. Box 927, Columbia, SC 29202, (803) 737-0400

TENNESSEE: Tennessee Technology Foundation, P.O. Box 23184, Knoxville, TN 37933, (615) 694-6772

TEXAS: Center for Technology Development and Transfer, ECJ 2.516 University of Texas, Austin, TX 78712, (512) 471-1653

UTAH: Utah Innovation Center, 419 Wakara Way, Suite 206, Research Park, Salt Lake City, UT 84108, (801) 584-2500

VIRGINIA: Center for Innovative Technology, The Hallmark Building, Suite 201, 13873 Park Center Road, Herndon, VA 22071, (703) 689-3000

WISCONSIN: Innovation Service Center, University of Wisconsin, 402 McCutchan Hall, Whitewater, WI 53190, (414) 472-1365

ENTREPRENEURIAL IDEAS FROM A TO Z | 15

The annals of American enterprise are full of success stories. While these stories vary greatly in the details of the approaches used, there are some recurring themes. Here are some of the common denominators in these brief examples:

- Drive
- Enthusiasm
- Ambition
- Hard work
- Analytical ability
- Innovativeness
- Perseverance
- Organizational ability
- Experience

Notice that in the above list, which is by no means exhaustive, one element that is absent is money. Neither the desire to be rich nor the availability of a lot of start-up money was among the leading factors characterizing successful innovators. Of course, money is necessary to run any new business. But in a surprising number of cases, amounts of $5000 or less were used to "bankroll" new ideas into viable businesses.

The following case histories also offer evidence that entrepreneurs are not simply born—they are made by dint of hard work and the skills acquired through experience. Whether these other qualities were inborn or acquired, they do, however, seem to have the following: a sixth sense—a vision that enables them to see an opportunity out of the corner of their eyes; reflexes like a downhill ski racer's which enable them to change pace or direction as needed; and a sense of confidence in their own abilities that rules out the word "can't."

Here, then, is a group of business opportunities—one for each letter of the alphabet—that have been put into action by "can do" capitalists.

A
ANTIQUES ON CONSIGNMENT

One of the popular methods of retailing today is via carts, kiosks, and mall displays in large enclosed shopping centers. An antique buff got an idea to arrange with a shopping mall to display good antiques on a particular weekend and to pay the mall management a percentage of all sales. Then he arranged with a number of antique dealers to "borrow" some selected pieces from their inventory that would be sold at the mall at a predetermined percentage. In addition, the "gypsy marketer" bought some antiques, such as jewelry, bric-a-brac, porcelains and other small, traffic-attracting items, and added them to the inventory. Each week another mall location within a 100-mile radius was chosen. Wherever possible, the antique seller would tie in with a larger mall event to ensure optimum traffic and promotional opportunities. The earlier part of the week was used to seek out merchandise and set up the two-way deals. Thus, the dealer enjoyed plenty of free time, but he also enjoyed the weekend opportunities for selling and profiting at minimal money investments—and in a business activity that he loved.

B
BIRD WATCHERS FROM HOME

Make money by watching birds? It seems improbable, but one entrepreneur did just that. There are tens of thousands of people who love our little feathered friends. They subscribe to bird magazines, buy bird feeders and bird foods, join the Audubon Society, go on bird-watching trips, buy costly binoculars to watch birds in the wilds from afar—and even buy video cassettes for $29.95 so that they can ogle the orioles from the comfort of their couches. The last item became the province of a writer-photographer from North Carolina. For five years he gave over his spare time to producing a five-volume videocassette library of bird lore. To give the project the wings of credibility and authority, he obtained a license from the National Audubon Society, agreeing to pay this group a percentage of all video sales. Promoting the five-volume video library through specialty publications and clubs of bird aficionados, he claims that business is good. Truly, his nest egg is growing.

C
COMPUTER PROGRAMMING

Few entrepreneurs in the computer field have been as successful as Charles B. Wang, a 45-year-old genius who was born in China and built a billion-dollar software company in Garden City, New York.

Wang's success came in four stages. The first one was to recognize that vast opportunities exist in computer programming. He noticed that the *New York Times* carried two-and-a-half pages of help wanted ads for programmers. When the young college graduate told his mother about this, she inquired what a programmer was. Wang said honestly, that he did not know, "but boy, do they need them." So he got a job as a programmer-trainee. The second stage was noting that the software that was available served only the hardware manufacturers, not the customers. Wang began talking and *listening to* the customers—the third step. Then, with very few resources, he started manufacturing the kind of flexible software customers wanted—the fourth stage. Today he still is entirely customer oriented.

He does not hire sales representatives for their technical knowledge, but for their empathy with people; he calls them "product owners" and makes them totally responsible for their customers and territory. "We're here to learn from our clients and from each other," says Wang. The formula has been wildly successful.

D
DIAPER MANUFACTURING

Perhaps you have seen Drypers on the store shelf. A national brand of disposable diapers may not sound like a "small business," but the two college-mate founders of this Houston-based business started smaller than small in a previous throw-away diaper company in Oregon. In fact, they started from below zero.

Just a year out of college, they had the idea for a unique low-cost, disposal diaper. The market, they reasoned, is forever; the modern economic climate with its high percentage of two-working-parent families, made such a convenience item almost mandatory. They reasoned right, and in a short time they were successful. There was only one fly in the ointment: In raising money they had given up too much control, and their outside investors owned 65 percent of the company. Whether it was due to personality conflicts or just plain avarice, the majority investors forced the two founding partners out. Because their home territory in Oregon had become inhospitable, the partners moved to Houston and found new investors, as well as friendly municipal officials. They started up again with Drypers, and are once more heading toward a $10 million company—but this time they are in charge. Wally Klemp and David Pitassi agree that they "had a dream," and they advise other entrepreneurs to "never give up on your dream."

E
EMPLOYMENT AGENCY

Adversity knocks some people down for good and spurs others to get up, dust themselves off, and start all over again. Perhaps this latter response is the essence of the successful entrepreneur. Marilyn

Ounjian, who heads Careers USA in Philadelphia, is an example. On her way to a $15 million employment agency she stumbled badly, but learned from her errors. She started a business training disadvantaged workers, based strictly on the contract promises of a friend in the government. The expected contract did not materialize, however.

Mrs. Ounjian did not have a written agreement, and her personal funds were insufficient to cover the business, so she had to close. It was a bitter lesson: Never launch any operation in business without written assurance that the project was ordered and would be paid for. When this entrepreneur started all over again and ultimately won out, she could say, "If you work hard, this country allows you to do whatever you want." Or as Michael Korda, a well-known author and entrepreneur, stated it: "The freedom to fail is vital if you're going to succeed."

F
FLOWERS ARE HIS FORTUNE

This flower vendor does not want his name used, nor his home base revealed. Yet his strategy is so ingenious that it needs to be told. His location is in an outlying, low-rent section of a major East Coast city. His original equipment was two used floral display cases, a large Rollodex directory, an assortment of floral containers, and some small gift envelopes. Later expenditures were made for promotional mailers, special-events cards to be attached to flower deliveries, and a small delivery panel truck that bore his unmistakable logo.

What is most striking about his example, however, is how he specialized his flower business as a promotional tool: His idea was to send companies' prospective business clients a single rose in a bud vase, with a card attached stating, "I would like to make an appointment with Mr. _____ to discuss something of great importance to him, and I will call you for confirmation within the next few days." This idea was pitched successfully to numerous companies that sold everything from insurance to computers to various systems. In addition, he offered birthday and anniversary services to executives, sending flowers and cards to their lists. Then he started a flowers-of-the-month subscription service. From what we are able to ascertain, everything about this entrepreneur's business continues to be green and to thrive.

G
GOURMET GROCERY DELIVERIES

How do you start a business without any cash? You use your head to come up with an idea that fills a need, that depends heavily on personal service, and that requires no overhead or inventory. PDQ Grocery Delivery was such a business. In this case, PDQ stood for "Phone & Delivery Quickly" and filled a need in the apartment-studded downtown area of a big city. The young entrepreneur who started and successfully ran it by himself—later adding several associates who would work after-hours and weekends—began by posting notices of his service on the bulletin boards of apartment houses around his neighborhood.

He visited every grocery store in the area and made "wholesale" arrangements with them, as well as with a couple of nearby distributors of gourmet comestibles, a bakery, and a wine shop. His posted "shopping lists" reflected competitive pricing, and his deliveries were made to the apartments during late afternoon and evening hours. The minimum order was $15, and each delivery had a $2 charge tacked onto the order. By "ganging up" his purchasing trips and deliveries, he was able to handle as many as 16 orders between 4 and 8 P.M. at an average of $4 profit per order—plus his profit on the groceries—a neat side business for a "retired" entrepreneur.

H
HOTELS/MOTELS

This is not your ordinary success story. Of course it *is* about success, but more than that, it is about perseverance. It is the story of the late Steve Rubell, who was the former owner of the famed Studio 54 club in New York. Briefly, he lost the club in 1980 due to huge tax delinquencies and was sentenced to federal prison. From the jet-set world of celebrities to the hostile world of a penitentiary was about as large a slide down as any person could make. It could have destroyed him. But being honest with himself and recognizing his mistakes, Rubell found the personal strength that would allow him later to bounce back from the bottom. When he was finally discharged, he and his former partner, Ian Schrager, were able to scrape together $30,000. They took a six months' option on a run-down hotel, and then they found that in order to get money to reopen it as an ultramodern, glitzy establishment, they had to give half of the equity away. However, the venture partner acted as a front for the bank that put up the mortgage money. Rubell's strategy worked, and, less than a decade later, the Manhattan hotel and several others the group bought and revitalized are worth an estimated $180 million.

I
THE IDEA SHOP

Ideas are generally carried around in our heads, where they take up little space, are infinitely replaceable, and cost nothing. However, they can be worth a great deal. Every major city has "ideators," who are sought out, or who become known through advertising, publicity, and networking; who sell advice and counsel in virtually all professions for substantial dollars. What is important is your own background, your own credibility: a reputation as an expert; experience in the "big city" or with a well-known company; making a good appearance; putting up an impressive front. These tangible and intangible assets combine to make an idea person successful.

One young college woman who was a whiz in economics and financing, through her academic reputation, landed a job as treasurer of a large, national organization. Within a year she had turned the group's flat finances around, and then, using this experience as a springboard, she was able to launch a successful financial consulting business. Now she sells ideas. You could, too. Capital investment? You need more confidence than cash. To get ahead, use your head.

J
JOB FAIRS

You can create a simple business out of others' employment needs. Growing in popularity from coast to coast are "job fairs" that bring employers and prospective employees together in a more efficient and effective manner than through the Help Wanted ads. Peruse these newspaper columns in many large cities and you will be struck by the profusion of ads. In some metropolitan markets the unemployment rate is so low that fresh employees—with the exception of high school and college graduates—are practically nonexistent and workers play musical chairs, switching jobs with other employed people. The Washington, DC, area is such a market. A job fair helps to take the pressure off both companies seeking personnel and employees searching out new opportunities.

To organize one of these events, you rent a prestigious hotel meeting hall or a portion of a civic or convention center; you lease chairs and tables; advertise and promote the fair, usually held on an evening or weekend; and place small, inexpensive classified ads in the Help Wanted sections of local newspapers. You charge fees to participating companies and invite organizations such as chambers of commerce, employment and executive search agencies, and even franchise operators (also for a fee, of course). You charge a small admission fee to those seeking jobs. Not only are you making money on both sides, but you are also providing a service.

K
KIDS' CARE SUPPLIER

This entrepreneur is really a modern, motorized peddler—but one who focuses on the needs of those providing child care. It all started with a woman who owned a small day-care center and found that it was sometimes difficult to get all the supplies she needed—drawing materials, paper goods, even mats and napping cots. She checked with other day-care providers and kindergartens, discovering that the problems were universal. Her question to them was: Would they purchase from a list of common everyday supplies if these were priced right and delivered to their doors? Yes, echoed the respondents, and the entrepreneur was in business.

She recruited her daughter, bought a second-hand van, got a good area map, and started the research and planning. The wholesalers were contacted for goods and prices; the area map was divided into manageable sections that would be canvassed once a week; circulars and price lists were printed; the van was decorated with a gay business sign—and the women were off. Their upfront cash investment was just a couple of thousand dollars. It took a while to generate the confidence that customers needed in the new mobile enterprise, but pretty soon the vendors took in as much as $500 a day—and that wasn't kids' stuff!

L
LEISURETIME ACTIVITIES

This entrepreneurial idea combines today's trend toward congregate living with these complex-dwellers' desire for organized leisuretime activities. Many people are not self-sufficient when it comes to filling their segments of idle time, a fact that applies especially to the fastest-growing segment of our population, the retirees. Large apartment and condominium developments often sell their properties on the basis of their recreational and entertainment facilities. In southern Florida, for instance, Century Villages have become meccas for tens of thousands of retirees, primarily because Red Buttons promises them great entertainment. Many smaller complexes, however, do not have the facilities or the money to employ in-house social directors.

So why not become a floating social director? Organize a show that can be put on within smaller apartment or condo complexes, or create outdoor entertainments—al fresco minishows, perhaps with audience participation and a barbecue. Fees could be charged to the tenant association, or advance tickets could be sold through local volunteer association chairpersons—perhaps even with a built-in discount or rebate for the sponsoring association. Customary advance payments usually take care of any out-of-pocket expenses. Developers, real estate agencies, and managers should welcome such a service, because it can help sell their properties. Your investment is virtually zero—as long as you have million-dollar talent and ideas.

M
MAGAZINE PUBLISHING

There is a fascination to magazine and newspaper publishing. It is like going on a stage. You, the publisher or editor, become the star. You can express your opinions and be creative; you can influence others.

There are more than 4000 known publishers of magazines of all sizes, kinds, and frequencies in the United States. They can vary from small newsprint editions run off on a photocopy machine to big four-color glossies costing several dollars per copy to produce. It is not a business to enter unless you know it backward and forward. It is also the kind of business that is pretty cash intensive. To compound the difficulty, neither banks nor the SBA generally finance magazine publishing, so that your own resources and those of privately solicited investors have to be tapped. With all these negatives, there are still hundreds of entrepreneurs entering this field every year. While almost an equal number fail at the task, there are enough successes to provide positive role models and galvanize other would-be publishers into action.

Take George Goldberg of Los Angeles. He saw a need for a singles magazine and started one. Of course he was not without experience or sources for capital. His new publication, named 2, started out with 25,000 copies being distributed to affluent singles in southern California. It is studded with the faces and bios of eligible men and women who pay from $110 for having a small black-and-white photo of themselves published to $4450 for a full page. Initial success was so great that Goldberg is planning a New York edition.

N
NOSTALGIA

The adage, "one man's junk is another man's treasure," has never been truer than during the past couple of decades. Attic disoveries and inheritances from Grandma have become fashionable. At fairs and shopping malls you can have your photo taken in Gay Nineties costume; shopping centers sell old-fashioned costumes; art deco designs are again all the rage; and Scott Joplin's ragtime music is played both by jazz and symphonic interpreters. Antique shops have a steady draw, and antique shows in shopping malls can attract thousands.

"Collectibles" is the term used today to dignify nostalgia items, and the category includes old political paraphernalia, baseball cards, stamps and coins, toys and banks; also books, photos, postcards, art deco china and glass, and "estate" jewelry. The Franklin Mint makes a mint of money on this trend. Why can't you? A good location (even a commercially zonable backyard), persistance in discovering your wares, and a little showmanship can put you into the nostalgia business with very little money.

O
OPTOMETRY

Some professions, like optometry and pharmacology, do not require you to be a licensed practitioner in that field. Many an astute entrepreneur has taken up these professions *as businesses* and hired the necessary professionals. Eric Kriss, a Boston management consultant, had an idea about eye-care centers. His investigations and background prepared him to raise the necessary capital from private investment sources. Now he runs 30 MediVision centers. They are all tightly organized, professionally managed, and subject to a strict accounting system that assures investor returns based on a highly productive—and profitable—operation. Each center has an ophthalmologist attached to it, as well as a dispensing optometrist. The patients get excellent care and streamlined professional treatment. The revenues for 1988 are reported to be in excess of $50 million. It's clear to see that a well-researched idea, combined with professional management, can spell success.

P
PHOTO STUDIO ON WHEELS

Even though this entrepreneur's occasional golf game was considerably over par, the idea he had one day on the ninth hole was right at par. He took some photos of his fellow players as they were putting that last hole on the short course. A photography hobbyist, he knew just how to frame the shot for optimum drama. The pictures were a success when he showed them, and they were displayed on the clubhouse wall. Soon other players asked to have their photos taken at the ninth or eighteenth hole. And so the heretofore amateur photographer snapped his way into a profitable weekend business.

He stationed himself each Saturday and Sunday at the ninth and eighteenth holes and shot away—with his camera. As money accumulated, he fixed up his van as a portable darkroom and developed the rolls of film as fast as they were exposed. While the photographed players were still regaling themselves in the "nineteenth hole" (the club lounge), the entrepreneur came in with pictures ready to show—and to sell. There were also reprint and enlargement orders. The addition to his repertoire of miniatures of the golfers' photos inserted in key-holder "telescopes" was another surefire money-maker.

Q
QUILTS

Have you priced a handmade quilt lately? Quilts, especially those that are, or look like, heirlooms, are hot items today. Gift shops and exclusive boutiques sell them for $250 to $550. If you are lucky, you might discover one—perhaps slightly used—at a farmer's market or country fair for below the going price.

To produce one takes very little in materials. Odds and ends of colorful cottons and fabrics can be bought up cheaply at fabric stores. Designs are available in pattern books or can be created on a quadrille-ruled pad (using an eight-to-one projection—that is, an eighth-inch square on your pad equals one inch of the actual quilt). You can develop wedding ring, patriotic, and random patchwork patterns, or anything more ingenious that you can think of and execute. Canvassing the area's gift shops, linen stores, bedding shops, and department stores with a handmade sample, a catchy business card, a pricing table, and an efficient delivery schedule, can put you into business. It would be wise then to line up some workers to help you—perhaps in homes where elderly women live who would like to keep busy and earn supplementary money. Remember that stores usually operate on a double markup, meaning, you'll only get half of the actual sales price. You can get a little more if you are willing to sell your quilts on consignment, meaning, collect your money only after they have sold the quilt.

R
RESTAURANT

Perhaps America's most popular, and most vulnerable, enterprise is a restaurant. It is one of those limited business categories that the SBA ordinarily will not back. Yet nearly half-a-million different restaurants are licensed. New ones open daily; old ones close up. Running a successful eating establishment requires money, labor, risk, patience, and optimism—not to mention getting through the red tape of permits.

Because of the high turnover of restaurants, it is quite easy to buy an existing location where a restaurant is about to close or has already closed. There are pros and cons to buying a defunct location. Was the problem management? Was the type of food wrong for that neighborhood? Was it a bad location? Was there too much competition? Were there sanitary problems that received notoriety in the press? Rick Cardin and Joe Sanfellipo of San Francisco found 17 factors contributing to restaurant's success or lack thereof. They applied scientific analysis and management to the creation of the O! Deli Corp. franchise restaurants; today the business is worth $6 million.

S
SENIOR SERVICES

A business that provides needed services to the fast-growing senior-citizen population should be assured of success. All available statistics point to it: People live longer; they want more services; they have higher disposable incomes with which to pay for these services. Altogether, it is a positive, optimistic picture. A college teacher in the Washington, DC, area thought so, too, and he developed an office where seniors—mostly widows—pay a modest $25 annual fee in order to receive many small services and referrals.

The professional services and businesses to whom members are referred also pay a fee for registering with the senior-services office. Such services could be as simple as getting some papers copied or notarized, or as complex as making up a will or filing tax returns. They could consist of shopping for a very special gift, finding appropriate medical attention for a member who is new to the area, writing a business letter, examining a lease, giving guidance with a car or appliance purchase, and planning a trip. The potential is endless and limited only by the imagination and ambition of the service's manager. It is also a business that can be staffed by seniors, or franchised to them.

T
TOY RECYCLING

If you have ever been to a big toy store, from a Toytown discount warehouse at the low end of the scale, all the way up to F.A.O. Schwartz, you know what today's toys cost. Their sophistication and price tags may make you wonder, how high is the sky? Your *second* thought might be, what happens to these $20, $50, and $100 toys once junior gets tired of them? Kids in the opulent suburbs, who have parents and grandparents heaping carloads of stuffed animals, dolls, and electronic games on them, have a blasé approach to toys: They tire of them quickly.

Ah—but in this sociological truth lurks an idea for an entrepreneur: Open up a toy store that stocks good-as-new toys, bikes, and other luxury kidstuff. The operating principle of such a store is like that of a secondhand clothing store that offers only designer clothes from rich ladies' closets. The latter have done very well, even in some fancy neighborhoods, such as upper Madison Avenue in New York. The most difficult aspect of this business would be the acquisition of good toys. But running clever little ads in suburban newspapers, posting notices on local bulletin boards, and pointing direct mail to selected neighborhoods might be just the ticket to building your own "Santaland II."

U
UNIQUE STAMP POSTERS

In a CPA's office hangs a large blowup of the U.S. Postage stamp that came out a couple of years ago to honor the country's certified public accountants. Underneath the blowup was the actual 22¢ stamp, and both items were nicely, and expensively, framed. The CPA had paid $200 for this vestibule attraction.

Instead of a signed and numbered lithograph, a poster of the stamp would serve the same decorative purpose at less than half the price of the fancier version.

For more than a century, new and colorful stamps have been issued each year to honor organizations, events, professions, famous people, and presidents. For each one there is a legion of potential poster customers. How many business and professional people are there whose name is Washington, Jefferson, Lincoln, Adams? How many who are bird watchers, animal protectors, antique car collectors, state capital workers, supporters of Boy and Girl Scouts? The list is endless, and so are the special-interest journals that could be used to reach the attention of these people. Stamps are beautiful, popular, and in the public domain. They are just one item in the vast arsenal of government-issue products that could become the basis of a tidy business.

V
VIDEO GAMES

It seems that every time a vacancy occurs in a neighborhood shopping center, another video store opens up. They persist, but there has been a decided change. While the mesmerizing video fad games of the past decade are fading, new high-quality video products are making their appearance. From the time when the industry, with the help of companies like Atari, swelled to a $2.5 billion volume in 1982, then plummeted to $90 million, till now, when it is nearly back to its peak, something good has happened. Japanese imports like Nintendo have surfaced with superior graphics and techniques,

177

and other software is light-years ahead of its primitive ancestors of a mere decade ago. Video stores are getting a shot in the arm, and those retailers who display and promote well should survive and thrive. If you plan to go into a high-tech business, look *ahead*. Remember, fads are fickle, and Hula Hoops once were all the rage.

W
WIFE ENTERTAINMENT

If this sounds like a chauvinist approach to a new business, it's only because the majority of conventioneers are still men. Many men's wives accompany them to other cities, enjoying this break in their routines. Once there, they seek diversion while their husbands are gassing at meetings. This leads to an opportunity; the entrepreneur who provides organized entertainment for the accompanying wives can make an interesting and lucrative living.

A suburban housewife near Washington, DC, turned her social skills to this need and built up a great convention-service business—showing her charges the White House, the Capitol, the Washington and Lincoln monuments, and countless other free attractions in the nation's capital. Her primary investment was her time and ingenuity, plus a smart brochure that went to convention planners and hotels.

In Atlanta another enterprising woman developed a series of bus trips and downtown walking tours to keep conventioneers' wives happy and occupied. You, too, could do this. Tours could be aimed at sightseeing, specialized shopping, architectural attractions, gardens, and a dozen other interests. London long has been famous for its walking tours. Just add a touch of Yankee imagination and go.

X
XEROX

Xerox is a trademark, and not every copy shop is equipped with Xerox machines. However, the word "Xerox" has become almost generic in its application to any kind of photo-reproducing equipment, and activity; it's even used informally as a verb. Like video stores, photocopying centers are proliferating all over the landscape. This is more than a passing fancy, and unless comparable, affordable home machinery is developed in the future—like cheap laser printers or optical scanner-printers—photo-copy centers will remain useful and even profitable enterprises.

Strangely enough, many small, conventional printers are still in business, which indicates that printing, as well as reproducing printed matter, is still a solid need among an increasingly marketing-conscious clientale. If photoreproduction has squashed anything, it is the use of carbon paper. Exemplary companies like Kinko, which is nationwide, and Staples, which is in the Washington, DC, area, do a landoffice business and bear studying—especially their auxiliary services that are evident profit centers—if you plan to go into this business.

Y
YOGURT

Who hasn't tasted this Middle-Eastern staple? It comes creamy on your supermarket shelf and frozen in specialty, franchised yogurt shops. There is now a growing taste for frozen tofu, which has no cholesterol and is made from the soy bean. Even ice-cream chain stores are adding the less-caloric frozen yogurt and no-cholesterol substitute for the health-conscious.

If you are planning to go into this dessert business, you can buy an existing shop from an owner who wants to go out of it (and you better find out *why*), or buy a brand new location from a franchise. You can study the making of the products, or find out where to buy them wholesale, and open your own store—if you know enough about the business. Location is important; low traffic flow can kill you quicker than thieving employees. The hours will be long, but the profit can be generous. You might get company financing, find silent investment partners, or even get bank financing if you can present a sound business plan that projects your future (and your payback) credibly. Your personal ingenuity in running an exceptionally attractive business will be as vital as the quality of your product.

Z
ZODIAC

Virtually all newspapers, and many magazines, carry a horoscope column. This popularity can be tapped further. How about opening a Zodiac Shop in a busy shopping mall? Think of the various possibilities: greeting cards for each sign of the Zodiac (if you cannot find good preexisting ones, produce your own—they could be a real money-maker at a 25 to 30¢ cost and $1 retail); jewelry with the Zodiac sign; key chains; pens; paperweights. Go to a novelty and gift show and see how many Zodiac items are available. How about a line of stationery; book plates and covers; books on the subject— especially those by well-known columnists like Jeanne Dixon, Sidney Omarr and Linda Goodman? Perhaps you could get some of the famed astrologists to make personal appearances for autograph sessions. Have an astrologer on the premises on busy weekends; properly publicized, this strategy could crowd your store to the stars. For some this is merely fun and games, but for millions, including the entrepreneur who makes the most of it, it is serious business.

> You may have a fresh start any moment you choose, for this thing that we call "failure" is not the falling down, but the staying down.
> —Mary Pickford

APPENDIX I: FORMS

SAMPLE FORMS

Low-Cost Business Booklets from the SBA

The U.S. Small Business Administration publishes several dozen booklets that can be obtained from local SBA offices, SCORE offices, the SBA's publication service, P.O. Box 15434, Fort Worth, TX 76119. A directory of all publications is available free at any of the above resources. The following reprint, "Business Plan for Small Service Firms," is of particular interest to small entrepreneurs. Included in this booklet are a personal financial statement form, 12-month cash-flow chart, start-up costs schedule, and expenses worksheet, among other forms.

Records Retention Checklist

It has been estimated that among the federal government, states, counties, and municipalities, about 250,000 forms have been created. The statutes of limitation pertaining to business records vary from state to state. However, an analysis of more than 900 federal and state regulations has created this brief guide. Your own personal requirements must also be taken into consideration. Obviously, customer lists, leases, contracts, annual financial statements, and legal documents should be kept for as long as you plan to be in business. These important documents are marked on the checklist by an asterisk (*).

LIST OF SAMPLE FORMS

SBA "Business Plan for Small Service Firms" (Booklet)
Typical Commercial Bank Loan Application
Monthly Cash Flow Projection (SBA Form 1100). For more details, see Gustav Berle, *How To Raise Money for Your Business* (Wiley, 1990).
Worksheet for Meeting Tax Obligations (SBA Management Aid 1.013)
Sole Proprietorship Tax Form (Form 1040, Schedule C)
Partnership Income Tax Return (Form 1065)
Corporation Short Form Income Tax Return (Form 1120-A)
Corporation Income Tax Return (Form 1120)
S Corporation Income Tax Return (Form 1120 S)
Corporation Estimated Tax (Form 1120-W)
Records Retention Checklist

Description of Documents	Years to be Retained
ACCOUNTING RECORDS	
Bank statements, deposit slips	3
Payroll records and time cards	3
Dividend checks (cancelled)	6
Expense reports	6
Subsidiary ledgers (incl. A/P and A/R)	6
Trial balances (monthly)	6
Checks (payroll and general)	8
Payroll earnings records	8
Vouchers for payment to vendors, employees)	8
*Audit reports	indefinite
*General ledgers and journals	indefinite

Description of Documents	Years to be Retained
CORPORATE RECORDS	
Mortgages, notes, expired leases	8
*Bylaws, charter and minute books	indefinite
*Cash books	indefinite
*Capital stock and bond records, stock certificates and transfer lists	indefinite
*Checks for taxes, property, fulfillment of important contracts	indefinite
*Contracts and agreements	indefinite
*Copyrights and trademark registrations	indefinite
*Deeds and easements	indefinite
*Labor contracts	indefinite
*Patents	indefinite
*Proxies	indefinite
*Retirement and pension records	indefinite
*Tax returns and work papers	indefinite
CORRESPONDENCE	
General	2
License, traffic, purchase	6
Production	8
*Legal and tax	indefinite
INSURANCE	
Policies (expired)	4
Accident reports	6
Fire inspection reports	6
Group disability reports	8
Safety reports	8
Claims (settled)	10
PERSONNEL	
Contracts (expired)	8
Daily time reports	8
Disability and sick benefit records	8
Personnel files (terminated)	8
Withholding tax statements	8

Description of Documents	Years to be Retained
PURCHASING AND SALES	
Purchase orders	3
Requisitions	3
Sales contracts	3
Sales invoices	3
TRAFFIC (Shipping and Receiving)	
Export declarations	4
Freight bills	4
Manifests	4
Shipping and receiving reports	4
Waybills and bills of lading	4

APPENDIX II: INFORMATION FROM THE U.S. SMALL BUSINESS ADMINISTRATION

SBA OFFICES BY STATES

What Information Do You Want from the U.S. Small Business Administration?

The SBA in Washington, DC, has an "Answer Desk" that receives 85,000 calls a year from all over the country. The majority of calls request information about SBA loans. It should be stated here that the SBA rarely makes direct loans anymore, except in cases of dire emergency or disasters. Loans are processed through commercial banks and, if warranted, are *guaranteed* by the SBA. However, there is a great deal of other information that the small start-up entrepreneur will want to know—information about SCORE and SBDC, about other government departments, about procurement and patents, laws and regulations. The one central source of information is the "Answer Desk," which can be dialed toll free from anywhere in the U.S. The number is 1-800-368-5855.

Other toll-free government assistance and information numbers follow, as well as telephone numbers of hundreds of other offices set up to aid the small business person all in alphabetical state order. Look up *your* state and find the bureau that can best assist you.

ALABAMA
Region IV

Small Business Administration

Management Assistance
Birmingham   205/254-1338

Financial Assistance
Birmingham   205/254-1344

Veterans' Affairs Officer
Birmingham   205/254-1338   James W. Allen

Women in Business Representative
Birmingham   205/254-1338   Donna Glenn

Small Business Development Centers

Auburn	205/826-4030	Mobile	205/460-6130
Florence	205/766-4100, ext. 420	Montgomery	205/293-4137
Huntsville	205/895-6407	Normal	205/859-7481
Huntsville	205/895-6303	Troy	205/566-3000, ext. 342
Jacksonville	205/435-9820, ext. 342	Tuscaloosa	205/348-7011
Livingston	205/652-9661, ext. 439	Tuskegee	205/727-8710
		University	205/348-7011

State Offices

Small Business Program	205/832-6980
Loan Information	205/832-3889
Procurement Information	205/832-3580
Minority Business	205/832-5633
Department of Revenue	205/269-6861 (Montgomery)
State Export	205/284-8722
Consumer Complaints	800/392-5658
Ombudsman	*

Other U.S. Government Offices

Internal Revenue Service	800/292-6300; 205/254-0403 (Birmingham)
Farmer's Home Administration	205/832-7077 (Montgomery)
Department of Commerce	205/254-1331 (Birmingham)
Department of Energy	205/826-4718 (Auburn)
Department of Labor, Wage/Hour Division	205/254-1305 (Birmingham) 205/832-7450 (Montgomery)
Occupational Safety and Health Administration	205/822-7100 (Birmingham) 205/690-2131 (Mobile)
International Trade Administration	205/254-1331 (Birmingham)
Federal Information Centers	**322-8591 (Birmingham) **438-1421 (Mobile)

*   None identified
** Number may be used only within this city.

186

================================

ALASKA
Region X

Small Business Administration

Management Assistance
Anchorage   907/271-4028
Fairbanks   907/452-1951

Financial Assistance
Anchorage   907/271-4022
Fairbanks   907/452-1951

Veterans' Affairs Officer
Anchorage   907/271-4022   Mike Siemion

Women in Business Representative
Anchorage   907/271-4022   Mary Huntingdon

State Offices

Small Business Program   907/465-2018
Loan Information:
    Alaska Resources Corporation   907/561-2210
                                         (Loan must be secured; limit $500,000 for small
                                         businesses with sales of less than $10 million.
                                         No service businesses.)

Procurement Information   *
Department of Revenue   907/586-5265
State Export   907/465-2500
Consumer Complaints   *
Ombudsman   *

Other U.S. Government Offices

Internal Revenue Service   907/276-1040
Farmer's Home Administration   907/745-2176 (Palmer)
Department of Commerce   907/271-5041 (Anchorage)
Department of Energy   907/276-0512 (Anchorage)
Department of Labor,
    Wage/Hour Division   206/442-4482 (Seattle, WA)
Occupational Safety and
    Health Administration   907/271-5152 (Anchorage)
International Trade Administration   907/271-5041 (Anchorage)
Federal Information Center   907/271-3650 (Anchorage)

*   None identified
** Numbers may be used only within this city.

187

ARIZONA
Region IX

Small Business Administration

Management Assistance
Phoenix   602/241-2205
Tucson (POD)   602/629-6715

Financial Assistance
Phoenix   602/241-2217
Tucson (POD)   907/629-6715

Veterans' Affairs Officer
Phoenix   602/241-2203   Vince Tammelleo

Women in Business Representative
Phoenix   602/241-2237   Mardel Newman

State Offices

Small Business Program   602/225-5705
Loan Information   *
Procurement Information   *
Department of Revenue   602/271-5537 (Phoenix)
State Export   602/255-5374
Consumer Complaints   800/352-8431
Ombudsman   *

Other U.S. Government Offices

Internal Revenue Service   800/352-6911; 602/261-3861 (Phoenix)
Farmer's Home Administration   602/261-6701 (Phoenix)
Department of Commerce   602/261-3285 (Phoenix)
Department of Energy   *
Department of Labor,
  Wage/Hour Division   602/261-4224 (Phoenix)
Occupational Safety and
  Health Administration   602/261-4858 (Phoenix)
International Trade Administration   602/261-3285
Federal Information Centers   602/261-3313 (Phoenix)
                                       602/622-1511 (Tucson)

*   None identified
**   Number may be used only within this city.

ARKANSAS
Region VI

Small Business Administration

Management Assistance
Little Rock   501/378-5813

Financial Assistance
Little Rock   501/378-5871

Veterans' Affairs Officer
Little Rock   501/378-5871   Walter Thayer

Women in Business Representative
Little Rock   501/378-5871   Mina Apple

Small Business Development Centers

Arkadelphia	501/246-5511	Monticello	501/268-6161
Conway	501/450-3190	Searcy	501/268-6161
Fayetteville	501/575-5148	State University	501/972-3517
Little Rock	501/371-5381		

State Office

Small Business Program	501/371-1121
Loan Information	501/374-9247
Procurement Information	*
Minority Business	501/371-1121
Department of Revenue	501/371-1476 (Little Rock)
State Export	501/371-7781
Consumer Complaints	800/482-8982
Ombudsman	*

Other U.S. Government Offices

Internal Revenue Service	800/482-9350; 501/378-5685 (Little Rock)
Farmer's Home Administration	501/378-6281 (Little Rock)
Department of Commerce	501/378-5794 (Little Rock)
Department of Energy	501/371-1370 (Little Rock)
Department of Labor, Wage/Hour Division	501/378-5292 (Little Rock)
Occupational Safety and Health Administration	501/378-6291 (Little Rock)
International Trade Administration	501/378-5794 (Little Rock)
Federal Information Center	**378-6177 (Little Rock)

* None identified
** Number may be used only in this city.

CALIFORNIA
Region IX

Small Business Administration

Management Assistance
Fresno	209/487-5605
Los Angeles	213/688-7173
Sacramento	916/440-2956
San Diego	619/293-5444
San Francisco	415/974-0590
San Jose (POD)	408/275-7584
Santa Ana	714/836-2494

Financial Assistance
Fresno	209/487-5605
Los Angeles	213/688-5543
Sacramento	916/440-2956
San Diego	619/293-5440
San Francisco	415/974-0617
San Jose	408/291-7584
Santa Ana	714/836-2494

Veterans' Affairs Officers
Fresno	209/487-5790	Warren Kightlinger
Los Angeles	213/688-2991	Dennis Aten
San Diego	619/293-6307	Alan Converse
San Francisco	415/974-0590	Don McMahan

Women in Business Representatives
Fresno	209/487-5789	Elodia Castro
Los Angeles	213/688-4894	Barbara Vint
Sacramento	916/440-2956	Teresa Ames
San Diego	619/293-6514	Darlene McKinnon
San Francisco	415/974-0590	Nell Klas

State Offices

Small Business Program	916/445-6545
Loan Information:	
California Office of Small Business Development	916/445-6545 (Sacramento)
Business and Industrial Development Corporations	415/557-3232
Alternative Energy Source Financing	916/445-9597
Procurement Information	*
Minority Business	916/322-5060
Department of Revenue	916/355-0370 (Sacramento)
State Export	916/324-5511
Consumer Complaints	800/952-5225
Ombudsman	*

cont.

190

Other U.S. Government Offices

Internal Revenue Service	800/242-4585; 213/572-7814 (Los Angeles)
	415/556-0880 (San Francisco)
Farmer's Home Administration	916/666-3382 (Woodland)
Department of Commerce	213/824-7591 (Los Angeles)
	714/293-5395 (San Diego)
	415/556-5860 (San Francisco)
Department of Energy	916/323-4388 (Sacramento)
Department of Labor,	
Wage/Hour Division	213/240-5274 (Glendale)
	916/484-4447 (Sacramento)
	714/863-2156 (Santa Ana)
	415/974-0535 (San Francisco)
	213/688-4957 (Los Angeles)
Occupational Safety and	
Health Administration	213/432-3434 (Long Beach)
	415/556-7260 (San Francisco)
International Trade Administration	213/209-6707 (Los Angeles)
	415/556-5860 (San Francisco)
Federal Information Centers	213/688-3800 (Los Angeles)
	916/440-3344 (Sacramento)
	619/293-6030 (San Diego)
	415/556-6600 (San Francisco)
	**275-7422 (San Jose)
	**836-2386 (Santa Ana)

*   None identified
** Number may be used only within this city.

COLORADO
Region VIII

Small Business Administration

Management Assistance
Denver   303/844-2607

Financial Assistance
Denver   303/844-2607

Veterans' Affairs Officer
Denver   303/844-6531   Paul Klinkerman

Women in Business Representative
Denver   303/844-6526   Marsha Summerline

State Offices

Small Business Program   303/492-5611 (University of Colorado)
Loan Information   *
Procurement Information   303/757-9011; 303/886-2077
Minority Business   303/866-2077
Department of Revenue   303/825-9061 (Denver)
State Export   303/866-2205
Consumer Complaints   *
Ombudsman   *

Other U.S. Government Offices

Internal Revenue Service   800/332-2060; 303/825-7041 (Denver)
Farmer's Home Administration   303/837-4347 (Denver)
Department of Commerce   303/837-3246 (Denver)
Department of Energy   303/839-2186 (Denver)
Department of Labor,
  Wage/Hour Division   303/837-4405 (Denver)
Occupational Safety and
  Health Administration   303/245-2502 (Lakewood)
International Trade Administration   303/837-3246 (Denver)
Federal Information Centers   303/234-7181 (Denver)
                                      **471-9491 (Colorado Springs)
                                      **544-9523 (Pueblo)

*   None identified
**   Number may be used only within this city.

CONNECTICUT
Region I

Small Business Administration

Management Assistance Hartford	203/722-2544		
Financial Assistance Hartford	203/722-3600		
Veterans' Affairs Officer Hartford	203/722-3603	Robert Young	
Women in Business Representative Hartford	203/722-2544	Maria Cirurgiao	

Small Business Development Centers

Bridgeport	203/335-3800	Stamford	203/323-1883
Hartford	203/525-4451	Storrs	203/486-4135
New Haven	203/787-6735	Waterbury	203/757-0701
New London	203/443-8332		

State Offices

Small Business Program   203/566-4051
Loan Information:
   Connecticut Product Development
     Corporation   203/566-2920
     (Risk capital to established manufacturing firms
     with a primary focus on job creation)

   Department of Economic
     Development   203/566-4051
     (Enterprise zone business start-ups)
Procurement Information   203/566-4051
Department of Revenue   203/566-8520 (Hartford)
State Export   203/566-3071
Consumer Complaints   800/842-2649
Ombudsman   203/566-7035
Department of Energy   203/566-5803
Product Development Corporation   203/566-2920

Other U.S. Government Offices

Internal Revenue Service   800/343-9000; 203/722-3064 (Hartford)
Farmer's Home Administration   413/253-3471 (Amherst, MA)
Department of Commerce   203/722-3530 (Hartford)
Department of Energy   800/424-0246 (Hartford)
Department of Labor,
   Wage/Hour Division   203/722-2660 (Hartford)
Occupational Safety and
   Health Administration   203/722-2294 (Hartford)
International Trade Administration   203/244-3530 (Hartford)
Federal Information Centers   **527-2617 (Hartford)
                                          **624-4720 (New Haven)

*   None identified
** Number may be used only within this city.

DELAWARE
Region III

Small Business Administration

Management Assistance
Wilmington   302/573-6294

Financial Assistance
Wilmington   302/573-6294

Veterans' Affairs Officer
Wilmington   302/573-6294   John J. Giannini

Women in Business Representative   *

Small Business Development Center
Newark, New Jersey   302/738-2747

State Offices

Small Business Program   302/736-4271
Loan Information   302/736-4271
Procurement Information   *
Department of Revenue   302/654-5111 (Wilmington)
State Export   302/736-4271
Consumer Complaints   *
Ombudsman   *

Other U.S. Government Offices

Internal Revenue Service   800/292-9575; 302/573-6083 (Wilmington)
Farmer's Home Administration   302/573-6694 (Newark)
Department of Commerce   215/597-2866 (Philadelphia, PA)
Department of Energy   302/736-5647 (Dover)
Department of Labor,
   Wage/Hour Division   301/962-2265 (Baltimore, MD)
Occupational Safety and
   Health Administration   *
International Trade Administration   215/597-2866 (Philadelphia, PA)
Federal Information Centers   *

*   None identified
**   Number may be used within this city only.

DISTRICT OF COLUMBIA
Region III

Small Business Administration

Management Assistance
Washington, D.C.   202/634-6200

Financial Assistance
Washington, D.C.   202/634-6200

Veterans' Affairs Officer
Washington, D.C.   202/634-6061   John Francis

Women in Business Representative
Washington, D.C.   202/634-1818   Dratin Hill

Small Business Development Center
Washington, D.C.   202/636-7187
                                    202/727-1051

State Offices

Small Business Program	*	
Loan Information	202/727-6600	
Procurement Information	202/727-0171	
Internal Revenue Service	202/488-3100, ext. 2222	
Department of Revenue	202/629-4665	
State Export	*	
Consumer Complaints	202/727-7000	
Telephone Consumer Hotline, Inc.	202/483-4100	
Ombudsman*		
Licensing	202/727-3645	

Other U.S. Government Offices

Internal Revenue Service	202/488-3100
Farmer's Home Administration	202/447-4323
Department of Commerce	202/377-2000
Department of Energy	202/727-1830
Department of Labor, Wage/Hour Division	202/576-6942
Occupational Safety and Health Administration	202/523-5224
International Trade Administration	202/377-3181
Federal Information Center	202/655-4000

*   None identified
** Number may be used within this city only.

FLORIDA
Region IV

Small Business Administration

Management Assistance
Jacksonville	904/791-3105
Miami	305/350-5521
Tampa (POD)	813/228-2594
West Palm Beach (POD)	305/689-2223

Financial Assistance
Jacksonville	904/791-3782
Miami	305/350-5521
Tampa (POD)	813/228-2594
West Palm Beach (POD)	305/689-2223

Veterans' Affairs Officers
Jacksonville	904/791-3107	Frederick W. Bethea
Miami	305/350-5833	Harry J. Perrin

Women in Business Representatives
Jacksonville	904/791-3782	Lucille Trotter
Miami	305/350-5521	Patricia Williams

Small Business Development Centers
Boca Raton	305/393-3174	North Miami	305/940-5790
Deland	904/734-1066	Orlando	305/275-2796
Elgin AFB	904/678-1143	Panama City	904/769-3556
Fort Lauderdale	305/467-4238	Pensacola	904/474-2908
Gainesville	904/377-5621	St. Petersburg	813/893-9529
Jacksonville	904/646-2476	Tallahassee	904/644-6524
Key West	305/294-8481	Tallahassee	904/599-3407
Miami	305/554-2272	Tampa	813/974-4264

State Offices

Small Business Program	800/342-0771; 904/488-9357
Loan Information	*
Procurement Information	904/243-7624
Minority Business	904/488-9575
Department of Revenue	904/488-2574 (Tallahassee)
Consumer Complaints	800/342-2176
State Export	904/488-5280; 904/488-6124
Ombudsman	*
High Tech	904/457-1880

Other U.S. Government Offices

Internal Revenue Service	800/342-8300; 904/791-2514 (Jacksonville)
Farmer's Home Administration	904/376-3218 (Gainesville)
Department of Commerce	305/350-5267 (Miami)
	813/461-0011 (Clearwater)
	904/791-2796 (Jacksonville)
	904/488-6469 (Tallahassee)
Department of Energy	904/488-2475 (Tallahassee)
Department of Labor,	
Wage/Hour Division	904/791-2489 (Jacksonville)
	305/527-7262 (Fort Lauderdale)
	305/350-5767 (Miami)
	813/228-2154 (Tampa)
Occupational Safety and	
Health Administration	305/527-7292 (Fort Lauderdale)
	813/228-2821 (Tampa)
	904/791-2895 (Jacksonville)
International Trade Administration	305/350-5267 (Miami)
Federal Information Centers	**522-8531 (Fort Lauderdale)
	**354-4756 (Jacksonville)
	305/350-4155 (Miami)
	**422-1800 (Orlando)
	813/893-3495 (St. Petersburg)
	**229-7911 (Tampa)
	**833-7566 (West Palm Beach)
	800/282-8556 (North Florida)
	800/432-6668 (South Florida)

*   None identified
** Number may be used only within this city.

GEORGIA
Region IV

Small Business Administration

Management Assistance
Atlanta   404/881-2441
Statesboro (POD)   912/489-8719

Financial Assistance
Atlanta   404/881-4325
Statesboro (POD)   912/489-8719

Veterans' Affairs Officer
Atlanta   404/881-2441   Hartsel Brady

Women in Business Representative
Atlanta   404/881-4325   Paula Hill

Small Business Development Centers
Albany   912/439-7232   Morrow   404/961-3414
Athens   404/542-7436   Rome   404/295-6327
Atlanta   404/658-3550   Savannah   912/233-3067
Augusta   404/828-4993   Statesboro   912/681-5194
Columbus   404/571-7433   Valdosta   912/247-3262
Macon   912/746-7601

State Offices

Small Business Program   *
Loan Information   *
Procurement Information   404/656-4291
Minority Business   404/656-1794
Department of Revenue   404/656-4291 (Atlanta)
State Export   404/656-4504
Consumer Complaints   800/282-4900
Ombudsman   *
High Tech   404/894-3575

Other U.S. Government Offices

Internal Revenue Service   800/222-1040
Farmer's Home Administration   404/546-2162 (Athens)
Department of Commerce   912/944-4205 (Savannah)
                                   404/881-7000 (Atlanta)
Department of Energy   *
Department of Labor,
  Wage/Hour Division   404/221-6401 (Atlanta)
                                   912/944-4222 (Savannah)
Occupational Safety and
  Health Administration   404/221-4767 (Tucker)
                                   912/746-5143 (Macon)
                                   912/354-0733 (Savannah)
International Trade Administration 404/881-7000 (Atlanta)
                                   912/944-4204 (Savannah)
Federal Information Center   404/221-6891 (Atlanta)

*   None identified
**   Number may be used only within this city.

HAWAII
Region IX

Small Business Administration

Management Assistance
Honolulu   808/546-3119

Financial Assistance
Honolulu   808/546-3151

Veterans' Affairs Officer
Honolulu   808/546-7336   Richard Waidzunas

Women in Business Representative
Honolulu   808/546-3119   Janet Nakasone

State Offices

Small Business Program   808/548-4172
Loan Information   800/367-5218; 808/548-4616
Procurement Information   *
Department of Revenue   808/548-2211 (Honolulu)
State Export   808/548-3048
Consumer Complaints   *
Ombudsman   *

Other U.S. Government Offices

Internal Revenue Service   808/546-2803
Farmer's Home Administration   808/961-4781 (Hilo)
Department of Commerce   808/546-8694 (Honolulu)
Department of Energy   808/548-2306 (Honolulu)
Department of Labor,
   Wage/Hour Division   213/688-4957 (Los Angeles)
Occupational Safety and
   Health Administration   800/546-3157 (Honolulu)
International Trade Administration   808/546-8694 (Honolulu)
   State Office   808/548-3048
Federal Information Centers   808/546-8620 (Honolulu)

 *   None identified
**   Number may be used only within this city.

199

IDAHO
Region X

Small Business Administration

Management Assistance
Boise   208/334-1780

Financial Assistance
Boise   208/334-1696

Veterans' Affairs Officer
Boise   208/334-1780   Lawrence Henderson

Women in Business Representative
Boise   208/334-1096   Janet Evans

State Offices

Small Business Program   208/334-1096
Loan Information   208/334-2470
Permits and Licensing   208/334-3598
Procurement Information   *
Department of Revenue   208/384-3159 (Boise)
State Export   *
Consumer Complaints   *
Ombudsman   *

Other U.S. Government Offices

Internal Revenue Service   800/632-5990; 208/336-1040 (Boise)
Farmer's Home Administration   208/334-1730 (Boise)
Department of Commerce   503/221-3001 (Portland, OR)
Department of Energy   208/334-3800 (Boise)
Department of Labor,
   Wage/Hour Division   503/221-3057 (Portland, OR)
                                             206/442-4482 (Seattle, WA)

Occupational Safety and
   Health Administration   208/384-1867 (Boise)
International Trade Administration   801/524-5116 (Salt Lake City, UT)
Federal Information Centers   *

*   None identified
**   Number may be used only within this city.

ILLINOIS
Region V

Small Business Administration

Management Assistance
Chicago   312/353-4528
Springfield   217/492-4767

Financial Assistance
Chicago   312/353-4528
Springfield   217/492-4767

Veterans' Affairs Officers
Chicago   312/353-5125   Stan Magiera
Springfield   217/492-4416   Keith Andrews

Women in Business Representatives
Chicago   312/353-5031   Delores La Velle
Springfield   217/492-4416   Jeanne Washburn

State Small Business Development Centers
Chicago   312/670-0434   S. Cook County   312-543-5000
Kane/DuPage/   S. Illinois   618-453-3307
  DeKalb   815-753-1243   S.W. Illinois   618-692-2929
Macon County   217/424-6297

State Offices

  Small Business Program   312/793-6885 (Chicago)
  Illinois Department of Commerce
    and Community Affairs - Small
    Business Development Center
    Network   1-800-252-2923
  Loan Information:
    Illinois Industrial Development
      Authority   618/997-6382 (Marion)
    Illinois Department of Commercial
      and Community Affairs   312/793-6304 (Chicago)
                                  217/782-1458 (Springfield)
  Procurement Information   217/782-4705
  Minority Business   312/793-6885
  Department of Revenue   800/252-8972; 217/782-3336 (Springfield)
  State Export   312/793-2086
  Consumer Complaints   *
  Ombudsman   *

cont.

201

Other U.S. Government Offices

Internal Revenue Service	800/972-5400; 312/886-4609 (Chicago)
	800/972-5400; 217/492-4288 (Springfield)
Farmer's Home Administration	217/398-5235 (Champaign)
Department of Commerce	312/353-4450 (Chicago)
Department of Energy	217/785-2009 (Springfield)
Department of Labor,	
Wage/Hour Division	312/775-5733 (Chicago)
	217/492-4060 (Springfield)
	312/238-8832 (Bridgeview)
Occupational Safety and	
Health Administration	312/891-3800 (Calumet City)
	312/896-8700 (North Aurora)
	309/671-7033 (Peoria)
	312/631-8200 (Niles)
International Trade Administration	312/353-4450 (Chicago)
Federal Information Center	312/353-4242 (Chicago)

*   None identified
**   Number may be used only within this city.

INDIANA
Region V

Small Business Administration

Management Assistance
Indianapolis   317/269-7264
South Bend (BO)   219/236-8361

Financial Assistance
Indianapolis   317/269-7272
South Bend (BO)   317/269-7272

Veterans' Affairs Officer
Indianapolis   317/269-7284   Paul R. Wyatt

Women in Business Representatives
Indianapolis   317/269-7278   Robert Gastineau
                                      317/269-2073   John Bates

State Offices

Small Business Program   317/634-8418
Loan Information:
    Corporation for Innovation
        Development   317/635-7325 (Indianapolis)
Procurement Information   *
Department of Commerce   1-800/824-2476 (Indianapolis)
Department of Revenue   317/633-6442 (Indianapolis)
State Export   317/793-8845
Consumer Complaints   800/382-5516
Ombudsman   317/232-3373
High Tech   317/635-3058

Other U.S. Government Offices

Internal Revenue Service   800/382-9740; 317/269-6326 (Indianapolis)
Farmer's Home Administration   317/269-6415 (Indianapolis)
Department of Commerce   317/269-6214 (Indianapolis)
Department of Energy   317/232-8940 (Indianapolis)
Department of Labor,
    Wage/Hour Division   317/269-7163 (Indianapolis)
                                      219/234-4045 (South Bend)

Occupational Safety and
    Health Administration   317/269-7290 (Indianapolis)
International Trade Administration   317/269-6214 (Indianapolis)
Federal Information Centers   **883-4110 (Gary/ Hammond)
                                      317/269-7373 (Indianapolis)

*   None identified
**   Number may be used only within this city.

IOWA
Region VII

Small Business Administration

Management Assistance
Cedar Rapids   319/399-2571
Des Moines   515/284-4760

Financial Assistance
Cedar Rapids   319/399-2571
Des Moines   515/284-6091

Veterans' Affairs Officers
Des Moines   515/284-6090   Vern Sampler
Cedar Rapids   319/399-2571   Roger Hoffman

Women in Business Representatives
Des Moines   515/284-4762   Cheryl Eftink
Cedar Rapids   319/399-2571   Carolyn Puntenney

Small Business Development Centers
Ames   515/294-8069   Des Moines   515/271-2655
Cedar Falls 319/273-2696   Iowa City   319/353-5340

State Offices

Small Business Program   515/281-8310; 800/532-1216
Loan Information: 515/281-4058
  Iowa Product Development
    Corporation   515/281-3925 (Des Moines)
Procurement Information   515/281-3089
Department of Revenue   515/281-5996
State Export   515/281-3655
Consumer Complaints   *
Ombudsman   515/281-3592
High Tech   515/294-3420

Other U.S. Government Offices

Internal Revenue Service   800/362-2600, ext. 4964
                                     515/284-4964 (Des Moines)
Farmer's Home Administration   515/284-4663 (Des Moines)
Department of Commerce   515/284-4222 (Des Moines)
Department of Energy   515/281-4420 (Des Moines)
Department of Labor,
  Wage/Hour Division   515/284-4625 (Des Moines)
Occupational Safety and
  Health Administration   515/284-4794 (Des Moines)
International Trade Administration   515/284-4222 (Des Moines)
Federal Information Centers   515/284-4448 (Des Moines)
                                     800/532-1556 (Other Iowa locations)

*   None identified
**   Number may be used only within this city.

SBA OFFICES BY STATES

KANSAS
Region VII

Small Business Administration

Management Assistance
Wichita   316/269-6273

Financial Assistance
Wichita   316/269-6571

Veterans' Affairs Officer
Wichita   316/269-6273   Ted Little

Women in Business Representative
Wichita   316/269-6426   Glenna Winningham

Small Business Development Centers
Emporia	316/343-1200	Overland Park	913/888-8500
Hays	913/628-4000	Pittsburg	316/231-7000, ext. 435
Lawrence	913/864-3117	Topeka	913/295-6305
Manhattan	913/532-5529		

State Offices

Small Business Program	913/296-3480
Loan Information	*
Procurement Information	913/296-2376
Minority Business	913/296-3480
Department of Revenue	913/296-0351 (Topeka)
State Export	913/296-3483
Consumer Complaints	800/432-2310
Ombudsman	*
High Tech	913/296-3480

Other U.S. Government Offices

Internal Revenue Service	800/362-2190; 316/263-2161 (Wichita)
Farmer's Home Administration	913/295-2870 (Topeka)
Department of Commerce	816/374-3142 (Kansas City, MO)
Department of Energy	913/296-2496 (Topeka)
Department of Labor, Wage/Hour Division	816/374-5721 (Kansas City, MO)
	402/221-4682 (Omaha, NE)
Occupational Safety and Health Administration	316/267-6311, ext. 644 (Wichita)
International Trade Administration	816/374-3142 (Kansas City, MO)
Federal Information Centers	913/295-2866 (Topeka)
	800/432-2934 (Other Kansas locations)

* None identified
** Number may be used only within this city.

205

KENTUCKY
Region IV

Small Business Administration

<u>Management Assistance</u>
Louisville   502/582-5976

<u>Financial Assistance</u>
Louisville   502/582-5973

<u>Veterans' Affairs Officer</u>
Louisville   502/582-5976   Forest Haynes

<u>Women in Business Representative</u>
Louisville   502/582-5976   Sally Deprez

<u>Small Business Development Centers</u>

Bowling Green	502/745-2901	Morehead	606/783-2077
Frankfort	502/564-2064	Murray	502/753-4134
Highland Heights	606/572-6558	Somerset	606/678-8174
Lexington	606/257-1751		

State Offices

Small Business Program	502/564-2064
Loan Information	502/564-4554
Procurement Information	502/564-2064
Department of Revenue	502/564-8054 (Frankfort)
State Export	502/564-2170
Consumer Complaints	800/432-9257
Ombudsman	502/564-4270

Other U.S. Government Offices

Internal Revenue Service	800/428-9100; 502/582-6259 (Louisville)
Farmer's Home Administration	606/233-2733 (Lexington)
Department of Commerce	502/582-5066 (Louisville)
Department of Energy	606/252-5535 (Lexington)
Department of Labor, Wage/Hour Division	502/582-5226 (Louisville)
Occupational Safety and Health Administration	502/564-2300 (Frankfort)
International Trade Administration	502/582-5066 (Louisville)
Federal Information Center	502/582-6261 (Louisville)

*   None identified
**   Number may be used only within this city.

LOUISIANA
Region VI

Small Business Administration

Management Assistance
New Orleans	504/589-2354
Shreveport (POD)	318/226-5196

Financial Assistance
New Orleans	504/589-2705
Shreveport (POD)	318/226-5196

Veterans' Affairs Officer
New Orleans	504/589-5976	Gerald Urpschot

Women in Business Representative
New Orleans	504/589-2288	Patricia Tooley

Small Business Development Centers
Baton Rouge	504/342-5366	Monroe	318/342-2129
	504/388-6282	New Orleans	504/948-4944; 286-6663
Lafayette	318/231-5745	Ruston	318/257-3537
Lake Charles	318/477-2520, ext. 531	Shreveport	318/797-5022

State Offices

Small Business Program	504/342-5366
Loan Information:	504/342-5367
	504/342-5382 (Baton Rouge)
Procurement Information	504/922-0074
Minority Business	504/342-6491
Department of Revenue	504/389-6667 (Baton Rouge)
State Export	504/342-5388
Consumer Complaints	800/272-9868
Ombudsman	*
High Tech	504/342-5361

Other U.S. Government Offices

Internal Revenue Service	800/362-6900; 504/589-2488 (New Orleans)
Farmer's Home Administration	318/473-7920 (Alexandria)
Department of Commerce	504/589-6546 (New Orleans)
Department of Energy	504/342-4594 (Baton Rouge)
Department of Labor,	
Wage/Hour Division	504/589-6171 (New Orleans)
Occupational Safety and	
Health Administration	504/589-2451 (New Orleans)
	504/923-0718 (Baton Rouge)
International Trade Administration	504/589-6546 (New Orleans)
Federal Information Center	504/589-6696 (New Orleans)

*   None identified
**   Number may be used only within this city.

MAINE
Region I

Small Business Administration

Management Assistance
Augusta   207/622-8242

Financial Assistance
Augusta   207/622-8378

Veterans' Affairs Officer
Augusta   207/622-8378   Carl L. Sullivan

Women in Business Representative
Augusta   207/622-8383   Susanne D. Pelletier

Small Business Development Centers
Augusta   207/622-6345   Machias   207/255-3313
Bangor   207/942-6389   Portland   207/780-4423
Caribou   207/498-8736

State Offices

Small Business Program   207/289-2656
Loan Information   207/289-2656 (Augusta)
Procurement Information   *
Department of Revenue   207/289-3695 (Augusta)
State Export   207/623-5700
Consumer Complaints   *
Ombudsman   *

Other U.S. Government Offices

Internal Revenue Service   800/452-8750;
                                  207/622-6171, ext. 466 (Augusta)
Farmer's Home Administration   207/866-4929 (Orono)
Department of Commerce   207/623-2239 (Augusta)
Department of Energy   207/289-3811 (Augusta)
Department of Labor,
    Wage/Hour Division   207/780-3344, ext. 344 (Augusta)
Occupational Safety and
    Health Administration   203/244-2294 (Hartford, CT)
                                  207/622-6171 (Augusta)
International Trade Administration 617/223-2312 (Boston)
Federal Information Centers   *

*   None identified
**   Number may be used only within this city.

MARYLAND
Region III

Small Business Administration

Management Assistance
Baltimore   301/962-2233

Financial Assistance
Baltimore   301/962-2150

Veterans' Affairs Officer
Baltimore   301/962-2150   Justin P. Palmisano

Women in Business Representative
Baltimore   301/962-2233   Joycelyn Johnson

State Offices

Small Business Program   **800/654-7336; 301/269-2621
Loan Information:
  Enterprise Zones   301/269-2624
  Short-term working capital for
    companies with procurement
    contracts   301/659-4270
  Industrial Development Financing
    Authority (not for retail or
    service businesses)   301/659-4262
  Established businesses   301/828-4711
Procurement Information   *
Minority Business   301/383-5555
Montgomery County - Steve Ames   301/984-0999
Department of Revenue   301/267-5981 (Annapolis)
State Export   301/269-2621
Consumer Complaints: Telephone
  Consumer Hotline, Inc.   1-800-332-1124
Ombudsman   *

Other U.S. Government Offices

Internal Revenue Service   800/492-0460; 301/962-2222 (Baltimore)
Farmer's Home Administration   302/573-6694 (Newark, DE)
Department of Commerce   301/962-3560 (Baltimore)
Department of Energy   301/383-6810 (Baltimore)
Department of Labor,
  Wage/Hour Division   301/962-2265 (Baltimore)
Occupational Safety and
  Health Administration   301/962-2840 (Baltimore)
International Trade Administration   301/962-3560 (Baltimore)
Federal Information Center   301/962-4980 (Baltimore)

*   None identified
**   Number may be used only within this city.

MASSACHUSETTS
Region I

Small Business Administration

Management Assistance
Boston   617/223-7991
Springfield   413/536-8770

Financial Assistance
Boston   617/223-3125
Springfield   413/536-8770

Veterans' Affairs Officer
Boston   617/223-3293   William Littlefield

Women in Business Representative
Boston   617/223-3212   Ethel Fredericks

Small Business Development Centers

Amherst	413/549-4930	Lowell	617/458-7261
Boston	617/734-1960	Salem	617/745-0556
Chestnut Hill	617/969-0100, ext. 4092	Springfield	413/737-6712
Fall River	617/673-9783	Worcester	617/793-7615

State Offices

Small Business Program   800/632-8181; 617/727-4005
Loan Information:
  New and expanding high-tec
    businesses with high
    employment and growth
    potential   617/723-4920
  Community Development
    Corporation Programs   617/742-0366
  Business expansions   617/536-3900
  Industrial finance   617/451-2477
Procurement Information   800/632-8181; 617/727-4005
Minority Business   617/727/8692
Department of Revenue   617/727-4393 (Boston)
State Export   *
Consumer Complaints   *
Ombudsman   *

Other U.S. Government Offices

Internal Revenue Service   800/392-6288; 617/223-5177 (Boston)
Farmer's Home Administration   413/253-3471 (Amherst)
Department of Commerce   617/223-2312 (Boston)
Department of Energy   617/727-4732 (Boston)
Department of Labor,
  Wage/Hour Division   617/223-6751 (Boston)
Occupational Safety and
  Health Administration   617/890-1239 (Waltham)
                                            413/781-2420, ext. 522 (Springfield)
International Trade Administration   617/223-2312 (Boston)
Federal Information Center   617/223-7121 (Boston)

MICHIGAN
Region V

Small Business Administration

<u>Management Assistance</u>
Detroit   313/226-6075
                                       313/226-7947 (SCORE)
Marquette (BO)   906/225-1108

<u>Financial Assistance</u>
Detroit   313/226-6075
Marquette (BO)   906/225-1108

<u>Veterans' Affairs Officer</u>
Detroit   313/226-3627   Allen Cook

<u>Women in Business Representative</u>
Detroit   313/226-4276   Linda Kuroz

<u>Small Business Development Centers</u>

| Detroit | 313/577-4431 | Kalamazoo | 616/383-8594 |
| Houghton | 906/487-2470 | Mount Pleasant | 517/774-3736 |

State Offices

Small Business Program   517/373-9039
<u>Loan Information:</u>
  Emphasis on high-tech and
    growth industries   517/373-4330 (Lansing)
  Community and private
    industrial development   517/373-6378
Procurement Information   517/373-8430
Department of Revenue   517/373-2910 (Lansing)
State Export   517/373-6390
Consumer Complaints   800/292-4204
Ombudsman and licensing   800/232-2727; 517/373-6241
  information
High Tech   517/373-0638

cont.

Other U.S. Government Offices

Internal Revenue Service	800/462-0830 (Detroit)
	800/482-0670 (Other cities)
Farmer's Home Administration	517/372-1910, ext. 272 (East Lansing)
	616/456-2337 (Grand Rapids)
Occupational Safety and	
Health Administration	313/226-6720 (Detroit)
International Trade Administration	313/226-3650 (Detroit)
Federal Information Centers	313/226-7016 (Detroit)
	**451-2628 (Grand Rapids)

* None identified
** Number may be used only within this city.

MINNESOTA
Region V

Small Business Administration

Management Assistance
Minneapolis   612/349-3574

Financial Assistance
Minneapolis   612/349-3559

Veterans' Affairs Officer
Minneapolis   612/349-3565   George Saumweber

Women in Business Representative
Minneapolis   612/349-3544   Cynthia Wright

Small Business Development Centers
Bemidji   218/755-2754   Moorhead   218/236-2289
Brainerd   218/828-5344   St. Cloud   612/255-3215
Duluth   218/726-7250   St. Paul   612/647-5840
Mankato   507/389-2963   Winona   507/457-2150
Marshall   507/537-7386

State Offices

Small Business Program   800/652-9747; 612/296-5011
Loan Information   *
Procurement Information   612/296-6949
Department of Revenue   612/296-3781 (St. Paul)
State Export   612/297-4659
Consumer Complaints   *
Ombudsman   *
Licenses   612/296-0617
High Tech   612/341-2222

Other U.S. Government Offices

Internal Revenue Service   800/652-9062; 612/725-7320 (St. Paul)
Farmer's Home Administration   612/725-5842 (St. Paul)
Department of Commerce   612/725-2133 (Minneapolis)
Department of Energy   612/296-8899 (St. Paul)
Department of Labor,
  Wage/Hour Division   612/725-6108 (Minneapolis)
Occupational Safety and
  Health Administration   612/725-2571 (Minneapolis)
International Trade Administration   612/349-3338 (Minneapolis)
Federal Information Center   612/349-5333 (Minneapolis)

*   None identified
**   Number may be used only within this city.

MISSISSIPPI
Region IV

Small Business Administration

Management Assistance
Jackson   601/960-4378

Financial Assistance
Biloxi   601/435-3676
Jackson   601/960-4378

Veterans' Affairs Officers
Jackson   601/960-4378   Tommy Traxler
Biloxi   601/435-3676   Jerry Haley

Women in Business Representative
Jackson   601/960-5328   Helen Hall

Small Business Development Centers
Jackson   601/982-3825   University   601/232-5001
Long Beach   601/868-9988

State Offices

Small Business Program   601/982-6457
Loan Information   *
Procurement Information   *
Minority Business   601/353-6855
Department of Revenue   601/354-6262 (Jackson)
State Export   601/359-3444
                                       800/468-1158 (In state toll free)
Consumer Complaints   800/222-7622
Ombudsman   *

Other U.S. Government Offices

Internal Revenue Service   800/241-3868; 601/969-4526 (Jackson)
Farmer's Home Administration   601/969-4316 (Jackson)
Department of Commerce   601/960-4388 (Jackson)
Department of Energy   601/961-2733 (Jackson)
Department of Labor,
  Wage/Hour Division   601/960-4347 (Jackson)
Occupational Safety and
  Health Administration   601/960-4066 (Jackson)
International Trade Administration   601/960-4388 (Jackson)
Federal Information Center   *

*   None identified
**   Number may be used only within this city.

214

MISSOURI
Region VII

Small Business Administration

Management Assistance
Kansas City   816/374-5868
Springfield (BO)   417/864-7670
St. Louis   314/425-6600

Financial Assistance
Kansas City   816/374-3416
Springfield   417/864-7670
St. Louis   314/425-6600

Veterans' Affairs Officers
Kansas City   816/374-5868   John Scott
St. Louis   314/425-6600   Joe Crump
Springfield   417/864-7670   Jim Laas

Women in Business Representatives
Kansas City   816/374-3416   Linda Rusche
St. Louis   314/425-6600   LaVerne Johnson

Small Business Development Centers
Kansas City   816/926-4572   St. Louis   314/534-7232
Rolla   314/341-4559   Springfield   417/836-5680

State Offices

Small Business Program   314/751-4982
Loan Information   314/751-2686
Procurement Information   *
Department of Revenue   314/751-2151 (Jefferson City)
State Export   314/751-4855
Consumer Complaints   800/392-8222
Ombudsman   816/274-6186
High Tech   314/751-3222

cont.

Other U.S. Government Offices

Internal Revenue Service	800/392-4200; 314/425-5661 (St. Louis)
Farmer's Home Administration	314/442-2271, ext. 3241 (Columbia)
Department of Commerce	314/425-3302 (St. Louis)
	816/374-3142 (Kansas City)
Department of Energy	314/751-4000 (Jefferson City)
Department of Labor,	
Wage/Hour Division	314/425-4706 (St. Louis)
	816/374-5721 (Kansas City)
Occupational Safety and	
Health Administration	816/374-2756 (Kansas City)
	314/425-5461 (St. Louis)
International Trade Administration	816/374-3142 (Kansas City)
Federal Information Centers	800/982-5808 (Area Codes 816 and 417)
	800/392-7711 (Area Code 314)
	816/374-2466 (Kansas City)
	314/425-4106 (St. Louis)

*   None identified
** Number may be used only within this city.

MONTANA
Region VIII

Small Business Administration

Management Assistance
Helena   406/449-5381
Billings (POD)   406/657-6047

Financial Assistance
Helena   406/449-5381
Billings   406/657-6047

Veterans' Affairs Officer
Helena   406/449-5381   Elwin Redding

Women in Business Representative
Helena   406/449-5381   Mary Bryson

State Offices
Small Business Program   406/444-3923
Loan Information   406/444-4324
Procurement Information   406/444-2575
Minority Business   406/444-4723
Department of Revenue   406/444-2460 (Helena)
State Export   406/444-4380
Consumer Complaints   800/332-2272
Ombudsman   *
Licensing/Ombudsman   406/444-3923
High Tech   406/444-3923

Other U.S. Government Offices

Internal Revenue Service   800/332-2275; 406/443-2320 (Helena)
Farmer's Home Administration   406/587-5271, ext. 4211 (Bozeman)
Department of Commerce   307/778-2220 (Cheyenne, WY)
Department of Energy   406/449-3780
Department of Labor,
   Wage/Hour Division   801/524-5706 (Salt Lake City, UT)
Occupational Safety and
   Health Administration   406/657-6649 (Billings)
International Trade Administration   303/837-3246 (Denver, CO)
Federal Information Center   *

*   None identified
**   Number may be used only within this city.

NEBRASKA
Region VII

Small Business Administration

Management Assistance
Omaha   402/221-3604

Financial Assistance
Omaha   402/221-3622

Veterans' Affairs Officer
Omaha   402/221-3626   Stephen Lewis

Women in Business Representative
Omaha   402/221-3626   Betty Raygor

Small Business Development Centers

Chadron	308/432-4451	Omaha	402/554-3291
Kearney	308/234-8344	Wayne	402/375-2004
Lincoln	402/472-3276		

State Offices

Small Business Program	402/471-3774
Loan Information	*
Procurement Information	*
Department of Revenue	402/471-2581 (Lincoln)
State Export	402/471-4668
Consumer Complaints	*
Ombudsman	402/471-2035
Patent Development Program	402/471-3786

Other U.S. Government Offices

Internal Revenue Service	800/642-9960; 402/221-3504 (Omaha)
Farmer's Home Administration	402/471-5551 (Lincoln)
Department of Commerce	402/221-3664 (Omaha)
Department of Energy	402/471-2867 (Lincoln)
Department of Labor, Wage/Hour Division	402/221-4682 (Omaha)
Occupational Safety and Health Administration	402/221-9341 (Omaha)
	308/534-9450 (North Platte)
International Trade Administration	402/221-3664 (Omaha)
Federal Information Centers	402/221-3353 (Omaha)
	800/642-8383 (Other Nebraska locations)

*   None identified
**   Number may be used only within this city.

NEVADA
Region IX

Small Business Administration

<u>Management Assistance</u>
Las Vegas   702/388-6611
Reno (POD)   702/784-5268

<u>Financial Assistance</u>
Las Vegas   702/388-6611
Reno (POD)   702/784-5268

<u>Veterans' Affairs Officer</u>
Las Vegas   702/385-6611   Robert Garrett

<u>Women in Business Representative</u>
Las Vegas   702/385-6611   Marie Papile

State Offices

Small Business Program   702/885-4420
Loan Information   702/323-3033
Procurement Information   *
Department of Revenue   *
State Export   *
Consumer Complaints   800/992-0900
Ombudsman   *

Other U.S. Government Offices

Internal Revenue Service   800/492-6552; 702/784-5521 (Reno)
                                         702/385-6291 (Las Vegas)
Farmer's Home Administration   801/524-5027 (Salt Lake City, UT)
Department of Commerce   702/784-5203
Department of Energy   702/886-5157 (Carson City)
Department of Labor,
  Wage/Hour Division   602/261-4224 (Phoenix, AZ)
Occupational Safety and
  Health Administration   702/883-1226 (Carson City)
International Trade Administration   702/784-5203 (Reno)
Federal Information Center   *

*   None identified
**   Number may be used only within this city.

NEW HAMPSHIRE
Region I

Small Business Administration

Management Assistance Concord	603/224-4041	
Financial Assistance Concord	603/224-4041	
Veterans' Affairs Officer Concord	603/224-4041	Robert C. Kelly
Women in Business Representative Concord	603/224-4041	Teresa Grove

State Offices

Small Business Program	603/271-2391
Loan Information	*
Procurement Information	*
Department of Revenue	603/271-1110 (Concord)
State Export	603/271-2591
Consumer Complaints	*
Ombudsman	

Other U.S. Government Offices

Internal Revenue Service	800/582-7200
Farmer's Home Administration	802/223-2371 (Montpelier, VT)
Department of Commerce	617/223-2312 (Boston, MA)
Department of Energy	603/271-2711 (Concord)
Department of Labor, Wage/Hour Division	207/780-3344, ext. 344 (Portland, ME)
Occupational Safety and Health Administration	603/224-1995 (Concord)
International Trade Administration	617/223-2312 (Boston, MA)
Federal Information Center	*

*   None identified
**   Number may be used only within this city.

NEW JERSEY
Region II

Small Business Administration

Management Assistance
Camden (POD)   609/757-5183
Newark   201/645-2434

Financial Assistance
Camden   609/757-5183
Newark   201/645-2434

Veterans' Affairs Officer
Newark   201/645-3251   Henry Harra

Women in Business Representative
Newark   201/645-6491   Janis Sullivan

Small Business Development Centers
Lincroft   201/842-1900   Trenton   609/586-4800
Newark   201/648-5621   Vineland   609/691-8600
New Brunswick   201/545-3300

State Offices

Small Business Program   609/984-4442
Loan Information:
  High Tech   609/984-1671
  General Business Loans   609/282-1800; 609/984-4442
Procurement Information   609/984-4442
Minority Business   609/292-0500
Department of Revenue   609/292-7592 (Trenton)
State Export   201/648-3518
Consumer Complaints   800/792-8600
Ombudsman   609/292--0700
High Tech   609/984-2444

cont.

Other U.S. Government Agencies

Internal Revenue Service	800/242-6750; 201/645-6478
Farmer's Home Administration	609/259-3136 (Robinsville)
Department of Commerce	201/645-6214 (Newark)
Department of Energy	201/648-3904 (Newark)
Department of Labor, Wage/Hour Division	201/645-2279 (Newark)
	609/989-2247 (Trenton)
Occupational Safety and Health Administration	201/645-5930 (Newark)
	201/359-2777 (Belle Mead)
	201/288-1700 (Hasbrouck Heights)
	609/757-5181 (Camden)
	201/361-4050 (Dover)
International Trade Administration	609/989-2100 (Trenton)
Federal Information Centers	201/645-3600 (Newark)
	**523-0717 (Patterson/Passaic)
	**396-4400 (Trenton)

*   None identified
**   Number may be used only within this city.

NEW MEXICO
Region VI

Small Business Administration

Management Assistance
Albuquerque   505/766-3588

Financial Assistance
Albuquerque   505/766-3430

Veterans' Affairs Officer
Albuquerque   505/766-1145   Deward Stegall

Women in Business Representative
Albuquerque   505/766-1143   Carolyn Rigirozzi

State Offices

Small Business Program   505/827-6204
Loan Information:
  New Mexico Research and
    Development Institute
    358 Pinon Building
    1220 South St. Francis Dr.
    Santa Fe, New Mexico 87501
  Business Development Corporation   505/827-6207
Procurement Information   *
Minority Business   505/827-6324
Department of Revenue   505/988-2290 (Santa Fe)
State Export   505/827-6200
Consumer Complaints   *
Ombudsman   *
Licensing   505/827-6318

Other U.S. Government Offices

Internal Revenue Service   800/527-3880; 505/243-8641 (Albuquerque)
Farmer's Home Administration   505/766-2462 (Albuquerque)
Department of Commerce   505/766-2386 (Albuquerque)
Department of Energy   505/827-5950 (Santa Fe)
Department of Labor,
  Wage/Hour Division   505/766-2477 (Albuquerque)
Occupational Safety and
  Health Administration   505/766-3411 (Albuquerque)
International Trade Administration   505/766-2386 (Albuquerque)
Federal Information Center   505/766-3091 (Albuquergue))

*   None identified
**   Number may be used only within this city.

NEW YORK
Region II

Small Business Administration

Management Assistance
Albany (POD)   518/472-6300
Buffalo (BO)   716/846-4517
Elmira   607/733-3358
Melville (BO)   516/454-0750
New York City   212/264-4314
Rochester (POD)   716/263-6700
Syracuse   315/423-5376

Financial Assistance
Albany (POD)   518/472-6300
Buffalo (BO)   716/846-4301
Elmira   607/733-4686
Melville (BO)   516/454-0750
New York City   212/264-1480
Rochester (POD)   716/263-6700
Syracuse   315/423-5364

Veterans' Affairs Officers
Buffalo   716/846-5664   Richard Keffer
Elmira   607/734-2673   Tom Agan
Melville   516/454-0750   Robert V. Miller
New York City   212/264-3525   Ernest D'Addario
Syracuse   315/423-5364   David Laveck

Women in Business Representatives
Buffalo   716/846-4517   Carol Kruszona
Elmira   607/734-3358   Yvonne Koury
Melville   516/454-0750   Walter Leavitt
New York   212/264-4349   Susan Fleming
Syracuse   315/423-5386   Shirley Burke

Small Business Development Center
Albany   518/473-1228

State Offices

Small Business Program   212/949-9300 (New York City)
                            518/474-7756 (Albany)
Loan Information   212/578-4150; 212/949-9300
Procurement Information   212/949-9300; 518/474-7756
Minority/Women in Business 212/949-9288; 518/473-0137
Department of Revenue   800/342-3536 (tax kit)
                            518/457-7177 (Albany)
State Export   212/309-0500
Consumer Complaints   212/488-7530; 212/577-0111
Ombudsman   212/949-9300
Licensing   800/342-3464; 518/474-8275
High Tech   518/474-4349

cont.

Other U.S. Government Agencies

Internal Revenue Service	800/343-9000 (Albany)
	800/462-1560 (Buffalo)
	212/264-3310 (New York City)
	212/330-7673 (Brooklyn)
Farmer's Home Administration	315/423-5290 (Syracuse)
Department of Commerce	716/846-4191 (Buffalo)
	212/264-0634 (New York City)
Department of Energy	518/473-4083 (Albany)
Department of Labor,	
Wage/Hour Division	716/846-4891 (Buffalo)
	516/481-0582 (Long Island)
	212/330-7662 (Brooklyn)
	212/264-8185 (New York City)
	212/298-9472 (Bronx)
	518/472-3596 (Albany)
Occupational Safety and	
Health Administration	212/264-9840 (New York City)
	518/472-6085 (Albany)
	315/423-5188 (Syracuse)
	716/263-6755 (Rochester)
	914/946-2510 (White Plains)
	716/846-4881 (Buffalo)
	516/334-3344 (Westbury)
International Trade Administration	716/846-4191 (Buffalo)
	212/264-0634 (New York)
Federal Information Centers	**463-4421 (Albany)
	716/846-4010 (Buffalo)
	212/264-4464 (New York City)
	**546-5075 (Rochester)
	**476-8545 (Syracuse)

*   None identified
**   Number may be used only within this city.

NORTH CAROLINA
Region IV

Small Business Administration

Management Assistance
Charlotte   704/371-6563

Veterans Affairs
Charlotte   704/371-6577   Thomas Rhodes

Financial Assistance
Charlotte   704/371-6563

Women in Business Representative
Charlotte   704/371-6587   Rachel Hughett

State Offices

Small Business Program   919/733-6254
Loan Information   *
Procurement Information   919/733-7232
Minority Business   919/733-2712
Department of Revenue   919/829-4682 (Raleigh)
State Export   919/733-7193
State Export   919/737-3793
Consumer Complaints   *
Ombudsman   *
High Tech   919/549-0671

Other U.S. Small Business Offices

Internal Revenue Service   800/822-8800; 919/378-5620 (Greensboro)
Farmer's Home Administration   919/755-4640 (Raleigh)
Department of Commerce   919/378-5345 (Greensboro)
Department of Energy   919/733-2230 (Raleigh)
Department of Labor,
   Wage/Hour Division   704/371-6120 (Charlotte)
                                   919/755-4190 (Raleigh)

Occupational Safety and
   Health Administration   919/755-4770 (Raleigh)
International Trade Administration 919/378-5345 (Greensboro)
Federal Information Center   **376-3600 (Charlotte)

*   None identified
**   Number may be used only within this city.

NORTH DAKOTA
Region VIII

Small Business Administration

   Management Assistance
   Fargo   701/237-5771, ext. 131

   Financial Assistance
   Fargo   701/237-5771, ext. 131

   Veterans' Affairs Officer
   Fargo   701/237-5771   James Floyd

   Women in Business Representative
   Fargo   701/237-5771   Carla L. Veitenheimer

State Offices

Small Business Program	701/224-2810
Loan Information	701/224-5600
Procurement Information	*
Department of Revenue	701/224-2770 (Bismarck)
State Export	701/224-2810
Consumer Complaints	800/472-2927
Ombudsman	*
Rural Development	701/237-7502

Other U.S. Government Offices

Internal Revenue Service	800/342-4710; 701/237-5771, ext. 5140 (Fargo)
Farmer's Home Administration	701/255-4011, ext. 4781 (Bismarck)
Department of Commerce	402/221-3664 (Omaha, NE)
Department of Energy	701/224-2250 (Bismarck)
Department of Labor, Wage/Hour Division	303/837-4405 (Denver, CO)
Occupational Safety and Health Administration	701/255-4011, ext. 521 (Bismarck)
International Trade Administration	402/221-3664 (Omaha, NE)
Federal Information Center	*

*   None identified
** Number may be used only within this city.

OHIO
Region V

Small Business Administration

Management Assistance

Cincinnati	513/684-2817
Cleveland	216/522-4180
Columbus	614/469-5548

Financial Assistance

Cincinnati	513/684-2814
Cleveland	216/522-4191
Columbus	614/469-6860 or 2359

Veterans' Affairs Officer

Cincinnati	513/684-2814	Steve Chapman
Cleveland	216/522-4194	Paul Turner
Columbus	614/469-2351	Louis Stevenson

Women in Business Representatives

Columbus	614/469-5548	Lisa Perrin
		Cheryl Bennett
Cincinnati	513/684-2814	Jerry Shapiro
Cleveland	216/522-4195	Jane Luxemburg
		Agnes Tilisky

State Offices

Small Business Program	800/282-1085; 614/466-4945
Loan Information:	800/282-1085; 614/466-4945
Loans funded by public	
employees' retirement system	614/466-2085
Procurement Information	800/282-1085; 614/466-4945
Department of Revenue	614/466-7910 (Columbus)
State Export	216/522-4750 (Cleveland)
	614/466-5017
Consumer Complaints	800/282-0515
Ombudsman	*
Licensing	800/248-4040
High Tech	614/466-3887

cont.

Other U.S. Government Offices

Internal Revenue Service
800/424-1040; 216/522-3414 (Cleveland)
800/424-1040; 513/684-2828 (Cincinnati)

Farmer's Home Administration
614/469-5606 (Columbus)

Department of Commerce
513/684-2944 (Cincinnati)
216/522-4750 (Cleveland)

Department of Energy
614/466-1805 (Columbus)

Department of Labor,
Wage/Hour Division
513/684-2942 (Cincinnati)
614/469-5677 (Columbus)
216/522-3892 (Cleveland)

Occupational Safety and
Health Administration
216/522-3818 (Cleveland)
513/684-3784 (Cincinnati)
614/469-5582 (Columbus)
419/259-7542 (Toledo)

International Trade Administration
513/684-2944 (Cincinnati)

Federal Information Centers
**375-5628 (Akron)
513/684-2801 (Cincinnati)
216/522-4040 (Cleveland)
**221-1014 (Columbus)
**223-7377 (Dayton)
**241-3223 (Toledo)

* None identified
** Number may be used only within this city.

OKLAHOMA
Region VI

Small Business Administration

Management Assistance
Oklahoma City   405/231-4491

Financial Assistance
Oklahoma City   405/231-4301

Veterans' Affairs Officer
Oklahoma City   405/231-4301   Frank Stegall

Women in Business Representative
Oklahoma City   405/231-4491   Peg Frandsen

Small Business Development Center
Durant   405/924-0121, ext. 431

State Offices

Small Business Program   405/521-2401
Loan Information   *
Procurement Information   *
Department of Revenue   405/521-3125 (Oklahoma City)
State Export   405/521-3501
Consumer Complaints   800/522-8555
Ombudsman   *

Other U.S. Government Offices

Internal Revenue Service   800/962-3456; 405/272-9531 (Oklahoma City)
                                  918/583-5121 (Tulsa)
Farmer's Home Administration   405/624-4250 (Stillwater)
Department of Commerce   405/231-5302 (Oklahoma City)
Department of Energy   405/521-2995 (Oklahoma City)
Department of Labor,
  Wage/Hour Division   918/581-7695 (Tulsa)
Occupational Safety and
  Health Administration   918/518-7676 (Tulsa)
                                  405/231-5351 (Oklahoma City)
International Trade Administration 405/231-5302 (Oklahoma City)
Federal Information Centers   405/231-4868 (Oklahoma City)
                                  **584-4193 (Tulsa)

*   None identified
**   Number may be used only within this city.

OREGON
Region X

Small Business Administration

Management Assistance
Portland   503/221-3441

Financial Assistance
Portland   503/294-5220

Veterans' Affairs Officer
Portland   503/294-5200   Wayne Carver

Women in Business Representative
Portland   503/294-5102   Mary Jo Witty

State Offices

Small Business Program	503/373-1200
Loan Information:	503/378-4111
	503/373-1215
Procurement Information	*
Minority/Women-owned Business	503/378-1250
Department of Revenue	503/378-3184 (Salem)
State Export	503/229-5625
Consumer Complaints	800/452-7813
Ombudsman	*
High Tech	503/373-1200

Other U.S. Government Agencies

Internal Revenue Service	800/452-1980; 503/221-3960 (Portland)
Farmer's Home Administration	503/221-2731 (Portland)
Department of Commerce	503/221-3001 (Portland)
Department of Energy	503/754-3004 (Corvallis)
Department of Labor, Wage/Hour Division	503/221-3057 (Portland)
Occupational Safety and Health Administration	503/221-2251 (Portland)
International Trade Administration	503/221-3001 (Portland)
Federal Information Center	503/221-2222 (Portland)

*   None identified
**   Number may be used only within this city.

PENNSYLVANIA
Region III

Small Business Administration

Management Assistance
Harrisburg (BO)   717/782-4405
Philadelphia   215/596-5834
Pittsburgh   412/644-5441
Wilkes-Barre   717/826-6495

Financial Assistance
Harrisburg (BO)   717/782-3846
Philadelphia   215/596-5889
Pittsburgh   412/644-5442
Wilkes-Barre (BO)   717/826-6498

Veterans' Affairs Officer
Harrisburg   717/782-3846   Kenneth J. Olson
Philadelphia   215/596-5842   Robert E. Light
Pittsburgh   412/644-5442   M. Allan Petrosky
Wilkes-Barre   717/826-6464   John F. Gallagher

Women in Business Representative
Philadelphia   215/596-5823   Willa Hunter
Pittsburgh   412/644-5441   Raymond Becki

Small Business Development Centers
Bethlehem   215/861-3980   Middletown   717/948-6031
Clarion   814/226-2626   Philadelphia   215/898-1219, 787-7282
Erie   814/871-7370   Pittsburgh   412/624-6435
Lewisburg   717/524-1249   Scranton   717/961-7588
Loretto   814/472-7000, ext. 231 Wilkes-Barre   717/824-4651, ext. 222

State Offices

Small Business Program   717/783-5700
Loan Information:
    State Department of Commerce 717/787-4147
    Pennsylvania Milrite Council 717/783-7408
    Pennsylvania Industrial
        Development Council   717/787-3300
    Pennsylvania Capital Loan Fund 717/787-3300
Procurement Information   717/783-8893
Minority Business   717/783-1127
Department of Revenue   717/787-8201 (Harrisburg)
State Export   717/787-7190 or 6500
Consumer Complaints   *
Ombudsman   *
High Tech   717/783-5053

cont.

Other U.S. Government Offices

Internal Revenue Service	800/242-0240 (Western)
	800/462-4000 (Eastern)
	412/644-6504 (Pittsburgh)
	215/597-0512 (Philadelphia)
Farmer's Home Administration	717/782-4476 (Harrisburg)
Department of Commerce	412/644-2850 (Pittsburgh)
	215/597-2866 (Philadelphia)
Department of Energy	717/783-8610; 800/822-8400 (Harrisburg)
Department of Labor,	
Wage/Hour Division	717/782-4539 (Harrisburg)
	412/644-2996 (Pittsburgh)
	215/597-4950 (Philadelphia)
Occupational Safety and	
Health Administration	215/597-4955 (Philadelphia)
	412/644-2905 (Pittsburgh)
	717/826-6538 (Wilkes Barre)
	717/782-3901 (Harrisburg)
	814/453-4531 (Erie)
International Trade Administration	215/597-2866 (Philadelphia)
	412/644-2850 (Pittsburgh)
Federal Information Centers	215/597-7042 (Philadelphia)
	**821-7785 (Allentown)
	412/644-3456 (Pittsburgh)
	**346-7081 (Scranton)

*   None identified
**   Number may be used only within this city.

PUERTO RICO
Region II

Small Business Administration

<u>Management Assistance</u>
San Juan   809/753-4572, 4683, 4978

<u>Financial Assistance</u>
No listing

<u>Veterans' Affairs Officer</u>
San Juan   809/753-4519   Raul Garcia

<u>Women in Business Representative</u>
San Juan   809/753-4519   Eldaa Conde

State Offices

Small Business Program   809/724-0542
Loan Information   809/726-2525; **726-4675
Procurement Information   *
Department of Revenue   809/724-9000
State Export   809/725-7254
Consumer Complaints   809/725-7555
Ombudsman   809/724-7373

Other U.S. Government Offices

Internal Revenue Service   *
Farmer's Home Administration   809/753-4308 (San Juan)
Department of Commerce   809/753-4555, ext. 555 (San Juan)
Department of Energy   809/727-0154 (Santurce)
Department of Labor,
   Wage/Hour Division   809/753-4463 (San Juan)
Occupational Safety and
   Health Administration   809/753-4457 (Hato Rey)
International Trade Administration   809/753-4555, ext. 555 (San Juan)
Federal Information Center   *

*   None identified
**   Number may be used only within this city.

RHODE ISLAND
Region I

Small Business Administration

Management Assistance
Providence   401/528-4583

Financial Assistance
Providence   401/528-4586

Veterans' Affairs Officer
Providence   401/528-7500   Anthony Ricci

Women in Business Representative
Providence   401/528-7500,
                                               ext. 4583   Linda Smith

State Offices

Small Business Program	401/277-2601, ext. 21
Loan Information	401/277-2601, ext. 13
Procurement Information	401/277-2601, ext. 24
Minority Business	401/277-2601, ext. 26
Department of Revenue	401/277-2934 (Providence)
State Export	401/277-2601
Consumer Complaints	*
Ombudsman	401/277-2080

Other U.S. Government Offices

Internal Revenue Service	800/662-5055; 401/528-5200 (Providence)
Farmer's Home Administration	413/253-3471 (Amherst, MA)
Department of Commerce	401/277-2605 (Providence)
Department of Energy	401/277-3370 (Providence)
Department of Labor, Wage/Hour Division	401/528-4378 (Providence)
Occupational Safety and Health Administration	401/528-4669 (Providence)
International Trade Administration	617223-2312 (Boston, MA)
Federal Information Center	**331-5565, Providence

*   None identified
**   Number may be used only within this city.

SOUTH CAROLINA
Region IV

Small Business Administration

Management Assistance
Columbia   803/253-5298

Financial Assistance
Columbia   803/253-5374

Veterans' Affairs Officer
Columbia   803/253-5377   Philip H. Black

Women in Business Representative
Columbia   803/253-5377   Theresa Singleton

State Offices

Small Business Program   803/758-7804
Loan Information   803/758-2094
Procurement Information   803/758-3150
Department of Revenue   803/758-2217 (Columbia)
State Export   803/758-3351
Consumer Complaints   800/922-1594
Ombudsman   *
High Tech   803/758-3208

Other U.S. Government Offices

Internal Revenue Service   800/241-3868; 803/765-5278 (Columbia)
Farmer's Home Administration   803/765-5876 (Columbia)
Department of Commerce   803/765-5345 (Columbia)
                                 803/677-4361 (Charleston)
                                 803/235-5919 (Greenville)
Department of Energy   803/758-5794 (Columbia)
Department of Labor,
  Wage/Hour Division   803/765-5981 (Columbia)
Occupational Safety and
  Health Administration   803/765-5904 (Columbia)
International Trade Administration 803/765-5345 (Columbia)
Federal Information Center   *

*   None identified
** Number may be used only within this city.

SOUTH DAKOTA
Region VIII

Small Business Administration

Management Assistance
Sioux Falls   605/336-2980, ext. 231

Financial Assistance
Sioux Falls   605/336-2980, ext. 231

Veterans' Affairs Officer
Sioux Falls   605/336-2980   Edward Wolfe

Women in Business Representative
Sioux Falls   605/336-2980
                                             ext. 231   Darlene Michael

State Offices

Small Business Program	605/773-5032
Loan Information	605/773-3181
Procurement Information	605/773-3405
Minority Business	605/773-4906
Department of Revenue	*
State Export	*
Consumer Complaints	800/592-1865
Ombudsman	*
Rural Assistance Program	605/688-4147

Other U.S. Government Offices

Internal Revenue Service	800/592-1870; 605/225-9112 (Aberdeen)
Farmer's Home Administration	605/352-8651, ext. 355 (Huron)
Department of Commerce	402/221-3664 (Omaha, NE)
Department of Energy	605/773-3603 (Pierre)
Department of Labor, Wage/Hour Division	303/837-4405 (Denver, CO)
Occupational Safety and Health Administration	605/336-2980, ext. 425 (Sioux Falls)
Federal Information Center	*

* None identified
** Number may be used only within this city.

TENNESSEE
Region IV

Small Business Administration

Management Assistance
Nashville   615/251-5881

Financial Assistance
Nashville   615/251-5881

Veterans' Affairs Officer
Nashville   615-251-7176   Chester Mason

Women in Business Representative
Nashville   615/251-5888   Mary Gibson

State Offices

Small Business Program   615/741-5020
Loan Information   *
Procurement Information   615/741-1035
Minority Business   800/342-8420; 615/251-7291 (Nashville)
Department of Revenue   615/741-2801 (Nashville)
State Export   615/741-5870
Consumer Complaints   800/342-8385
Ombudsman   *
High Tech   615/741-5070

Other U.S. Government Offices

Internal Revenue Service   800/342-8420; 615/251-7291 (Nashville)
Farmer's Home Administration   615/251-7341 (Nashville)
Department of Commerce   901/521-3213 (Memphis)
                                   615/251-5161 (Nashville)
Department of Energy   615/741-6677 (Nashville)
Department of Labor,
   Wage/Hour Division   615/251-5452 (Nashville)
                                   615/525-7176 (Knoxville)

Occupational Safety and
   Health Administration   615/251-5313 (Nashville)
International Trade Administration 901/521-4826 (Memphis)
                                   615/251-5161 (Nashville)
Federal Information Centers   **265-8231 (Chattanooga)
                                   901/521-3285 (Memphis)
                                   **242-5056 (Nashville)

*   None identified
**   Number may be used only within this city.

TEXAS
Region VI

Small Business Administration

Management Assistance
Austin (POD)	512/482-5288
Corpus Christi (BO)	512/888-3306
Dallas	214/767-0605
El Paso	915/541-7560
Ft. Worth (BO)	817/870-5457
Harlingen	512/423-8934
Houston	713/660-4420
Lubbock	806/743-7481
Marshall (POD)	214/935-5257
San Antonio	512/229-6270

Financial Assistance
Austin (POD)	512/482-5288
Corpus Christi (BO)	512/888-3331
Dallas	214/767-0605
El Paso	915/541-7586
Fort Worth (BO)	214/767-0605
Harlingen	512/423-8934
Houston	713/660-4453
Lubbock	806/743-7466
Marshall (POD)	214/935-5257
San Antonio	512/229-6250

Veterans' Affairs Officers
Corpus Christi	512/888-3304	Jesse Sendejo
Dallas	214/767-0605	David Long
El Paso	915/541-7560	Rudy Ortiz
Harlingen	512/423-8934	Phillip Nelson
Houston	713/660-4409	Eugene Black, Jr.
Lubbock	806/743-7481	Tony Barnett
San Antonio	512/229-6280	Anthony Reyna

Women in Business Representatives
Corpus Christi	512/888-3302	Diane Fuertes
Dallas	214/767-0382	Carol Silverstrom
El Paso	915/541-7590	Molly Rios
Harlingen	512/423-8934	Graciela Guillen
Houston	713/660-4460	Laura Sanders
Lubbock	806/743-7471	Barbara Hunt
San Antonio	512/229-6250	Geraldine Cook

cont.

State Offices

Small Business Program	512/472-5059
Loan Information	512/472-5059
Procurement Information	512/472-5059, ext. 654
Minority Business	512/472-5059
Department of Revenue	*
State Export	512/472-5059
	713/229-2578 (Houston)
State Export	512/472-5559
Consumer Complaints	*
Ombudsman	512/472-5059
High Tech	409/845-0538

Other U.S. Government Offices

Internal Revenue Service	800/492-4830; 512/397-5314 (Austin)
	713/226-5142 (Houston)
	214/767-1428 (Dallas)
Farmer's Home Administration	817/774-1301 (Temple)
Department of Commerce	713/226-4231 (Houston)
	214/767-0542 (Dallas)
Department of Energy	512/475-5407 (Austin)
Department of Labor, Wage/Hour Division	214/767-6294 (Dallas)
	817/334-2678 (Fort Worth)
	512/888-3156 (Corpus Christi)
	713/226-4304 (Houston)
	512/229-6125 (San Antonio)
Occupational Safety and Health Administration	713/226-4357 (Houston)
	806/762-7681 (Lubbock)
	512/397-5783 (Austin)
	817/334-5274 (Fort Worth)
	512/425-6811 (Harlingen)
	214/767-5347 (Irving)
International Trade Administration	214/767-0542 (Dallas)
Federal Information Centers	**472-5494 (Austin)
	**767-8585 (Dallas)
	817/334-3624 (Fort Worth)
	713/229-2552 (Houston)
	**224-4471 (San Antonio)

* None identified
** Number may be used only within this city.

UTAH
Region VIII

Small Business Administration

Management Assistance
Salt Lake City   801/524-3212

Financial Assistance
Salt Lake City   801/524-3215

Veterans' Affairs Officer
Salt Lake City   801/524-5800   Gerald Randall

Women in Business Representative
Salt Lake City   801/524-5800   Bonnie Miller

Small Business Development Centers
Cedar City   801/586-4411   Salt Lake City   801/581-7905
Logan   801/750-2283

State Offices

Small Business Program	801/533-5325
Loan Information:	
High Tech, R&D, Emerging	
Businesses	801/533-6899
New Product Development	801/583-4600
Funding through state	
employees' pension fund	801/355-3884
Procurement Information	801/533-4000
Minority Business	801/965-4208
Department of Revenue	801/328-5111 (Salt Lake City)
State Export	801/533-5325
Consumer Complaints	801/530-6601
Ombudsman	*

Other U.S. Government Offices

Internal Revenue Service	800/662-5370; 801/524-5767 (Salt Lake City)
Farmer's Home Administration	801/524-5027 (Salt Lake City)
Department of Commerce	801/524-5116 (Salt Lake City)
Department of Energy	801/533-5424 (Salt Lake City)
Department of Labor,	
Wage/Hour Division	801/524-5706 (Salt Lake City)
Occupational Safety and	
Health Administration	801/524-5080 (Salt Lake City)
International Trade Administration	801/524-5116 (Salt Lake City)
Federal Information Centers	**399-1347 (Ogden)
	801/524-5353 (Salt Lake City)

*   None identified
**   Number may be used only within this city.

VERMONT
Region I

Small Business Administration

Management Assistance
Montpelier   802/229-9801

Financial Assistance
Montpelier   802/229-0538

Veterans' Affairs Officer
Montpelier   802/229-0538   Ora H. Paul

Women in Business Representative
Montpelier   802/229-0538   Joan Innes

Small Business Development Centers
Brattleboro   802/257-7967   Rutland   802/773-3349
Burlington   802/656-2990   St. Johnsburg   802/748-8177
Montpelier   802/223-2389   Winooski   802/656-4420

State Offices

Small Business Program   802/828-3221
Loan Information   *
Procurement Information   *
Department of Revenue   802/828-2509 (Montpelier)
State Export   802/828-3221
Consumer Complaints   800/642-5149
Ombudsman   *

Other U.S. Government Offices

Internal Revenue Service   800/642-3110; 802/951-6370 (Burlington)
Farmer's Home Administration   802/223-2371 (Montpelier)
Department of Commerce   617/223-2312 (Boston, MA)
Department of Energy   802/828-2768 (Montpelier)
Department of Labor,
   Wage/Hour Division   617/223-6751 (Boston, MA)
Occupational Safety and
   Health Administration   603/224-1995 (Concord)
International Trade Administration   617/223-2312 (Boston, MA)
Federal Information Center   *

*   None identified
**   Number may be used only within this city.

VIRGINIA
Region III

Small Business Administration

<u>Management Assistance</u>
Richmond   804/771-2410

<u>Financial Assistance</u>
Richmond   804/771-2765

<u>Veterans' Affairs Officer</u>
Richmond   804/771-2765   Guy R. Cooter

<u>Women in Business Representative</u>
Richmond   804/771-2765   Nancy Smith

State Offices

Small Business Program	804/786-3791
Loan Information	*
Procurement Information	*
Minority Business	804/786-5560
Department of Revenue	804/770-4494
State Export	804/786-3791
Consumer Complaints (State	
agencies only)	800/552-9963
Telephone Consumer Hotline, Inc.	1-800-332-1124
Ombudsman	*

Other U.S. Government Offices

Internal Revenue Service	800/552-9500; 804/771-2289 (Richmond)
Farmer's Home Administration	804/771-2451 (Richmond)
Department of Commerce	804/771-2246 (Richmond)
	703/560-6460 (Fairfax)
Department of Energy	804/745-3305 (Richmond)
Department of Labor,	
Wage/Hour Division	804/771-2995 (Richmond)
Occupational Safety and	
Health Administration	804/782-2864 (Richmond)
International Trade Administration	804/771-2246 (Richmond)
Federal Information Centers	**244-0480 (Newport News)
	804/441-3101 (Norfolk)
	**643-4928 (Richmond)
	**982-8591 (Roanoke)

*   None identified
** Number may be used only within this city.

243

WASHINGTON
Region X

Small Business Administration

Management Assistance
Seattle   206/442-5534
Spokane   509/456-3786

Financial Assistance
Seattle   206/442-4518
Spokane   509/456-5346

Veterans' Affairs Officer
Seattle   206/442-5645   David Morado
Spokane   509/456-5346   Dan Mitchell

Women in Business Representatives
Seattle   206/442-8404   Fran Quick
Spokane   509/456-3786   Kathleen B. Simmons

Small Business Development Centers
Bellingham   206/676-3896   Spokane   509/456-4259
Pullman   509/335-1576

State Offices

Small Business Program   206/753-5614
Loan Information   206/753-2219
Procurement Information   *
Minority Business   206/753-4243
Department of Revenue   *
State Export   206/464-6283
Consumer Complaints   800/552-0700
Ombudsman   *
Licensing   800/562-8203
High Tech   206/753-5614

Other U.S. Government Offices

Internal Revenue Service   800/732-1040; 206/442-5515 (Seattle)
Farmer's Home Administration   509/662-4353 (Wenatchee)
Department of Commerce   206/442-5615 (Seattle)
Department of Energy   206/754-0725 (Olympia)
Department of Labor,
  Wage/Hour Division   206/442-4482 (Seattle)
Occupational Safety and
  Health Administration   206/442-7520 (Washington)
International Trade Administration   206/442-5616 (Seattle)
Federal Information Centers   206/442-0570 (Seattle)
                                       **383-5230 (Tacoma)

*   None identified
**   Number may be used only within this city.

Other U.S. Government Offices

Internal Revenue Service	800/452-9100; 414/291-3302 (Milwaukee)
Farmer's Home Administration	715/341-5900 (Stevens Point)
Department of Commerce	414/291-3473 (Milwaukee)
Department of Energy	608/263-1662 (Madison)
Department of Labor, Wage/Hour Division	414/291-3585 (Milwaukee)
	608/264-5221 (Madison)
Occupational Safety and Health Administration	414/291-3315 (Milwaukee)
	414/734-4521 (Appleton)
International Trade Administration	414/291-3473 (Milwaukee)
Federal Information Center	608/271-2273 (Milwaukee)

*   None identified
** Number may be used only within this city.

WYOMING
Region VIII

Small Business Administration

Management Assistance
Casper   307/261-5761

Financial Assistance
Casper   307/261-5761

Veterans' Affairs Officer
Casper   307/261-5761   Henry Ise

Women in Business Representative
Casper   307/261-5761   R. Jean Micek

State Offices

Small Business Program   307/777-7287
Loan Information:
    Industrial Development Corp.   307/234-5351
Procurement Information   *
Department of Revenue   307/777-7971
Consumer Complaints   *
Ombudsman   *

Other U.S. Government Offices

Internal Revenue Service   800/525-6060;
                                                307/772-2220, ext. 2162 (Cheyenne)
Farmer's Home Administration   307/265-5550, ext. 5271 (Casper)
Department of Commerce   307/778-2220, ext. 2151 (Cheyenne)
Department of Energy   307/766-3362 (Laramie)
Department of Labor,
    Wage/Hour Division   303/837-4405 (Denver, CO)
                                                801/524-5706 (Salt Lake City, UT)
Occupational Safety and
    Health Administration   303/234-4471 (Lakewood, CO)
International Trade Administration   303/837-3246 (Denver, CO)
Federal Information Centers   *

*   None identified
** Number may be used only within this city.

GLOSSARY

GENERAL BUSINESS TERMS*

A

Account. A record of a business transaction or "deal." When you buy something on credit, the company you are dealing with sets up an "account," which means a record of what you buy and the amount you pay. You will do the same thing with any customers to whom you extend credit. At the bank, you will also have an account, a record of what you deposit and withdraw.

Accountant. One who is skilled at keeping business records. The term "accountant" usually refers to a highly trained professional rather than to one who keeps books. An accountant knows how to set up the books needed to operate a business, and he or she can help a business owner understand what the business records mean.

Accounts receivable. A record of what is owed to you. All of the credit accounts—what each customer owes you taken together—are your "accounts receivable." Even though you don't have the money in

---

* These terms are used in the SBA Prospective Small Business Owners Workshop script, "Keys to Business Success." The simple definition given for each term is not intended to be the only or complete definition but rather to clarify the term in the context of the Workshop presentation.

hand, money that is owed to you is an asset, like property you own. You have to know your accounts receivable in order to know what your business is worth at any time. Of course, your accounts receivable must be collected to become a real asset.

Analysis. The breaking down of an idea or a problem into its parts. In business you must "analyze" a problem before you can decide on the best solution. Let's say your problem is some item that isn't selling well. You make a list of things that might be wrong and ask questions like, is the price right? What have customers said about the item? Etc. An analysis includes gathering facts that might help explain the problem and indicate its solution.

Appraisal. An estimated value set after inspection of a business or property. It is used as a starting point for negotiations in borrowing funds, severing a partnership, defending a lawsuit, or making an insurance settlement.

Articles of incorporation. A legal document that sets forth the purposes and regulations of a corporation. These papers must be approved by the appropriate state office before a corporation legally exists and can do business. Each state has different requirements and the procedures are complicated, so it is usually necessary to hire a lawyer specializing in corporate law for this process.

Asset. Anything of worth that is owned. Your personal assets (not counting your abilities) are the money you have in your pocket or in the bank, whatever is owed to you, any securities and property you own, your furniture and appliances, and all the miscellaneous things that you personally own. The assets of a business are just the same: money in the bank, accounts receivable, securities held in the name of the business, real estate, equipment fixtures, merchandise, supplies, and all the real things of value that the business owns.

B

Bad debt. Money owed to you that you can't collect. The risk of "bad debts" is why a business should carefully consider giving credit and lending money. When it is apparent that an account is not collectible, that account should not be kept on the books as an asset. An accountant can advise when and how to enter such accounts as bad debts.

Balance. As a noun, the amount of money remaining in a bank account after accounting for all transactions (deposits and withdrawals). Also, the amount of money you owe a creditor, or a customer owes. As a verb, when the amounts of money in a positive (credit) account and a negative (debit) account are made equal. Think of an account as an old-fashioned set of scales. When there is nothing on either side, they are "balanced." When credit is extended, it is like putting an amount of money on one side—the weight makes that basket go down. When money is paid on the account it is like putting weight on the opposite side. When enough money is paid back, the scales will equal or balance again.

Balance sheet. An important business record that shows what a business owns and owes at any one time. A "balance sheet" lists business assets and their present value on one side of a ledger and liabilities on the other. The liabilities include the net worth of the business, which the business "owes" the owner. If the balance sheet has been figured correctly, it must balance.

Business Development Corporation (BDC). A business financing agency, usually made up of the financial institutions in an area or state, and organized for assisting industrial concerns that are not able to obtain such assistance through normal channels. The risk is spread among various members of the BDC, and interest rates may vary somewhat from those charged by member institutions.

Business venture. A financial risk taken in a commercial enterprise. Successful businesspeople have learned that they can control the risk by practicing good management and getting advice from bankers, accountants, lawyers, and business associates.

C

Capital. Available money to invest or the total accumulated assets you can make available for starting a business and for living on while the business is in the early stages. If you are successful, the business will accumulate "capital" in the form of property, goods, and money (including securities).

Capital requirement. A list (or schedule) of expenses that must be met to establish a business—i.e., how much capital must be invested to start the business and keep it operating. One item of importance that is often forgotten is the amount of money that will be needed for living expenses until the business starts earning a profit.

Cash. Currency—hard money, bills, and negotiable securities (like checks)—in your cash drawer or readily available. The money you can draw on demand—your bank accounts or savings accounts— also represents "cash." You must have it to keep a business going, and even a very successful business can run out, particularly as the business is growing. So good managers plan ahead on their needs for cash.

Cash receipts. The money received by a business from customers. "Cash receipts" are to a business what food and water are to living things. A business can survive just so long on its stored-up capital. Businesspeople preserve their capital as much as possible and try to have a regular, sufficient flow of cash.

Certified Development Corporation (SBA 503 Program). A local or statewide corporation or authority that packages SBA, bank, state, and private money into a financial assistance package for existing business capital improvement (both for profit and nonprofit concerns). Each state has at least one CDC. The SBA holds the second lien on its maximum share of 40 percent involvement; this is called the "503 Program."

Certified lenders. Banks that participate in the SBA's guaranteed loan program, have a good track record with the SBA, and agree to certain conditions set forth by the SBA. In return, the SBA agrees to process any guaranteed loan application within three business days. District offices of the SBA can provide lists of certified banks in their areas.

Chain of command. The proper lines of authority among the head of an organization, its manager, supervisors, and workers. In every well-organized business, there should be a line of authority that everyone understands. Sometimes a "chain-of-command" graph is useful in making this clear. A good manager will make sure employees understand the order of authority and the method of communicating with management.

Contract. A legally binding agreement regarding mutual responsibilities between two or more parties. In business law, a "contract" exists whenever there has been a meeting of minds—whether or not the contract is written. However, contracts are usually made in written form and should never be taken lightly. Any business contract should be examined by a qualified lawyer. It should also be read thoroughly by the parties and signed only after its meaning is clearly understood. Note that many sales forms are binding contracts and should not be signed unless the terms of the agreement are clearly understood.

Controllable expenses. Costs of doing business that can be restrained, meaning postponed or spread out over a period of time. For example, depreciation on equipment is a "controllable expense" in that it isn't required. A businessperson can put off obtaining new equipment until the business can support the purchase and its depreciation.

Corporation. A business structure, created by a state charter, comprising a group of individuals or objects treated by the law as an individual. Thus, a corporation is an artificial personage; acting through its officers, it can do business as a separate entity the way individuals can in a sole proprietorship or a partnership. Unlike the case with other types of ownership, a corporation may be owned by a number of persons, who hold shares.

Cosigners. Joint signers of a loan agreement, pledging to meet the obligations in case of default. When you ask someone to "cosign" a note, you are asking that person to share a debt with you and guarantee that the loan will be paid back. The lender can take legal action against cosigners' property if they refuse to pay. This arrangement should not be entered into lightly by either borrowers or cosigners.

D

Debit. Debts recorded. Bookkeeping deals with "credits" and "debits" in putting down the additions and subtractions of business capital; debits are the minus or negative entries in the books—the money that is taken out of a particular account. Usually, books are set up so that debits are recorded in the left-hand column of an account.

Debt. That which is owed. If you borrow money, buy something on credit, or receive more money on an account than is owed, you have a "debt"—an obligation to pay back whatever amount is involved. Going into debt was once considered a sin, but it can be useful and is often a necessary way of doing business. A debt is bad business when it is larger than the ability of the borrower to repay.

Default. Failure to pay a debt or meet an obligation. Any debt is a trust, and failure to pay it is a violation of a serious kind. To "default" is to demonstrate that you are untrustworthy and do possibly irreparable damage to your reputation. In business such a poor reputation can, and probably will, restrict your credit and cost you valuable creditors and business friends; ultimately, it may cost you your business.

Depreciation. A decrease in value through age, wear, or deterioration. It is said that an automobile "depreciates" as soon as it is driven off the lot, it immediately becomes a "used" car and is worth something less to the owner than when it was brand new. In the same way, all the equipment you buy for a business begins to depreciate immediately and is worth increasingly less as it continues to be used. Depreciation is a normal expense of doing business, but it is a real expense that must be taken into account. When a new piece of equipment is purchased, it is set up as an item in a "depreciation account" whereby it can be expensed over a period of time. There are regulations governing the manner and periods of time that may be used for depreciation, in that the rate of depreciation affects a business's taxable income.

Direct loans. Financial assistance provided through the lending of federal monies for a specific period of time, with a reasonable expectation of repayment. Such loans may or may not require the payment of interest.

Disaster loans. Various kinds of physical and economic assistance available to individuals and businesses who have suffered losses due to natural disaster. This is the only SBA loan program available for residential purposes.

E

Economics. The management of financial resources, whether of nation, city, and business or of an individual. A small-business owner does well to have a basic understanding of "economics" because it is such an important matter in the conduct of business.

Embezzle. To steal or take by fraud another's property for one's own use. One of the great perils of doing business is that seemingly trustworthy people sometimes are moved to steal from their employers and associates. Many businesses have been unable to survive the effects of such acts. There are three ways to protect a business against "embezzlement": careful selection of those people who are the best risks, business procedures that make the practice difficult, and insurance or bonding against any loss that may occur.

Enterprise. A business firm or a business undertaking. In a general sense, "enterprise" refers to any hard, dangerous, or important project, which makes the term apt for business, because a successful business has all these attributes.

Entrepreneur. A person who organizes and manages a business. This is a French word that has been accepted into the English language. Its popularity probably has something to do with its grand sound which befits anyone who has the initiative to create and run a business.

Equity capital. Venture money. In order to go into business you will certainly have to lay it on the line. You put up savings or property when you go into business in hopes of getting a good return. Unfortunately, some people who have worked hard and protected their savings magnificiently still make foolish investments. It is very important to consider carefully before investing in your own business and to take all the steps you can to protect your "equity capital."

F

Factor. Generally, something that contributes to a result; in business, a finance company specializing in short-term, high-risk loans (usually at high interest rates). The first meaning has to do with "facts" or "factual things" that are a part of any subject. When we speak of the "factors" involved in borrowing money, we mean the facts that the banker or loan officer must know in order to approve a loan. The second meaning of "factor" is specific to the finance business. Factors who lend money to a high-risk enterprise usually require collateral and may exercise control of the enterprise.

Financial statement. A record of total assets and liabilities. Knowing what you or your business is worth is rather important. It's a way to find out whether you are advancing or retreating in the conduct of your affairs, and, as such, is an aid to making business decisions. In a sense, the financial statement is the certificate of success or failure. In order to borrow any appreciable amount of money, the lender will require an accurate financial statement.

Financing. Obtaining money resources. Businesses usually have to obtain financing at some time—either to get started or to expand operations (hopefully not just to stay in business). The time to set up relationships with those who might provide financing is before you need the money. Maybe you won't ever need financing, but that would be most unusual, so you would be well advised to lay the groundwork early.

Fixed expenses. Costs that don't vary from one period to the next—i.e., that are not affected by the volume of business. Rent, for example, must be paid whether or not any business is conducted. "Fixed expenses" are the basic costs that a businessperson has each month.

Franchise. A right or privilege to deal in a certain line or brand of goods and services. A franchising company (franchisor) is in the business of "selling" businesses or brands to small entrepreneurs (franchisees). Usually, the franchisor and the franchisee enter into a binding contract providing that the franchisor will supply the product, materials, and a certain amount of know-how, and the franchisee will handle the product exclusively and run the business according to certain standards prescribed by the franchisor. Such a relationship may be mutually advantageous, but it is a long-term arrangement that should be examined carefully before being accepted.

Functional. Relating to a function or a characteristic action. In a general sense, the term is used to describe an object that is useful rather than ornamental. In business, a "functional" organization means an organization structured around the activities of the business, in contrast with the more formal "line management" organization. A functional organization has specialists who serve as managers rather than managers who only manage and are not specialists.

G

Gross. The whole amount of income, before deductions and expenses. One has to learn early the difference between "gross" and "net" figures, for many new businesspeople get fooled by the gross figures. These may show a business making a substantial "gross" profit, but by the time all the expenses are deducted, the "net" or real profit is small. Another meaning of "gross" is "very wrong," and that's exactly how it is if a businessperson confuses gross with net.

Guaranteed/insured loans. Loan programs in which the federal government makes an arrangement to indemnify lenders against part or all of any defaults by those responsible for repayment of the loans.

I

Income. Money coming in. "Income" means essentially the same for a business as for an individual. It is all the money received before anything is taken out. See "gross."

Incubators. Facilities for encouraging entrepreneurship by housing in one place a number of fledgling enterprises that share an array of services. These shared services may include meeting areas, secretarial services, accounting, research library, on-site financial and management counseling, and computer word-processing facilities. "Incubators" facilitate new business formation and growth, particularly for high technology firms.

Industrial Development Authority. The financial arm of a state or other political subdivision established for supporting economic development in an area. This is usually done through loans to nonprofit organizations, which in turn provide facilities for manufacturing and other industrial operations.

Industry Ratio. The average percentage of income spent by firms in the same industry on various cost items. These "industry ratio" figures are very important guidelines for a business. The point is not that a businessperson ought to adhere rigidly to the industry averages, but by comparing costs with what similar businesses spend, he or she can look for areas that seem to be out of line. If for example, a business's expenditures are only half of the industry ratio, the business owner would do well to consider additional advertising.

Interest. The cost of borrowing money. Banks and loan companies are businesses like any others. They have to receive a profitable income or they can't attract money, expand, and provide the services that banks must provide. Of course, any "interest" or price you pay comes right off the top of your income and is subtracted from your profit. Shop for a good interest rate as you would for anything you buy.

Inventory. A list of present or current material assets. If you are in a retail business, the stock you have on the shelves is "inventory," but so are your available supplies, goods received or stored, and any expendable items on hand. As a regular part of the bookkeeping process, inventory must be counted periodically because it is needed to figure what the business is worth.

Invest. Lay out money for any venture from which a profit is expected. One way to evaluate whether investing in a business is worthwhile is to consider what you would make by putting that money into a low-risk investment. The prospects should be for a much greater return if money is risked in a business.

L

Labor Surplus Areas. Places that are designated as "labor surplus" have high unemployment. This information is requested on procurement bid sheets, and firms bidding for jobs are given extra points.

Lease. A long-term rental agreement. A "lease" arrangement is mutually advantageous to both the lessor owner and the lessee (renter). The agreement assures the landlord that the property will be rented, and assures the renter that the business property will not be taken out from under the business. It is a good idea to have a lease option for extending the rental period, but be careful. Businesses often find that they did not plan on sufficient space and are bound by a lease they cannot get out of.

Liability. That which is owed. This is one of the business words that have more than one application and can be confusing. There is "liability" insurance, which is insurance to cover any claims that are brought against the policy holder (see below). But the term "liabilities" usually refers to the obligations of the business as opposed to its assets. Of course, the business also has a liability toward its owner, so with the list of what the business owes there is always an ownership liability, which is the difference between what a business owns and what it owes to those other than the owners.

Liability insurance. Protection a business carries to cover the possibility of loss from lawsuits in the event the business or its agents are found to be at fault if an accident occurs. It protects the business investment.

Limited partnership. A legal arrangement in which some owners are allowed to assume responsibility only up to the amount invested. The idea in a "limited partnership" is that investors may put up money for a business venture without being directly involved in its operation and so are not held responsible for the debts of the other partners beyond the possible loss of the money they have invested.

Line position. A place of authority in a "line" organization. Having a "line position" means being responsible only to the person directly above you in the organization.

Liquidate. To settle a debt or to convert to cash. This word literally means "to do away with"; in a business sense, "liquidate" means to do away with a debt by paying it, or to do away with material assets by selling them and thus turning them into cash.

Loan. Money borrowed with an interest charge.

Local development corporation. An organization, usually made up of local citizens, whose aim is to improve the economy of the area by inducing business and industry to locate there. A "local development corporation" usually has financing capabilities.

M

Management. The art of conducting and supervising a business. It isn't enough just to invest money in a business; someone—a manager—must nurture, protect, and help the business along to success. Another way to look at it is that "management" is the exercise of judgment in business affairs.

Marketing. All the functions involved in buying and selling. It is often said about business that nothing happens until somebody sells something, so "marketing" is really the heart of a business operation. Marketing includes advertising, sales promotion, and even public relations.

Merchandise. Goods bought and sold in a business. "Merchandise" or stock is a part of inventory. In usage, merchandise has come to mean anything movable that can be sold or traded.

Minority businesses. The Small Business Administration defines minorities as those who are "socially or economically disadvantaged." Social disadvantage has to do with membership in one of several different racial or ethnic categories as defined by regulation (or on a case-by-case basis for others who feel they are socially disadvantaged, like the physically handicapped). Groups that are considered to be socially disadvantaged include Black Americans, Hispanic Americans, Native Americans (American Indians, Eskimos, Aleuts, and Native Hawaiians), Asian Pacific Americans (people originating in Japan, China, the Philippines, Vietnam, Korea, Samoa, Guam, U.S. Trust Territory of the Pacific Islands, Northern Mariana Islands, Laos, Cambodia, and Taiwan), and Subcontinent Asian Americans. Economic disadvantage has to do with the barriers that social disadvantage has placed in the way of an individual's employment and participation in business. In most cases, being a woman does not by itself qualify a person for minority status.

Minority Enterprise Small Business Investment Company (MESBIC). MESBICs are licensed by the SBA as federally funded, private venture capital funds. They are comparable to SBICs, except that the MESBICs are targeted toward socially or economically disadvantaged individuals.

Motivation. Strong influence or incentive. "Motivation" is the force that moves a person to do whatever he or she does. It may be something that the person is not even aware of, and a whole field of business psychology has grown up around motivation research—the study of why people buy things, including hidden reasons.

N

Net. What is left after deducting all charges. See "gross."

Nonrecurring. One time, not repeating. "Nonrecurring" expenses, like those involved in starting a business, only have to be paid once and will not occur again.

O

Objective. A goal toward which effort is directed; something to accomplish. Note that "objective" also means "realistic"; we could say that "objectives" are aims set to produce some realistic result.

Obsolescence. Decline in value because of replacement by newer or better things. People have a way of wanting whatever is the latest style or development, so a businessperson will do well to guard against "obsolescence" and not overstock items that tend to change style.

Office of Small and Disadvantaged Business Utilization (OSDBU). Each agency of the federal government has an office located in Washington that is a watchdog over it—assuring that the agency complies with federal regulations to purchase a certain percentage of products and services from small and minority-owned-and-operated businesses. If small businesses can't get help from one of these, they can contact the OSDBU in Washington.

Operating costs. Expenditures arising out of current business activities. Your "operating costs" for any period of time are simply what it costs you to do business—the salaries and charges for electricity, rental, deliveries, etc., that were involved in performing the business dealings.

Operating organization. The management structure as opposed to legal structure of a firm.

Operating ratios. The relationship among costs arising from business activities, such as the percentage of costs that went for rent. How does that compare with other businesses like yours? These are facts that a business needs to operate efficiently and not waste resources.

Organize. To put in order. A good manager can make order out of just about anything—a work force, a payment schedule, or a merchandise display plan. There is a logic to every task, and using that logic is what it means to "organize."

Owner-manager. One who operates his or her own business. One of the greatest assets an "owner-manager" has is flexibility in meeting problems. There is no need to call a committee together or consult the board of directors to take action. Being a good owner-manager is one of the most satisfying of endeavors.

Ownership organization. The legal as opposed to management structure of a business. How a business is organized legally depends upon how it is owned. If one person owns it it's usually a proprietorship; if several people own it jointly as owner-managers, it's a partnership (unless incorporated). If many people own a business, it almost certainly is some form of a corporation.

P

Partnership. A legal business relationship in which individuals share responsibilities, resources, and profits. Partnerships are built on mutual trust, but trust should be backed up with a firm agreement in writing.

Payable. Ready to be paid. One of the standard accounts kept by the bookkeeper is "accounts payable." This is simply a list of bills that are current and due to be paid.

Pay on demand. An order to comply with an obligation. Contracts are often written with a "pay-on-demand" clause, which means the debtor must pay the balance when asked, even if the terms of the contract agreement have been met.

Personnel. Collective term for all people in the employ of a business. As a small business grows, it will need "personnel" to handle the expansion of the business and carry out its work.

Pledge. To bind by a promise; to give possession of something of value as security for a loan. There has to be a great deal of trust between parties doing business—indeed, it seems doubtful that business could proceed without it, for it is the basis for all credit transactions, most business agreements, and the general conduct of commerce. For the most part, we accept the first kind of "pledge" from other people, and usually they keep their promises. However, the second kind of "pledge" is sometimes called for, particularly when sizable amounts of money are involved, and is a more formal arrangement. The borrowing party then pledges (usually in writing) to give possession of some capital assets if he or she is unable to meet the terms of the obligation.

Post. To enter an account in the books.

Pricing. Setting a value upon something. How well a small businessperson handles "pricing" may determine if there is a profit and how much. An operation as important as pricing should not be left to "what the traffic will bear" or "what the other outfits are charging." It is far better to establish prices scientifically by figuring out all the costs involved and adding a fair profit—*then* comparing your prices with the market.

Principal. Property or capital assets as opposed to income; also, one who is directly concerned in a business enterprise. If you consider that the word means "the first in importance"—whether referring to people or capital assets—the usage becomes clearer. The money you invest in a business is the first in importance—"principal." And if you are investing money and effort in business you are a "principal."

Procurement assistance. A kind of contract from the Government offering special opportunities to qualifying businesses. Small businesses should be particularly interested in two types of "procurement": (1) small-business set-asides, which are required by law to be on all contracts under $10,000, or a certain percentage of an agency's total procurement expenditure; and (2) the SBA 8(a) program, in which small and minority-owned-and-operated businesses can negotiate on special contracts.

Profit. Financial gain—return over expenditures, or, most simply put, what you've got left after paying for everything. Hopefully, the "profit" represents a good return on the investment in a business, plus reward payment for good management; but never take profit for granted—it can be disappointing.

Profit & loss statement. A list of the total amount of sales less expenses and costs, to show the amount of "profit or loss" for doing business. It is sometimes called an "income statement."

Profit margin. An allowance above expenditures made in setting a price. A businessperson plans for profits by building them into prices (see "pricing").

Prompt pay. A ruling that if federal government agencies do not pay invoices for goods and services within 45 days of billing, they have to pay interest to the vendor on any amount overdue.

Proprietorship. Exclusive ownership. A "proprietor" is one who owns a business, and a business owned by one person is called a "proprietorship."

R

Ratio. The relationship of one thing to another expressed as numbers or degrees. For example, we say that a greengrocer has a 10 to 1 loss ratio on lettuce, which is a short way of saying that for every 10 heads of lettuce he or she buys, the grocer loses one head that either doesn't sell or spoils before it can be sold and has to be thrown away. "Ratios" of this kind are established by keeping figures over a period of time. The ratio here is figured by dividing the number lost into the number sold.

Receivable. Unpaid and ready for payment. See "accounts receivable." In accounting, a "receivable"—money that is owed to you—is an asset; it is listed as a current asset in the balance sheet.

Regulations. Rules of law. It is accepted in our system of government that the state has the obligation to protect citizens, so the government has established laws to prevent injury. Some of these have to do with business practices and must be followed to avoid penalties. Of course, many such regulations benefit the small businessperson.

Reserve. That which is held back and stored for future use or in case of emergency. The success or failure of many young businesses depends upon their ability to weather a financial crisis. There should be something in "reserve" to meet an emergency.

Retail. Selling in small quantities directly to the consumer, in contrast with selling in large quantities to dealers for resale, which is a "wholesale" activity. There is some confusion brought about by advertising that says "discount," "cut-rate," or "wholesale prices," but these operations are really "retail" as long as they are selling in small amounts to the general public.

S

SCORE/ACE. The Service Corps of Retired Executives and the Active Corps of Executives, a combined volunteer management assistance program of the SBA. SCORE and ACE volunteers provide one-on-one counseling free of charge and offer workshops and seminars for a small fee.

Secured loans. A loan that is protected or guaranteed. To "secure" means to make an object safe, so a "secured loan" is one that is made safe by something of value put up as collateral.

Service business. A retail business that deals in activities for the benefit of others. If you go to a doctor or lawyer, he or she will send you a bill marked "for services rendered." Other examples are a laundry, an auto repair shop, a beauty salon, etc.

Share. One of the equal parts into which the worth of a corporation is divided for sale. Thus, "share" represents a part ownership in a corporation. The more shares one holds, the more ownership one has.

Site. A plot of ground set aside for a particular use. The business "site" may or may not be owned by the business, and it is often better to rent a "site" when getting started.

Small Business Investment Corporation (SBIC). Federally funded, private venture capital firms licensed by the SBA. Money is available to small businesses under a variety of agreements. This money is usually, but not always, expansion capital for new, risky, or high-tech firms.

Stabilizing. Becoming less subject to ups and downs. Like a ship on the ocean, a business may run into a "rough sea" of changing conditions. Successful businesspeople look for "stabilizing" methods to smooth out these conditions—whether by diversifying into products that are more "stable," by eliminating the factors that cause the fluctuations, or by operating on a level that minimizes the effects of the fluctuations.

Stock. An ownership share in a corporation (another name for share); also, accumulated merchandise, a merchant's wares. Putting merchandise out for display is called "stocking the shelves."

Surety bond. A guarantee of reimbursement to an individual, company, or the government if a firm fails to complete a contract. The SBA backs "surety bonds" in a program much like its guaranteed loan program.

T

Trade credit. Permission to buy from suppliers on an open account. When you buy business supplies on credit, you are really borrowing from the supplier—you have the loan of whatever he or she is selling you until it is paid for. Suppliers usually extend this service for a period of time (often 20 to 30 days) without charging interest, but it is not uncommon to charge interest sooner if the amount is large and the time to repay is extended. "Trade credit" is useful to small businesspeople, who should keep their reputations bright so they may continue the privilege.

Transfer. To move from one place to another or from one person to another. One of the main services of banks is to provide the efficient "transfer" of funds. The practice of using checks is to accomplish the transfer of money without the need for moving the money physically.

Tangible. Real. The literal meaning is "can be touched," but the business meaning refers to something that can be seen and evaluated. "Tangible" assets are those that have a real value and can be converted, if necessary, into cash. The "intangible" assets of a business are attributes that may be of value but can't be measured or objectively evaluated—for example, the good will that a business has built up.

Tax number. A number assigned by a state revenue department that enables a business to buy goods wholesale without paying the sales tax.

V

Venture capital. Money used to support new or unusual undertakings; equity, risk, or speculative investment capital. This funding is provided to new or existing firms that exhibit above-average growth. See "business venture."

Volume. An amount of quantity. The "volume" of a business is the total it sells over a period of time.

W

Wholesale. Selling for resale. See "retail."

TERMS OF SALE (TERMS OF PAYMENT)

Date of invoice. All terms originate from date of invoice. The date cannot be prior to day of shipment. Note: Terms may expire prior to receipt of goods.

Dated, or As of. Terms do not begin with the date of the invoice but at a later specified date. If an invoice is "dated" May 1 and reads "2% 10 days net 30 plus 30 days," the terms become effective June 1. If the invoice says "2% 10 days net 30 as of April," terms of payment begin April 1.

Discount. Usually expressed as a percentage of the net. Discounts cannot be taken on taxes or freight shown separately on invoices.

E.O.M. End of month. The buyer can wait until the end of the month during which purchases are made before credit terms (or discount terms) become effective. Example: The buyer received an invoice dated June 20; terms of payment do not begin until July 1.

Net. No discount; bottom figure on invoice including tax. The "net" is usually accompanied by terms of when due—i.e., "on receipt of invoice," "10 days," "30 days," "10th Prox.,"etc. If date terms are shown, the amount is due on receipt of invoice and no discount is allowed.

Prox. Abbreviation for "proximo," which means "next following."

2% 10th Prox, Net 30th Prox. If an invoice is dated on or before the 25th, a discount of 2% is allowed if the bill is paid by the following 10th. Otherwise, the net is due July 30th. If an invoice is dated after the 25th, then the 2% discount is allowed by the 10th of the second month and the net is due by the 30th of the second month.

TERMS FOR INTERNATIONAL TRADE

A

Advising bank. A bank operating in the exporter's country that handles letters of credit for a foreign bank by notifying the exporter that the credit has been opened in his or her favor. The advising bank fully informs the exporter of the conditions of the letter of credit without necessarily bearing responsibility for payment.

Arbitrage. The process of buying foreign exchange, stocks, bonds, and other commodities in one market and immediately selling them in another market at higher prices.

B

Barter. Trade in which merchandise is exchanged directly for other merchandise without the use of money. Barter is an important means of trade with countries using currency that is not readily convertible.

C

Collection paper. Any document (commercial invoice, bill of lading, etc.) submitted to a buyer for the purpose of receiving payment for a shipment.

Commercial attaché. The commerce expert on the diplomatic staff of a country's embassy or large consulate.

Consular declaration. A formal statement, made to the consul of a foreign country, describing goods to be shipped.

Consular invoice. A document, required by some foreign countries, describing a shipment of goods and showing information such as the names of the consignor and consignee and the value of the shipment.

Convertible currency. A currency that can be bought and sold for other currencies at will.

Correspondent bank. A bank that, in its own country, handles the business of a foreign bank.

Countertrade. The sale of goods or services that are paid for in whole or in part by the transfer of goods or services from a foreign country. See "barter."

Customhouse broker. An individual or firm licensed to enter and clear goods through customs.

Customs. The authorities designated to collect duties levied by a country on imports and exports. The term also applies to the procedures involved in such collection.

D

Destination control statement. Any of various statements the U.S. Government requires to be displayed on export shipments that specify the destinations authorized for shipment.

Drawback. Refund of duty related to articles manufactured or produced in the United States for export with the use of imported components or raw materials. Manufacturers are entitled to a refund of up to 99 percent of the duty charged on the imported components.

E

Exchange permit. A permit sometimes required by the importer's government enabling the importer to convert his or her own country's currency into foreign currency with which to pay a seller in another country.

Exchange rate. The price of one currency in terms of another—i.e., the number of units of one currency that may be exchanged for one unit of another currency.

Export broker. An individual or firm that brings together buyers and sellers for a fee but does not take part in the actual sales transactions.

Export commission house. An organization that acts as a purchasing agent for foreign buyers, for a commission.

Export license. A government document that permits the licensee to engage in the export of designated goods to certain destinations. See "general export license" and "validated export license."

Export management company. A private firm that serves as the export department for several manufacturers. It solicits and transacts export business on behalf of its clients in return for a commission, salary, or retainer plus commission.

Export trading company. A firm similar to an export management company, but with a broader range of services, including the taking of title to goods.

F

Foreign sales agent. An individual or firm that serves as the foreign representative of a domestic supplier and seeks sales abroad for the supplier.

Free port. An area such as a port city into which merchandise may be moved without payment of duties.

Free trade zone. A port designated by the government of a country for duty-free entry of any nonprohibited goods. Merchandise may be stored, displayed, used for manufacturing, etc., within the zone and reexported without duties being paid. Duties are imposed on the merchandise (or items manufactured from the merchandise) only when the goods pass from the zone into an area of the country subject to the customs authority.

G

General Agreement on Tariffs and Trade (GATT). A multilateral treaty intended to help reduce trade barriers between the signatory countries and to promote trade through tariff concessions.

General export license. Any of various export licenses covering commodities for which "validated export licenses" are not required. No formal application or written authorization is needed to ship goods under a "general export license."

L

Letter of credit (L/C). A document, consisting of instructions by a buyer of goods, that is issued by a bank to the seller, who is authorized to draw a specific sum of money under certain conditions (i.e., the receipt by the bank of certain documents within a given time). An "irrevocable L/C" provides a guarantee by the issuing bank in the event that all terms and conditions are met by the buyer (or drawee). A "revocable L/C" can be canceled or altered by the drawee after it has been issued by drawee's bank. A "confirmed L/C" is one that is issued by a foreign bank and validated or guaranteed by a U.S. bank for a U.S. exporter in the case of default by the foreign buyer or bank.

P

Private Export Funding Corporation (PEFCO). Lends to foreign buyers to finance exports from the United States.

Purchasing agent. An agent who purchases goods in his or her own country on behalf of foreign importers, such as government agencies and large private concerns.

Q

Quota. The quantity of goods of a specific kind that a country permits to be imported without restriction or imposition of additional duties.

S

Schedule B. Refers to Schedule B Statistical Classification of Domestic and Foreign Commodities Exported from the United States. All commodities exported from the United States must be assigned a seven-digit Schedule B number.

Shipper's export declaration. A form required by the U.S. Treasury Department for all export shipments. It is prepared by a shipper and indicates the value, weight, destination, and other basic information about the shipment.

V

Validated export license. A document issued by the U.S. Government authorizing the export of commodities, covering a specific transaction or time period in which the exporting is to take place.

INDEX